# Praise for L

Technology is moving at li̟ _ _ _ ̲u̲. It seems like every day we are living more in an episode of *Star Trek,* but technology for aging is more like *The Flintstones.* This simple guide for Boomers breaks down the tech talk into what works as we age. It offers hope and a clear path that will allow you to live life easier. This practical guide is a must-read!

—Jack Canfield
Co-Founder, *NY Times*
Best-selling Book Series,
*Chicken Soup for the Soul,*
*The Success Principles,* and
*How to Get from Where You Are*
*to Where You Want to Be*

Lisa is my go-to expert on multigenerational living, opportunities for seniors, and the Baby Boomer lifestyle. She brings a wealth of wisdom, experience, and empathy to this important topic. I trust her, and I follow her. You should too.

—Kary Oberbrunner
CEO, Igniting Souls
Award-winning author of *Unhackable*

*BOOM* is a beacon of hope! This guide will change how you think about aging and your options for living life to the fullest. Lisa has created a simple yet comprehensive guide to understanding which tools and technologies will be most valuable to you as you age. A must-read for any Boomer.

—Dr. Benjamin Hardy
Author of *Personality Isn't Permanent* and *Who Not How*

# BOOM

# BOOM

## THE BABY BOOMERS' GUIDE TO PRESERVING YOUR FREEDOM AND THRIVING AS YOU AGE IN PLACE

## LISA M. CINI

ethos
collective

Published by **Ethos Collective** ™
PO Box 43, Powell, OH 43065
ethoscollective.vip

LCCN: 2020922653

ISBN: 978-1-63680-015-8 (paperback)
ISBN: 978-1-63680-016-5 (hardback)
ISBN: 978-1-63680-017-2 (ebook)

Available in paperback, hardback, e-book, and audiobook.

## To My Tribe

Thank you for believing in me and not letting me rest before my mission is complete. I'm updating this book frequently with more value, interviews, resources, and information based on feedback you share. I would love to meet and chat with you about any new or amazing technology you use that I may not have in the book.

Connect with me at **LisaMCini.com** where you'll also find more tips, updates, and resources.

At **BestLivingTech.com** you'll find products that will help you to age in place.

To find out more about our design work, visit **MosaicDesignStudio.com** to see beautiful, engaging, senior living homes.

• • •

The latest surveys reveal Baby Boomers are more scared of being unable to care for themselves than they are of dying.

*BOOM: The Baby Boomers' Guide to Preserving Your Freedom and Thriving as You Age In Place* is filled with key insights and actions to live a safer and less stressful life while saving tens of thousands of dollars per year. The book outlines how to leverage the latest state-of-the-art technologies to facilitate aging in the right place and traveling with freedom while also accounting for the challenges of aging (e.g., declining memory, vision impairment, etc.).

• • •

Note: If you're reading this book on a Kindle app, please make sure it's the latest version of the book. To get the latest and greatest, just open your app, click or press the "More" icon in the lower right-hand corner, then press "Sync," and you'll always be updated with the most recent version.

# CONTENTS

INTRODUCTION                                              XI

LAYING THE GROUNDWORK                                      1

TECHNOLOGY & THE KID CONNECTION                            7

YOU'VE HEARD OF THE SIX SENSES, BUT HAVE YOU
HEARD OF THE 6 DS?                                        23

AI, DATA MINING, & SENSORS                                34

IOT (INTERNET OF THINGS) & CROWDSOURCING                  51

3D PRINTING & ON DEMAND MANUFACTURING                     76

ROBOTS, EXOSKELETONS, & DRONES                            89

WELL-BEING, MIND, BODY, & SPIRIT                         139

CANNABIS & AGING                                          201

SMART HOUSE                                               221

THE "LOVE" DESIGN METHOD                                  287

UNIQUE HOUSING OPTIONS FOR BOOMERS                        315

GAMIFICATION, AUGMENTED REALITY (AR)/
VIRTUAL REALITY (VR), & LIFELONG LEARNING                 334

PETS                                                      374

THE CRAZY, BUT VERY POSSIBLE FUTURE                       434

SUMMARY, BONUS, & RESOURCE LINK                           462

ABOUT THE AUTHOR                                          471

REFERENCES                                                480

# INTRODUCTION

As we start this journey together, I need to confess that this book is written out of frustration. It's a typical response from an entrepreneur. When I can't find a solution to a problem, I create the solution. The solution to the problem culminates in a clear and thorough but not overwhelming guidebook that will help you successfully age on your terms.

Imagine never being introduced to silverware, dishes, and drinking glasses. You go through life eating with your hands and cupping your hands to drink water (There are no drinking fountains either.). You survive, but you don't thrive. Life is much harder because you don't have the proper tools to handle the simple tasks of daily living.

Then someone introduces you to silverware and teaches you how to use it. Life is much better, but eating soup and drinking is still a messy, time-consuming proposition. You have some tools but haven't been exposed to the ones that can really impact your life.

This guidebook is intended to not only expose you to the best tools out there to age on your terms, but it is also set up for you to know what you should use and when. Imagine eating soup with a fork. It wouldn't be very helpful, right? Unfortunately, the information that we've been provided regarding technology is a lot like discovering a lost king's tomb from a highly advanced society where we're guessing as to what this or that's used for, and we're overwhelmed by the shiny gold everywhere. We might guess right, but it can be exhausting trying to analyze all that's out there and understand what will be useful or not.

Having said all this, I bet you'll be surprised to know that this book—the one that you're reading right now and bought thinking it is all about technology—is actually a book that's all about freedom. We can't stop the clock, but we can stop our limiting beliefs on aging. When we embrace aging on our terms, we become free.

As you enter a new season of your life, I believe there's a key out there. This key won't only let you unlock the gifts and talents that you'll take with you in this season; it will also support you all the way through it. That key? Just like in the *Raiders of the Lost Ark* it's technology, this time it's not ancient technology of a world forgotten; it's available to us right now, today! Ultimately, it's what will let you age on your terms.

Think of *BOOM* as your own treasure map. It's tying together all the systems, ideas, and advancements, showing you what works with what and giving you simple, clear information that will help you to decide what works for you in your life.

To be clear, there's no one out there who's really doing this. Vendors aren't very helpful because it's in their best interest if you buy their whole package. Then a little later, it's still in their best interest and not *yours* if you buy their whole new, newer, newest package. And very quickly, every tech-related item becomes very overcomplicated or outdated.

But it doesn't have to be. Simplification is possible. **BOOM** is simplification! And with it, you'll discover the tech tools to bring you to the best living you can possibly have as you age. My hope is *knowing* the tools that are out there will let you create smart strategies, and those strategies are what will put you in command of something I feel is critical to aging: *the way you want to make decisions yourself before someone else makes them for you.*

Having smart strategies helps you mitigate the aging process. We're all aging and will continue to age, if we're lucky enough. The loss of our personal freedom—or, if you want to call it something else, call it "the loss of our independence"—often comes with the gift of aging. The gift of aging is being old enough to not care what others think and live on our terms. Smart strategies lessen the loss of personal freedoms that we spent years earning. Some of the strategies are quite simple: a memory rescue diet can help you avoid becoming memory impaired. A personal assistant robot can keep you on track with your schedule and remind you to take your medications. Technology makes both things easier. It helps track your memory diet and keeps you out of the hospital because it helps you not forget to take your blood pressure pills. These are only the tip of the iceberg.

If you want to go the route of aging in a *home,* technology can aid in your understanding of which of those homes will be the best fit for you. Freedom is making the choice yourself, so you don't have it made for you and end up living out your life in a place where you don't feel you belong.

Where health decisions are concerned, **BOOM** explains how using technology moves you away from being reactive and towards being proactive. We'll look at AI (Artificial Intelligence), data mining, and sensors and how they can help you accomplish that. Stay with me on this journey, and this book will take both of those terms and make them feel like your familiar friends as opposed to your scary, science fiction, dystopian, future nightmare.

For the last 20 years, I've been the CEO of the Mosaic Design Studio, one of the country's largest senior living design firms. So as you can imagine, I've spent a lot of time thinking about the topic of how we age. I've thought about aging from the 30,000' macro perspective and from an extremely up close and micro perspective. I've talked to the owners and developers of senior living facilities. I've been inspired by the leading thinkers in the field of aging. I've had moving conversations about the topic from people in the thick of it. Finally, I've experienced it in the most personal and intimate ways. For the last few years, I've been living my life in the middle of my family's social experiment where we have four generations living under one roof, and the eldest generation is my 96-year-old grandmother, who deals with (and so we *all* deal with) Alzheimer's/Dementia.

What I've learned from all of this is that you can only have freedom if:

- You have made decisions about who you are. *(How do I want to age?)*
- You have the right tools. (*What are my technology options?*)
- You have the right options. (*What do I need right now? What do I have access to right now? What do I anticipate needing in my future?*)

What else helps is knowing your personal definition of retirement. My old buddy Webster defines it like this: "To withdraw from use or service, to take out of use."[1]

But is that how you define it? Do you feel that when you retire, you're done contributing? Do you think, *That's it; now I'll just sit on the front porch in my rocker until I die?* Or will you choose to see your gifts and talents and use them to redefine your life in this new season?

It's been said that you should plant your seeds before you need the harvest. That rings true as we discuss freedom. Wisdom to me is planning what *you* determine is best for you today so that you won't be dealing with crisis management in the future. I've seen crisis management from close up; it's never easy, never pretty, and rarely brings happiness to anyone involved. No matter where you are in your season, you are ahead of where you'd be if you hadn't taken the time to read **BOOM**. It will serve you well.

So let's plant some seeds and make our harvest one that's beautiful and self-determined.

# CHAPTER 1
## LAYING THE GROUNDWORK

The world is changing at exponential speeds in all directions. It's exciting but a little scary, kind of like your first kiss, roller coaster ride, or learning to drive a car. Looking back, it was always worth it. It's what makes me know I'm alive.

Let's start with what I'll call **The Big 3**. These big questions will frame the conversation—pretty much any conversation—this book takes on.

1. How are you going to be able to live your life with freedom and confidence?

2. where will you be living your life?

3.  How are you going to care for your mind, body, and spirit?

## 1. HOW ARE YOU GOING TO BE ABLE TO LIVE YOUR LIFE WITH FREEDOM AND CONFIDENCE?

This is all about technology. Technology is any tool that makes our lives easier. Hunting tools were created long, long ago so we could eat. Then we created more tools called "nets" so we could expand our diets and eat fish. And now we've created another new kind of net tool, the "Internet." Once again, technology has given us a tool to make our lives easier. Technology isn't limited to the things that we have to plug into the wall. Technology is all around us.

Technology is nothing new. As human beings, we have a drive to create things, and technology is our way to fulfill this drive. My goal in my professional career and with this book is to merge our drive to create with our process of aging. If that happens, technology will let us age gracefully (whenever possible), on our terms, and enjoy life up to our last moment.

## 2. WHERE WILL YOU BE LIVING YOUR LIFE?

This question is one about *Health Care vs. Well Care*. You don't want to be sent to a *prison*, do you? And yes, *prison* is exactly the way I've heard a lot of people describe their idea of senior homes. Now don't get me wrong. At my firm, Mosaic Design Studio, we design beautiful, award-winning senior living homes that are like the Ritz, but the statistics say that 90% of United States seniors still don't want to live in senior living no matter how beautiful my team and I make it.[2] Senior living is a lot like sushi. It's not for everyone, but for those who enjoy it, it's expensive but wonderful. Are you in the 90% or the 10%?

If you're a Boomer, the chances are good that you've been living your life right *where you want to live it*. And chances are also good that no one's told you where (or how) to live it before, so why in the world would you start letting them tell you where to live it *now?*

And probably, you don't want them to tell you. Most likely, *you* want to remain the one who's driving and steering your life bus, and that makes sense. But there's also a chance that as you look around today, you're seeing choices regarding your where that don't seem like you at all.

That's because they're not.

Those choices were right for the *silent generation*, the people who were born from around 1925–1945. Their choices look like: Home Health, Independent Living (IL), Assisted Living (AL), Memory Care (MC), and Skilled Nursing (SN). That was then; this is now.

Your choices are flexible but can seem complex. Imagine their flexibility like women's fashion today. It used to be you could tell the year by the length of a skirt. If you had a miniskirt on and the fashion of that time was to be below the knee, you wouldn't fit in very well.

Aging used to be like this with a very siloed view of where you were allowed to live, depending on your age and your health needs. But as with women's skirts, you can now wear anything you want. Thank gosh, because those right below the knee skirts cut me at the worst possible place. They made my already short frame of 4'11" look even shorter, and they made me look 10 lbs heavier! Now, with Home Healthcare, telemedicine, crowdsourcing, and personalized medicine, you have tons of options. Whatever you choose doesn't have to be a lifelong decision. So as your needs change, you can change where and what you want.

## 3. HOW ARE YOU GOING TO CARE FOR YOUR MIND, BODY, AND SPIRIT?

Healthcare is about the body only, and that's fine; we all have bodies, and they absolutely need care. But what about the rest of what makes us who we are? What about our minds? What about our souls?

That's a whole other part of what I mean when I say, "aging on your own terms." It's looking at all of what you can and want to do for your body, mind, and spirit. Put them all together, and you've got a whole, full, real person. Take them apart, and it all starts to unravel.

Lucky for us, there are tools to keep us together. We will look at the physical needs of our bodies with sensors, data mining, personalized supplements, fitness programs, and medicines. We will also look into the power of connection, adding value, meditation, brain scans and brain food, and what drives your spirit or passion to keep you engaged, resilient, and happy.

With the recent advances in personalized medicine, AI, nanotechnology, and our connections, the experts are saying if you can survive the next 10 years, then you can break the 120-year mark or even longer. When this happens, a mind shift takes place. Imagine the age you think you'll live to. Now, what if I could guarantee you'd live another 50 years? How would this change your thoughts on how you'd take care of your mind, body, and spirit? Would you write that book you always wanted to or leave Wall Street and go back to school to become a teacher? What legacy would you want to leave by living a full life and giving to all those you know and love with your gifts and talents? This might seem like a big bomb to drop, but it's happening, and as I mentioned before, wisdom is creating a plan before the crisis.

The speed at which technology is improving can be completely overwhelming. But it also gives us almost unlimited options and autonomy in deciding how we want to live and how we want to age. Consider about how quickly we went from no cell phones to huge, bulky cell phones. Then we had phones that fit in our pockets, and now we have access to the entire world. We now have access to so many things and while the ride is fast, it is worth exploring how it can help us keep our freedom, keep us safe, and keep us healthy.

# CHAPTER 2
## TECHNOLOGY & THE KID CONNECTION

Kids don't care about technology in terms of its social aspects, its barriers, or the issues that might be wrapped up in it. What they care about is whether or not it serves them. If it does, they'll tell everyone about it; they'll preach loud, clear, and forever. *American Idol*? Yeah, its success was largely due to tween girls. *Twilight*? Yep, it was pretty much the same demographic: girls between the ages of 8-12 or 9-13 (depending on the resource), in case you were wondering what a tween was, like I was. Tweens have an estimated spending power of two hundred billion dollars—that's BILLION. And if a specific technology doesn't serve them? They'll quit it and adopt something new.

Take the iPhone, for example. The percentage of tweens girls with an iPhone was 76% but dropped to 53%.[3] When the iPhone first emerged, it quickly became a fashion statement. Fashion is something that always grabs the younger generation first. But as time marches on, the iPhone is no longer a fashion statement, but it has become a tool. As a tool, it doesn't create the same need-to-have feeling as when it was a fashion statement because there are more options to work with between Android and Windows phones.

In my work, I look at what kids are doing and adopting, and I think about how maybe those things could help Boomers as they move forward and make decisions about the future. My reasoning for this is if a kid can use it, then it's intuitive. They typically don't whip out a user manual and start reading from step one. If the product isn't useful, they'll discard it, and it'll die a quick, cold death and find its way to the technology graveyard. If it's a winner in their eyes like Google, Facebook, DoorDash, Uber, and Instagram, then I'm willing to get on the bus and figure out how to use the tech tool to make my life better. You can count on one thing with kids and technology, they NEVER adopt technology that makes their life harder. They're brand agnostic and value-driven. They're the best, cheapest research team we've got, and we just have to watch and wait.

What do kids use? They have tablets and smartphones that parents put into their hands to entertain them, let them collaborate with others, and to communicate with friends. What do Boomers use? They use a tablet (iPad) or smartphone for entertainment, collaboration, and communication. The similarities are amazing.

What's the next tech that the kids are using and we need to leverage? 3D printing and Augmented Reality/Virtual Reality (AR/VR).

To explain, VR (Virtual Reality) is like being inside of a dream or a video game. You don't have full movement, but you experience the situation you're seeing through goggles that are connected to a computer. The scientific data states that if you're placed in a scary or horrific VR environment, your body will react in a stressed way, but if you're placed in a happy VR environment, you'll react in a happy, non-stressed way. Virtual Reality (VR) is used to help those with PTSD who served in the military and people with phobias. They're using the technology to reduce stress to that situation until it's all gone. Likewise, being in a happy situation makes you happier. Imagine being in a peaceful scene (your favorite vacation spot), and you can go there whenever you put on the goggles, or sculpting in 3D right in your living room without having to get all supplies ready or clean up afterward.

Augmented reality is similar, but it adds to glasses you already wear (with an adapter) to help you see items that may be of benefit. For example, when you're in your kitchen and you look at the refrigerator, it may remind you that you're out of milk. If you have ever watched a professional football game on TV, they use augmented reality to superimpose the lines on the field to show where the first down has to be. These tools are a blend of entertainment, education, and having a 24/7 personal assistant.

It may sound crazy to you now, but imagine driving on a trip without GPS. Eventually, these tech tools will become so integrated into our lives; they'll seem as necessary as indoor plumbing or electric lights.

It's an exciting place to be, right here, right now, leveraging the past and the present while peeking into the future.

This may come off like I'm a geek or nerd, but it's critical to *geek out* a little bit so that you can fully understand the changes coming. If we can successfully hang around for the next 10 years, the positive exponential world changes will be larger than we could ever imagine for our lives and health.

When I say the word exponential, what I mean is a huge shift in our reality. Think of it like this: When you have one child, you deal with the issues that come with having one child. It's challenging but manageable. Millions of people throughout time have done it. Now think about having twins; it's not earth-shattering, but the work doubles. You have to modify your plans and maybe even get some help. I remember my cousin having twins and just feeding them was quite the challenge. Her mother and husband helped because it was more than a 24-hour job keeping the twins satisfied. Now let's move to an exponential change, 10 kids . . . at one time. Basically, a human litter. What worked in the past will no longer work. A completely new strategy has to be implemented. You probably would have to get a new car, house, and definitely would have to enlist assistance or help from others. Just think of feeding time and trying to handle feeding 10 babies at once. It's impossible, even if you developed skills like those circus performers who spin plates in the air all at the same time. If you run back and forth, making sure one didn't drop, eventually you'd tire out, and something would fall.

Now imagine that but in a positive way. The exponential isn't about having to do more things and run from plate to plate, hoping that nothing will fall and break. It's exponential change that allows computers, robots, and teams to anticipate your needs before you even see them, and it helps you handle what used to be a chore or very difficult. This type of change creates not just an evolution; it creates a revolution.

The best way to explain it is if you could go back to the United States prior to home appliances. Washing your clothes required capturing rainwater, then using a washing board or paddle contraption that you had to turn to agitate the mixture of water, lye, and clothes to clean them. Then you had to rinse the clothes and hang them on the clothesline to dry. Cooking required a garden (Let's not even go into that effort.), getting fuel for the stove, starting the fire, gathering the eggs, preparing the bread, food, etc. Then it was cooking and cleaning the dishes and then starting all over again. Then let's move on to sweeping the floors and rugs—not an easy task. Rugs needed to be removed from under the furniture and dragged outside, hung on a line or fence, and the dirt was beaten out of them. They were then drug back into the house and the furniture was moved back onto them. There was also this little thing about having to light all the lamps in the house and deal with no indoor plumbing. In most cases, until the 1930s in rural America, indoor plumbing and electricity didn't exist. Unless you lived in N.Y.C., Chicago, or Philly, a bowl for washing your face and a chamber pot were the bathroom in your house. Of course, if you were rich enough to have domestic servants, none of this would have mattered to you.

Taking care of your home was such a chore prior to household appliances. My 96-year-old grandmother's school book on *Foods and Home Making* by Greer (1928) had a whole section in the Modern Housewifery chapter on "Stoves and Fire building." It explained wood and coal ranges, the supply of air needed, and more. Basically, she was an expert in HVAC (Heating, Ventilation, and Air Conditioning) for her family. She made sure they were comfortable, well-fed, and the home was clean and functioning properly.

Move forward to when appliances started to become mainstream. The Hoover vacuum cleaner was one appliance that was sold starting in 1908 and touted, "It beats … as it sweeps … as it cleans."[4] It was an amazing time and back saver.

In the 1930s, things changed due to a government program called the Rural Electrification Administration (REA). Its goal was to bring electricity to the rural areas of the U.S.. Instead of heating an iron on your coal or wood stove, you could plug it in and voila! It was heated so no more starting a fire, stoking it, and then heating the iron. Time was being won back for the modern housewife of the late 1930s.

Now let's think about kids and how their interaction with technology has created new opportunities. Entertainment is one of the top areas of growth, and much of it aims to please a younger demographic. We went from listening to the radio to watching TVs in every home. This made way for Saturday morning cartoons that everyone remembers fondly. The next step was computers for commercial use. Think about how quickly computers expanded once they were used for more than only business processing. They were also used for games and programs for kids. Now, we've gone from computers to tablets, where we can bring everything with us in our backpacks from spreadsheets to games to Netflix (online movies). And the newest jump has been the use of Augmented Reality (AR). The games created under the AR platforms are only getting better, which means they're always becoming more useful and educational.

To understand the past and the present in technology, you need to understand Moore's Law and its impact on exponential growth. Moore's Law basically states that computing power doubles every 24 months. Peter Diamandis presents the following data in his book *Abundance.*[5]

> *In 1971, the Intel 4004 integrated circuit had 2,300 transistors costing one dollar each with .00074GHz of processing power. Today, an Nvidia GPU has over 7.1 billion transistors, which cost less than $0.0000001 each and has over 7GHz of processing power. This is 10,000 times faster, 10 million times cheaper, and 100 billion-fold improvement.*

This explains how computers can get smaller and smaller yet be faster and smarter. It is said that a kid in Africa with a smartphone has more technology than President Bill Clinton had at his disposal when in office. Everything we use that has a computer in it has been impacted by Moore's Law.

Take a moment and make a list, either mentally or on a piece of paper, of all of the technology you currently use daily. Given the definition that technology is the application of scientific knowledge for practical purposes, what did you come up with? In a couple of seconds, I came up with over 45 technologies that I use on a daily basis, and I didn't include software or apps. If I had, I'm sure the list would have been twice as long.

1. Phone
2. Cell phone
3. Car
4. Electric curling iron
5. Sonic toothbrush
6. Hair dryer
7. Indoor plumbing
8. Alarm system
9. GPS
10. Cloud computing
11. Laptop computer

12. Tablet

13. Digital camera

14. Fax

15. Copier

16. Vacuum sweeper

17. Clothes washer

18. Clothes dryer

19. Dishwasher

20. Refrigerator

21. Electric auto-dimming lighting

22. Heated flooring

23. Thermostats to electric heat

24. Gas hot water tank

25. Blender

26. Juicer

27. Stove

28. Oven

29. Microwave

30. Coffee pot

31. Food processor

32. Electric bed

33. Massage chair

34. Scooter

35. Personal printer

36. Glasses

37. Electric iron

38. Safety cameras on car

39. Heated electric Bidet toilet

40. Wi-Fi

41. TV

42. Alexa / Google Home

43. DVR/DVD

44. Outlook calendar

45. Wi-Fi speakers

These technologies are average to most consumers. The point is when you were growing up, could you ever have imagined having a microwave in your kitchen, a printer in your home office, and a cell phone? It would have been impossible then to dream up the technology, let alone understand how it would change our lives for (mostly) the better.

Current technologies that should be leveraged by the Baby Boomers are those that impact your ability to live your life with freedom and confidence.

In designing for thousands of senior living homes over the past 25 years and visiting many more, I'm still shocked by the lack of technologies used to make the environment better, cheaper, and more connected. It seems there's a distrust of technology that being connected or watched will open the potential for lawsuits and make it even harder to provide care for seniors while staying profitable. Dignity is the other factor that gets brought up as a stumbling block to adopting new technology in senior living. The key is appropriate permission-based use of technology. Great technology is hardly noticeable, as you'll see, and it solves problems that improve dignity, safety, outcomes, compliance, and risk. It's like adding in the

Typically, technology is first adapted by those with the lowest mental barriers to using it. Tweens and teens usually fit the bill. When I was having trouble doing research on the Internet in 1998, I asked the 9-year-old neighbor kid to help. He told me to type in the word, "Google." I said, "Google? What is it?" He told me, "Just do it and stop asking questions."

seat belt to cars back in 1984. At first, it felt restrictive, but then it was comforting to know you wouldn't fly through the window if, God forbid, you were in an accident.

The easiest way to approach this discussion will have to be twofold. First, you need to define your categories of technology that you'll need, and then second, these technologies will need to be married to the impact they have on how you want to live your life. Basically, the cost of the technology both in dollars and outcome has to outweigh the pain of doing things the old way.

Technology does require an investment, and this is usually the first and largest objection. But I ask you, can you imagine using an out-house vs. indoor plumbing? Can you imagine using a pail to get your water out of your well vs. turning the lever on your sink? It sounds ridiculous to us now. The amount of time wasted in villages without running water keeps girls from education, not to mention the safety issues involved. Can you imagine going back to a non-electric typewriter? I can't comprehend how long and how many rewrites it would take me to write what you're reading.

Or let's go a step further. Let's say you have access to the Internet, but you choose not to use the technology because it's silly with all the Facebook stuff and the costs to have it. Now imagine you need to research something, so you go to the library (Yes, they still exist.). You search through the system to find out which books may be of value. You then get their Dewey Decimal numbers, and you're off on a hunt. The books are all over the library and intermixed. They're heavy, but that means value, right? You then look at each one for a hidden treasure of evidence. Finally, you find your nuggets. When the information is short, you hand-copy it down, but when it's large, you mark the page and then copy it at the copier. After all the research is completed, you have to return the books. If you missed something and can't remember which book it came from, you have to start all over. There's no cookie history to lead you back to where you were. It was exhausting to write. It felt like a waste of time just detailing it out, yet some Baby Boomers are very much like what I just described, using archaic systems because they exist and are familiar. My mother-in-law won't get on Facebook and complains that she's not as connected to the kids as she'd like. She has Internet and instant access but feels it's silly and is stuck in her old ways. My 78-year-old mother, on the other hand, is very connected. She Facebooks, Instagrams, and Snapchats with her grandkids and keeps a very open, real-time, up-to-date relationship with them. They both have the same access to the same tools; one just chooses not to move into the future and use them.

Let's go back to the library scenario. Recently, Google introduced a book search called *Talk to Books* that allows you to search millions of books in a second. You search not only the title but every word in all of these books for exactly what you're searching for. Just as the Dewey Decimal system allowed us to save time then, this newest Google search technology will make things even faster and more accurate. Millennials will be able to say to their kids, "Back in my day, Google only gave you book titles. We still had to read all those books."

The point is, we can't imagine the future, but we can be mentally prepared to take advantage of it. Talk to your grandkids or neighbor kids about what they're using and how it may help you. Have fun with this; you're not going to break anything.

Technology can help increase your quality of life and freedom.

# CHAPTER 3

## YOU'VE HEARD OF THE SIX SENSES, BUT HAVE YOU HEARD OF THE 6 DS?

Understanding Peter's 6 Ds of Tech Disruption—Digitize, Deceptive, Disruptive, Demonetize, Dematerialize, and Democratize[6]—will help you find your footing in the world of technology. He explains the seasons of technology so that you won't be caught off guard, or at the very least, you'll know the next stage and that there will be a shift happening.

## 1. Digitize.

*The Idea:*
Digitize—anything that becomes digitized becomes disruptive. Think of the time when books had to be hand-copied and then along came the printing press. All of a sudden, books and Bibles were given to the masses. Being able to mass distribute information changed the whole world. Now you can carry 10,000 books on your phone or tablet.

Remember back when music could only be heard live? Then it was recorded and distributed on an album, and people were able to enjoy music where and when they liked. Millions more had access to the best musicians in the world.

Photos were another example when the film was developed. But when they went digital (taking a photo on your phone, for example, and sending it via your phone to another), our lives forever changed. We record and share our lives now as every moment is captured.

When you digitize something—books, music, images—it allows everyone to have access anywhere at any time.

*Why is this important to you?*
Our medical records and all the testing and imaging are currently being digitized. This will allow artificial intelligence and data mining to help us be our best us by tailoring all our health care into Well Care. Telemedicine will now be possible with everything being digitized, which should break the insurance industries' locks on how portable our insurance is. This, in turn, will drive down all the healthcare costs. Basically, you'll be able to be in control and *own* your music, books, photos, and medical records. This will allow you to travel as you wish with all of your favorite things in your pocket and not have to worry if you get sick or need a prescription filled. The local doctor will have immediate access to your entire medical history and will be able to video in your personal doctor for a consultation, if needed, all seamlessly.

## 2. Deceptive.

*The Idea:*
When it starts being digitized, its growth is deceptive. When it starts out, it's hard to even see it's getting traction. Then the law of compounding comes into play, and everyone thinks it's an overnight success, but really, it's been

building and building, and then finally, like a plane on a runway, it takes off.

### *Why is this important to you?*
Blockchain and Bitcoin are perfect examples of *deceptive*. These are digital currency (money that's real, but it's existing only on the Internet) that no government can control or tax. Several online retailers will take Bitcoin as payment, and it'll only get larger. By the time it comes out of deceptive, the entire economics system of the world will be changed.

Remember when banks started with debit cards? Bitcoin is a new form of money that's universal. Popular companies like Travelocity accept Bitcoin. We may not understand how it works yet, but the world is moving in a direction to make money easier for us to understand. It will also help us when traveling as your Bitcoin currency in the future would be like using your credit card now, except there isn't need to convert the dollars to Euro, for example. The Bitcoin price would be the same no matter where you are—Africa, Italy, Mexico, or the United States.

## 3. Disruptive.

*The Idea:*
When digitizing moves from deceptive into disruptive, it knocks out the existing technology. Think about how we used to consume music. You'd go to the record store and buy it, but now you download the music right to your phone, and records are considered an antique novelty. Cell phones did the same thing to landline phones. In *our* house, we don't have a landline; even my parents use only their cellphones.

*Why is this important to you?*
Today, Wi-Fi connects us to the Internet and one another wherever we are in the world. The local coffee shop, library, beauty salon, and senior living all have Wi-Fi because customers demand it. The status quo has been disrupted!

This is where we're heading with VR/AR, too, and probably by the time you're reading this, it will have already disrupted life and will be part of the normal or accepted way of life.

Remember the Periodic Table of Elements from your high school chemistry days? Remember thinking you'd parted ways, maybe even somewhat amicably? Well, who thought it *wasn't* done, and who thought it, like some of its gases, was inactive? I did. But on Dec 2, 2016, I learned I was wrong. That's when four new elements were added—one was *graphene*. Are you wondering how this fits into disruptive?

Graphene is an allotrope of carbon and also a new kid on the Periodic Table of Elements block! And it's also 200 times stronger than the strongest steel. In car manufacturing, first it was "*Steel, steel, steel.*" And then they realized that aluminum was better. "*Aluminum, aluminum, aluminum.*" Those poor car manufacturers and developers just finished retooling everything again, and along comes graphene. Now it's "Shove over aluminum. Here comes graphene."

The key to our future is flexibility. Disruption will continue to happen faster and faster. This is great for aging because it means even if something worked in the past, that doesn't mean something in the future won't disrupt it and make it even better. While it's not a disruptor yet, some doctors I have spoken to feel that stem cell therapy will be the next disruptor. Imagine getting a couple of knee or hip injections, and your body heals itself instead of having to do surgery or rehab! This disruption would be a huge blessing for all of us as we age, increasing our confidence and freedom.

## 4. Demonetize.

### *The Idea:*
Reaching this D means that money is no longer a barrier between the first adapters—or whom I'll call "the Richie Riches"—and the rest of us normal folk who are now getting it.

### *Why is this important to you?*
Remember back to the day of those big, clunky cell phones? If that's not enough to trigger your memory, then do you remember that they had antennae? Well, back then, only super rich people had one, like maybe a president and a few kings. Now little kids in the poorest countries can afford to have as much access as only the elite had before.

When money is no longer an object, we experience de-monetization. This means the technology that's reached this point will be super cost-effective and improve your life as you age, providing you more confidence and freedom.

## 5. Dematerialize:

*The Idea:*
We're not carrying a lot of *stuff* anymore.

*Why is this important to you?*
I used to carry a camera, phone, pager, separate GPS, and a Franklin planner, which to this day, I still miss! And for my work as a designer, I had a level too! Back then, I carried six or seven things with me every time I traveled for work. Now I no longer do that because I have it all in a phone.

When material goods fall to the wayside because they're encompassed by one thing, that's dematerialization. Recently, research has been looking at the ear as the new wrist. What I mean by that is the ear is a great place to measure your balance, brain, and heart. Overlay the fact that most people use earbuds with their phones to listen to podcasts, books on tape, music, or have phone calls, and the ear becomes the perfect place to measure all of your health data, help you connect, and also hear better. Marry this with Augmented Reality (AR) glasses, and you can say goodbye to your smart watches and cell phones. Imagine wearing a hearing device and glasses to take photos, have access to all of your data, and connect, relax, and listen to whatever you need.

## 6. Democratize:

### *The Idea:*
The day comes where everyone can have it—access is open to anybody and available to all. Not too long ago, using a public toilet (not an outhouse) was not for everyone. As the standards have risen, everyone gets access. In other parts of the world, you still have to pay to use the toilet facilities.

### *Why is this important to you?*
With the rise of the Internet and access for anyone, the world is at your fingertips in seconds. What used to be only for the rich and the elite of the society is now free to everyone and instantly available.

With Data Mining and AI, you can now invest for yourself, read the latest medical breakthroughs, and know what's happening in every part of the world. When you democratize, the best of the best is available to everyone, no matter your age or economic standing.

## 7. Delocalize:

Peter has recently introduced a 7th disruption, **Delocalization.** Basically, with all of the 6 Ds happening, the world is getting smaller. We can reach anyone anywhere with the above disruptions. We will no longer have boundaries, which will open up our lives to so much more fullness and aid in technologies to improve our lives as we age. To learn more about delocalization, please go to Peter's website: (diamandis.com).

## MOORE'S LAW:

*What is it?*
Computing power doubles every 24 months.

*Why is this important to you?*
We can't anticipate what comes next. And because of this, you have to be able to have *future flexibility,* because we don't really know what ideas are going to hit and which ones aren't.

And to complicate it further, very often something else is going to piggy-back off the new thing, and it's going to go pretty far off the charts. We don't know which technology is going to take off; there could be 50 things going until it reaches the disruptive phase and starts to skyrocket. It's a little bit like playing the stock market.

As I write this, I'm thinking that AR (augmented reality) and VR (virtual reality) are going to hit and skyrocket. Have some fun learning about all of these technologies and imagine the possible, positive impact on improving your life, then try them out.

# CHAPTER 4

## AI, DATA MINING, & SENSORS

Alexa is our personal assistant, personal shopper, DJ, patron saint of lost phones, temperature and light controller, newsman, weatherman, and comedian. The Amazon Echo—powered by Alexa—is the newest member to our family. Alexa is the persona you talk to similar to iPhone's Siri persona. She's connected to Amazon, so she can do more and more each day. I'm thinking about getting a Samsung Family Smart Hub refrigerator and if I do, she'll be connected to my fridge and help me get groceries. Alexa is a mashup of Rosie the Robot from *The Jetsons* and Jarvis from *Iron Man*.

One technology that surrounds you every day that you may not be aware of is data mining. Facebook and Google use it every day. When you get on the Internet, whether you're aware of this or not, they target you. They send things that you've already looked at, so it's specifically targeted toward your likes. Think of it in old school terms. If I want to date a certain person, I'd find out what their interests are in terms of food, sports teams, music, and movies. I'd then drop hints about these things to the person I like so that we had a common bond. I would be much more successful getting a date with this data—it might prevent me from asking them to a steak dinner when they are vegan. Data mining is collecting data and making it useful. Why see 1,000 ads for something you don't care about when data mining can help you see two ads that relate exactly to what you need?

Companies use data mining to learn your behaviors and patterns and reduce the amount of digital noise so you can purchase and buy from them faster and easier. That's their ultimate goal. If you've recently looked up how to quit smoking, this gets mined, and then you see ads scrolling on the side of Facebook for e-cigarettes, patches, and any other means to help you quit smoking. It's really quite brilliant but also a little unnerving.

If you have ever stayed at a Four Seasons Hotel, they're known for data mining as a way to improve customer service. It goes something like this: When a guest arrives, they have an idea of when they'll be coming. They use clues like a spy would figure out who they are and, if need be, the bellman will ask their name. The bellman then radios the front desk and lets them know Mr. Smith is coming. The guest is greeted with a warm, "Welcome to the Four Seasons, Mr. Smith. We're so glad you're staying with us." This process keeps happening throughout the whole stay.

How awesome would it be if your house could be as customer-focused as the staff at a Four Seasons Hotel? As I mentioned previously, please remember, not all technology involves fancy space-age computers; some technology that we already have access to needs to be better utilized.

The best way to explain the practical applications of data mining and artificial intelligence is to meet IBM's Watson. Watson is a supercomputer that can learn. One of the most

difficult things for a computer to do is to recognize natural language or human speech and
be able to respond appropriately to it. It has to
understand the context and the double mean-
ings that can be confusing even for us humans.
This is one of the main reasons why it was such
a breakthrough when Watson, in 2011, beat the
top Jeopardy winners on national TV.

In 2013, WellPoint, IBM's Watson, and
Memorial Sloan-Kettering Cancer Center
started working together on the first AI application for treatment decisions in lung cancer. WellPoint (Anthem) has utilized the supercomputer to increase patient outcomes and
reduce costs. While this may seem scary and
out of a sci-fi movie (the merger of the evil
health insurance company with the evil artificial intelligence computer), it's actually quite
the opposite. There's constant improvement to
Watson's knowledge base by participating doctors and nurses: "Watson's successful diagnosis
for lung cancer is 90%, compared to 50% for
human doctors."[7] Now, let me ask you a simple
question: If you or a loved one was thought to
have lung cancer, who would you rather get
your diagnosis from? A doctor who could diagnosis the patient as well as I could with the
toss of a coin or Watson, that's 90% accurate?

Earlier, better diagnosis not only improves outcomes but saves money. Now imagine this type of technology in senior living, especially memory care. Add in sensor technology to improve medication compliance and increased feedback for medical data so that you could know in an instant how Mom is doing.

To further the case for AI and Data Mining, one of the largest issues for healthcare is the immense amount of data constantly updated in the world of healthcare. Healthcare professionals are expected to read, analyze, and apply this information in the form of correct diagnoses and treatment for their patients. Watson, however, cannot only process one million books in seconds but can also take this information and apply it to help physicians with complex patient diagnoses.

Part of the reason Watson is able to happen is infinite computing. Infinite computing used to be only for the governments, for the big corporations. You needed enough money to build a supercomputer and then get a whole team to run it. Now you can rent vs. own. Basically, rent the supercomputer that someone else built, only use what you want or need, and only pay for that very small amount. That means you can have access to faster, cheaper, and more accessible computing.

Say you want to create a program, or somebody out there has a great idea. The individual can have access to the largest and fastest computer mainframes in the world and only pay for what they need. This is similar to movie stars renting a five-million-dollar necklace to wear to the Oscars to look fabulous. Things are going to continue to go faster and faster because now anyone has access to the mainframes. The super computers are getting even smaller. The fastest supercomputer in the world is in China, and it takes up half of a football field. There's new tech that will be released soon that will take all that computing power (half a football field) and shrink it to the size of a hot water tank for a lot less money. This change will open the doors for millions of new products to be economically developed. While it will be difficult to sort through the opportunities, imagine the time it took to read through the want ads in your local newspaper and search for your job description. Compare that to an online Craigslist post with all the filters and the

"30% of $2.3 trillion dollars spent on healthcare in the U.S. annually is wasted" per Reuters.[8]

ability to see 100 times the amount in exactly what you qualify for. Tools will be developed to help you find the solutions and the providers you need.

All of this supercomputing power, data mining, and sensors have allowed AI to move from science fiction to the nightly news. Meet Sophia, the world's first AI that's been given citizenship by Saudi Arabia. She's a humanoid social robot that can display 62 expressions and carry on conversations. She looks like a robot Audrey Hepburn and even seems to have a sense of humor. Hanson Robotics, along with Alphabet Inc. (Google's parent company), and Singularity Net designed the robot to be a companion for the elderly living alone or in nursing homes.

When researching Sophia, I found a weird, okay, creepy coincidence. Sophia doesn't seem like her name was randomly drawn out of a hat. Sophia in the Gnostic tradition means the human soul—let that sink in for a moment.

## Sensors

The technologies I use include Fitbits, Kardia, Nest, NuHeara IQbuds, Toto, and BioBidet toilets seats. These technologies help to keep me and my family healthy and increase independence. The Fitbits help to encourage us to move more and keep healthy. Kardia is an FDA approved EKG device (the size of a credit card) that you place your fingers on, and it will help to predict five days prior if you're going to have a heart attack or a stroke. I recommended it to someone who was healthy, and when they used it, they had triple bypass surgery the next day, which saved their life. Nest helps to regulate the temperature in the home and has cameras to ensure my grandma's safety when we aren't at home. IQbuds are earbuds that help to hear in noisy situations and connect directly with the TV or phone. The best technology in this category that we've used by far is the Bidet toilet seats. They are heated, antibacterial, wash your bum, and blow dry it. It's like living at the Ritz and allows you to maintain control of your privacy as you age.

Infrastructure limits technology adoption, adaptation, and access (AAA). Infrastructure Triple A, in this sense, is your worst enemy. In the early days of my career, even in skilled nursing, oxygen was hard-plumbed into the wall in a patient room as was nurse call (the device you use to call the nurse to come help you when you're in the hospital or nursing home). If you had a patient who needed oxygen, your options on a new building were to pay the excess cost of plumbing oxygen into every room to ensure flexibility, or there were only certain rooms with oxygen, which meant rejecting a patient if you didn't have what they needed. Now with portable oxygen machines, we don't even use it in a wall if someone needs it in a nursing home. Utilizing portable machines has allowed an estimated 2.5 million seniors in the U.S. alone to stay in their homes who would otherwise need senior living.[9]

Remember the old payphones you saw around town? These have gone by the wayside due to the easy access and low cost of cell phones. Cell phones are now priced so low they can cost about the same per month as two gallons of gas for your car. With Wi-Fi, you can even call free internationally with apps like Viber and WhatsApp.

The point is technology has finally broken through the infrastructure barrier. The best way to explain this is to imagine if all of our transportation was still restricted to trains. You could only go where the tracks were and when and where the train stopped. Now imagine your car, and it's not just a car, but it's one of those off-road cars you see on the commercials that allows you to go over boulders, through creeks, and still drive on streets. Freedom is endless as to where you can go, at what time, and what you want to see along the way. A whole new world is opened up for you to discover and possibly create better, faster, cheaper solutions. A mode of transportation without rails gives you complete control vs. being bound by what the train barons set as the schedule, path, and stops.

The Pro: The Boomers can get off the tracks and go wherever and whenever they want.

The Con: Knowing where you want to go can be extremely confusing and overwhelming without the right roadmap or guide.

Technology and the people who use it are now free from infrastructure. From trains to cars, phones to cell phones, cable to Wi-Fi, plumbed oxygen to O2- making machines, and hard-wired electricity to batteries—it's all portable, chargeable, and wireless, which gives us freedom to make choices.

Studies cite that 90% of us want to age in place in our homes; we don't want to move into senior housing.[10] The key is utilizing all the available infrastructure and free technology out there to stay in our homes longer, without whining, confusion, or thinking it's a fad. This type of thinking will only take away your freedom. My suggestion from personal experience is to select one or possibly two technologies that you find attractive and dip your toes in the water of technology. Learn what works and then, only then, add more.

Progress won't be stopped; it is like a river, and it will find a way to get downstream via the path of least resistance. Allow yourself to discover the possibilities with an open mind and learn what will best work for you.

Sensors are nothing new, and we don't even realize it, but we already live in a world of sensors. The canary in the coal mine was a sensor, letting the miners know when it was time to get out of the mine for safety's sake. The first cars were without sensors. Imagine no gas gauges or speedometers. Folks soon realized it was very helpful to know when you were going to run out of gas prior to doing so in the same way it was helpful to know when you needed oil, how fast you were going, and so on. I remember my first car was always on empty because the gas gauge was broken. I had to calculate what I thought was my gas mileage constantly. I was scared to drive on the highway for fear I'd miscalculated, and I'd be stuck. A gas gauge is such a basic thing, yet so valuable. Basic sensors are used on our hot water tanks, heating, and air-conditioning units in the form of a thermostat and temperature controls for the oven. Some sensors are for convenience, others for safety, and some to save energy. Safety sensors alert you to a fire, break-in, or a tornado coming. Energy sensors may turn off the lights after no movement for a period of time. Sensors are part of our everyday life in one form or another.

One of the simplest, most cost-effective sensor technologies on the market rarely gets discussed, and most people in the U.S. don't have them. I bet if I gave you hints, it wouldn't even cross your mind. I first discovered this technology in Japan 14 years ago. While visiting a public restroom, I was astonished to experience a heated toilet seat that had a night-light, was a Bidet and blow dryer, and was antimicrobial and antibacterial. This was a public restroom! In the U.S., I'm happy to see a toilet seat and toilet paper. While this story may seem crude to you, it shouldn't. Toileting is a major concern as you age. As soon as I got back home, I ordered a Japanese-style Bidet toilet seat with all the bells and whistles for my master bath.

A weird phenomenon started to happen at my home. No matter how many available bathrooms there were in my house, my children's friends, our family, and even guests would find themselves drawn like a magnet to my bathroom. At first, I thought it had to be my incredible taste ☺ or maybe the heated floor, but on further investigation, I discovered it was the toilet seat!

When we moved to a larger house to be able to have my parents and grandmother move in with us, my only requirement was that we'd have these Bidet toilet seats on every toilet so that I could have some privacy in my master bath. I have to admit I was also performing a home experiment. I've been pitching these seats to clients for 11 years with no luck and wanted to see firsthand how my parents and grandmother with early stage Alzheimer's would respond. I couldn't imagine having access to an available technology that would ensure the dignity and independence of my family and not using it.

The results speak for themselves. My 90 plus year-old grandmother didn't know what it was until it was explained to her, but now she loves it and also uses it as she put it "in-between showers" for her bottom. My parents, at 78 and 80, think it's the greatest thing since sliced bread and feel the need to tell all the family and their friends about it.

Who knew for less than $400 per toilet, I could make everyone so happy, increase their independence and dignity, and decrease the chances of having to assist in toileting in my home? It's a real win-win. They require no infrastructure and fit on top of an existing toilet. You simply hook the water up and then attach the electricity (which your bathroom should already have). The seat tends to be higher than a normal toilet seat, which is perfect as you age. With the night-light, it's easier to find the bathroom at night and increases the chances of a better hit ratio if you're male.

As a note, there are many different manufacturers and styles of these toilet seats. I've tried five different ones. Most allow you to control the seat and water temperature and then the intensity of the water, direction, and the intensity of the blow dryer. My recommendation would be to get the toilet seat that allows the controls to be mounted on the wall so that they don't accidentally get used to steady a family member or loved one. One final note is they are pressure-sensitive, meaning they'll not spray unless someone is sitting on the seat to avoid someone pushing the controls and water spraying everywhere. These have been tried and tested in other countries and have stood the test of public restrooms—I think it's high time we give them a shot in our homes.

Recently, we were all introduced to sensors integrated with the home environment through our smartphones. Users can integrate with

Nest to turn the heat up or down before they get home, lock doors, and even view who was at their door right on their phone or iPad. You could get a notification that your kids are home from school, they locked the house back up, and are safe and sound. This technology centers on peace of mind and has proven to have been what consumers were looking for.

In Chapter 9, we will dive into smart homes, but it's appropriate to talk about this now with our discussion on sensors.

Lowe's Home Improvement Smart Home Monitoring System (a sensor device) named Iris has taken this a step further by integrating a system that can be used with any smartphone and has a low monthly fee. Iris has kits that are divided into Safe and Secure, Comfort and

Control, and the Smart Kit. Care, which is an add-on to the system, is specifically for the senior in your home. The system will allow for you to set rules and let you know if Mom hasn't been in the refrigerator in the past 24 hours (or whatever time span you choose), which may indicate she's not doing well. Cameras can be used inside the home and operated remotely. A notification can be sent to you if the front door opens in the middle of the night.

The system is intended to provide greater independence and dignity, but it also keeps the children from worrying when, through sensors, they can know everything is fine or when the four-hour drive is necessary. It's Freedom and Confidence for the whole family. We will go into this in much more detail on smart homes with other technologies such as Ring, security devices, connected locks, and much more. The technology wouldn't be possible without AI, data mining, and sensors.

While this may all seem complicated, don't worry. As I always say, you don't have to know how to fix a car to drive one. Just be open to the freedom and confidence that technology will give you and then try it out. What's the worst that could happen?

# CHAPTER 5
## IOT (INTERNET OF THINGS) & CROWDSOURCING

**IOT?** **"What's this?"** I hear this question a lot. And if I said, "It's a global description of everything that's going on," would you wonder if I lost my mind or worry that you're about to? Sorry, but it is that big.

Think of it as everything that's *smart,* meaning: your phones, your tablets, your GPS, your TVs, and of course, your computers. And all of these smart things are making your physical environments *smart.*

Even your refrigerator, for instance, is becoming smarter and smarter. If you're not able to program it when you're reading this now, you might be able to in your very near future. Think of it like your fuel gauge on your car. When you get a smart refrigerator, it will know when you're low on eggs, milk, or any number of things. And then beyond that, it'll order those things for you, and it will set up your delivery time too.

Technology is seeping into everything we do and into the fabric of all our lives. I mean that very literally—the fabric of our clothes, our shoes, and our security.

While clothing that conceals cords and holds your smart devices have become popular, we will see in the next couple of years that our clothing will become a diagnostic computer of our health data—taking our heart rate, temperature, perspiration, EKG, sugar levels, O2, and sleep patterns. It will even predict when we may be getting sick in enough time to take supplements so that we don't get sick. Can you imagine your Victoria Secret bra as your personal health doctor and coach? Or your Hanes underwear letting you know that blood pressure has been climbing the last three days and you need to see a doctor? I know this sounds funny, but underwear is worn by most people daily, and you have less of them than you do your outer clothes, so it makes perfect sense to integrate health devices right there by your underwire.

**Crowdsourcing** is a fancy name for getting someone else to help you for a small price. It may be using Uber to get a ride to the doctors or pharmacy or finding someone to help clean, cook, take care of the yard, or pay the bills.

There are so many different options available now from the likes of: Task Rabbit, Fiverr, Uber, Lyft, and even good old-fashioned Craigslist. You can employ these folks safely and increase your freedom all the while paying for only what you need.

What's the difference between a taxi and a crowdsourced vehicle, besides the smell of every passenger who's sat in that back seat over the last three days? A company with employees runs the taxies; crowdsourced cars are folks using their car and a smartphone to pick up extra money. The real difference is, in this example, the Uber driver can rate you low if you're a jerk, and if you get too many of these low ratings, you'll no longer be able to take advantage of working with the crowd. I actually have a friend that was banned. You also rate the Uber driver, so if he was rude, you can let them know, and if they get too many bad ratings, they'll no longer be able to drive. Another feature is that all the payments are done through the app, so no whipping out your credit card and having the taxi driver tell you he only accepts cash. The last item of attraction and why I've switched to a no taxi policy is that I can see the Uber driver on my phone, what he looks like, where his car is, can track him along the way, and call or text him if needed. There's comfort and confidence that he's on his way, even if he's taking a bit longer because I can see on the app that he's just stuck at the light.

Lyft has also developed a program for seniors who need more help getting in and out of the car or need someone to wait for them at doctors' appointments—a pretty neat solution the crowd has provided with zero employees as drivers and zero cars.

Crowdsourcing seems like a new concept, but it's really quite an old one. Before technology, when it was time to harvest the crops or build a barn, family, friends, and neighbors would join forces to help one another to get large amounts of work completed that would otherwise be impossible. These *crowds* would come together for the greater good, or crops would go bad, or help wouldn't come when you needed your barn raised.

Now with harvest machines and other technologies, we're no longer dependent upon our family, friends, and neighbors to bring in the harvest or raise our barns, but we have new problems—more work than we can handle and micro-expertise that's required to build and create. The solution to these new problems comes in the form of crowdsourcing. With access that's now been created through the Internet, we instantly can hire minions or micro-experts from anywhere in the world for a fraction of the cost previously available. Angie's List is a great example of crowdsourcing. You can hire folks for tasks, and their work is reviewed by the buyer, so you know they accomplish what they say they will. Not only do you have access to a crowd of potential minions, but you become a part of the crowd by providing feedback on the services you bought.

Airbnb is another great example of crowdsourcing. Basically, you can rent your home or a room in your home on a website called Airbnb. I've rented homes in Cinque Terra, Rome, Croatia, N.Y.C., Toronto, Barcelona, Scottsdale, and more. I find them wonderful, less expensive than a hotel, and in real neighborhoods. It's probably not the thing you want to do if you're attending a conference and need to have direct access, but if you want to get to know a city, it's the way to go. The rating system works similar to Uber, so don't trash the place or you won't be able to rent again. I can typically cut my costs in a city by half using Airbnb.

Now that we understand the basics of crowd-sourcing, let's get into the specifics and review different types, how you access it, and give you some examples. Crowdsourcing takes advantage of connecting specific experts or interested parties to solve challenges in either a competitive or collaborative format.

Crowdsourcing has become huge in the fields of task-related work and specialty creative work, such as graphic design, video, social media, writing, and coding. Companies such as Fiverr, Task Rabbit, Upwork, 99designs, Crowdspring, Waze, Lego Ideas, and Crowdmed are just a few and have been growing exponentially year after year.

I use these companies on a daily basis and save approximately 90% on costs I would normally spend if we hadn't crowdsourced. Don't get me wrong—crowdsourcing requires your effort and engagement, but once you get the hang of it, it's like having a clone. For example, I used to spend anywhere from $2,500 to $4,000 for logo development. I would get two or three versions, and these would be in that particular graphic artist's style. If the artist was not getting what I was trying to accomplish in look or feel, I would be out the money and have to research and find another designer and then start the process all over again and spend another $2,500 to $4,000.

When I had a client that was starting a new senior living company, we used Crowdspring to create a contest to develop a name for their company and ensure it was not used by others. The contest cost $239 and gave us 434 entries to choose from! Then we launched a contest to develop the logo for that same company through 99designs for $499. We received 283 entries (different designs). Compare this to two or three versions from one graphic artist, and you start to see my point. I had 93 different designers competing for the $499!

How it works is you describe in detail what you're looking for, and then designers, without being paid, send you their designs; you give feedback and then select a final round of the top entries. All the way through, the designs improve based on your feedback. Sometimes, a designer watches vs. participates and then jumps in close to the end with an awesome design, similar to how you bid at an auction.

It's very much like the show, *The Voice*. At the end, you select the winner, and they transfer the logo and all of its rights over to you. One of the largest benefits that I've found in using this format, besides the costs, is what I had in my head as the right direction didn't end up being the winner. By seeing so many different options, it helps you to really understand what you like and don't like with little risk. The book cover for *BOOM* was crowdsourced, and then I ran a Facebook contest to see which cover of the 12 finalists everyone liked the best, and I did it all for under $500!

Another example is transcription. When we have a conference call meeting with a client, for $5.00 on Fiverr, it can be transcribed and ready to be put into meeting minutes. I don't know about you, but my team can't transcribe, and it costs us a lot more than $5.00 to type up the audio from a half-hour meeting. My last personal example for you is Fiverr. For $5.00, I was able to have my website analyzed, and I found out I had tons of broken links that we were unaware of.

You may wonder how this is all possible. Well, some people do it to get their foot in the door with you, and for others, it's a way to make additional income after their day job. For others, it is their actual income. While $5.00 in the U.S. will hardly buy you lunch at a fast-food restaurant, five U.S. dollars is the daily wage for some countries and $499 for one contest equates to their typical monthly wage. One of the best ways to see if you could utilize crowdsourcing is to have your team list out all their activities in detail and then see which ones you could outsource through crowdsourcing.

One of the basic crowdsourcing platforms is called Task Rabbit. It's basically a handyman on steroids. You sign up, then create a task— let's say bring the Christmas decorations down from the attic. It will then give you profiles of people that can do the task, their ratings and references, their availability, and their hourly rate. Then you choose one. It's as easy as that.

I just hired someone to clean up all my garden beds after winter. It was a huge relief as I've been traveling and couldn't seem to get to it. Their network is so large that IKEA, the furniture company, recently purchased them as they noticed that seniors liked their furniture but hated putting it together. Now IKEA has a network of Task Rabbits all over the world who will do it for you. They don't have to deal with it, and the best part—they get more sales.

Uber, Airbnb, and Task Rabbit are typically cheaper than hiring a company as these individuals have no overhead, 401K, insurance, HR manager, etc. They're barebones on the corporate side, and you and I get to take advantage of it.

Essentially, there are three formats that prevail:

1.  Creative Competitions
2.  Bid for Task
3.  Reward-Based

**<u>Creative competitions</u>** work great for when you need a logo developed, website designed, article written, or software developed. These systems work by signing up to a provider and basically placing a want ad for the work you need completed with as much detail as possible. You can either choose a site where you select how much you're willing to pay, then the creator submits their work and competes for the winning bid, or you allow creators to bid on the work. Then you choose the creator that best matches your price point and has the background or portfolio you like the best. The key is feedback: Creators need constant feedback to improve, which is easy to do through the secure portal of the crowdsourcing company you have selected.

The upside is that instead of going with your local marketing company and getting the same designer with the same ideas, you could have 60 different designers from all over the world providing you with fresh and sometimes off-base designs. You're able to shorten the design process substantially and reduce your cost. Most crowd creators have a primary job, so this is to make extra money, to be creative, or build a reputation.

Utilizing these services can improve your look to the community and keep your events fresh and exciting, all at a low cost.

On a larger scale, The XPRIZE, created by Peter Diamandis, showed the world that competition creates solutions that were otherwise thought impossible. With NASA downsizing its program and retiring the shuttle, Peter decided to launch a competition similar to the one that Charles Lindbergh and the *Spirit of St. Louis* won by making the first solo non-stop flight from New York to Paris. This contest changed how the world viewed air travel forevermore. Peter created a contest to get a vehicle into space for $100K with three people, and that could replicate the trip in two weeks to prove durability for ten million dollars. Teams from all over the world entered the contest. 26 teams entered and spent over $100 million! Private space travel was born for a fraction of the investment and time that NASA could have done it for.

While Peter has created many other XPRIZE contests, the one to watch for in Well Care living is the QualComm Tricorder XPRIZE. The QualComm Tricorder XPRIZE will soon be awarded, and its main goal is to put minor health diagnosis in the hands of the consumers at a higher accuracy rate than that of the current medical profession. Once this takes place, senior living will have to run to catch up to the level of quality and speed in regard to how fast the general public will be able to self-diagnose.

**Bid for Task** works differently than the creative competitions we've discussed. Basically, it can be anything from hiring a handyman, to organizing your bills, to ensuring quality assurance programs.

You can even make money doing bid for task. Let's say a company wants to shop their competition and see what someone who isn't an expert would find, in multiple cities, without hiring a large secret shopper company that would entail a large contract and travel and reimbursable expenses. They could hire you as one of their secret shoppers on a task site and create a template for exactly what you needed to do, where, and how you were to report back to the company.

There's one company that will pay you to send inventory data back to them via your camera phone in stores you already shop in. Let's say you're a customer of a national drug store chain, and on your visit, you notice they're out of your favorite lipstick. You pull up their app and snap a photo of the shelf. You then notice that the cough drops are in the wrong location, so you snap a photo and upload it to their app. Kids earn $80 a week through direct deposit into their accounts for simply being aware in places they already visit and providing valuable asset management data in real-time to the store.

Or say you want to have an engraving done, custom cookie cutters made, a phone answering machine message recorded by Elmer Fudd or James Earl Jones, etc. There are millions of people that have used task crowdsourcing to do these gigs. Easyshift and Field Agent are great sites for this type of work.

**Reward-Based Crowdsourcing** can be more altruistic and collaborative, but in nature, it's about the work, not a monetary reward.

You could be collaborating with the crowd to identify a DNA sequencing to help find a cure for cancer or contributing to open-source code development for new software. This category sometimes gets mixed in with gamification and data mining, which we will discuss in greater detail in those chapters. The point is that if you have a problem and want to solve it, don't try to do it by yourself or just with your team; rather, allow others to work with you.

An example of reward-based crowdsourcing is Cellvation[11] (gamified crowdsourcing), a project that was completed in 24 hours to see the possibilities of what kind of impact a reward-based crowdsourcing app could have. Cellvation states that 428 million hours are spent playing online games each day. Their idea was to play a game and save lives in the process.

Cellvation decided to figure out how to use gamification and crowdsourcing to solve malaria and cancer. Every day there are 600,000 cases of malaria. It takes 30 minutes for a clinician to look at a slide. That's 300,000 man-hours spent every day just on diagnosing malaria. Malaria is easily resolved if it's able to be diagnosed properly and quickly. To further complicate the issue, most of the cases are in Africa where there aren't as many clinicians as in developed nations.

The solution is to play a game where you identify malaria. With 22 amateur people looking at the slide, they can get 99% accuracy, and these people are just having fun playing the game. After one minute of training, they can go down to 13 people and get a 99% accuracy rate.

It's the same thing with cancer. Based on my extensive research, prescreening of cancer is said to help prevent the deaths of somewhere between 3 to 35% of Americans. Even if they can get prescreened, there's just not enough time or clinicians to do the prescreening.

Imagine if we could potentially avoid between 3 to 35% of cancer fatalities through prescreening, just by playing a game. There's no money involved, but there are rewards (gaming rewards), fun, and the knowledge that you're doing something good.

Almost everyone I know has lost someone to cancer . . . 609,640 people are estimated to have died of cancer in the U.S. in 2018. 3% equates to 18,289 lives who could have been saved on the low side and 213,374 lives on the high side of 35%! How awesome would this be? Not to mention the savings in medical costs to the families and system.

Foldit, on the other hand, isn't a test but a real game that's helping to save lives. Drugs get tested on computer simulations of human proteins (amino acids), and in a lot of cases, the limitations of computers to fold these proteins makes this a better task for humans (score one for the humans). Per Foldit's website, protein structure is the key:

> *Protein structure prediction: As described above, knowing the structure of a protein is key to understanding how it works and to targeting it with drugs. A small protein can consist of 100 amino acids, while some human proteins can be huge (1,000 amino acids). The number of different ways even a small protein can fold is astronomical because there are so many degrees of freedom. Figuring out which of the many, many possible structures is the best one is regarded as one of the hardest problems in biology today, and current methods take a lot of money and time, even for computers. Foldit attempts to predict the structure of a protein by taking advantage of humans' puzzle-solving intuitions and having people play competitively to fold the best proteins.[12]*

The concept of dealing with disease and drug creation is very similar to a war strategy. The more you have intel on the enemy, know where they are, how many troops they have, and what type of flexibility, weapons, and weaknesses they may have, the better chance you have at winning the war. Folding proteins helps scientists better understand how proteins function, and they can then design strategies or drugs to combat them if they've gone to the dark side and now cause disease.

Per Foldit's site, they explain the relevance to not only cancer but also Alzheimer's, which most of us are all too familiar with:

- **Cancer:** Cancer is very different from HIV in that it's usually our proteins to blame, instead of proteins from an outside invader. Cancer arises from the uncontrolled growth of cells in some part of our bodies, such as the lungs, breasts, or skin. Ordinarily, there are systems of proteins that limit cell growth, but they may be damaged by things like UV rays from the sun or chemicals from cigarette smoke. But other proteins, like **p53 tumor suppressor**, normally recognize the damage and stop the cell from becoming cancerous—unless they too are damaged. In fact, damage to the gene for p53 occurs in about half of human cancers (together with damage to various other genes).
- **Alzheimer's:** In some ways, Alzheimer's is the disease most directly caused by

proteins. A protein called **amyloid-beta precursor protein** is a normal part of healthy, functioning nerve cells in the brain. But to do its job, it gets cut in two pieces, leaving behind a little scrap from the middle—amyloid-beta peptide. Many copies of this peptide (short protein segment) can come together to form clumps of protein in the brain. Although many things about Alzheimer's are still not understood, it is thought that these clumps of protein are a major part of the disease.

Why does this matter to you? Most of the major breakthroughs in medicine have come from crowd collaboration of researchers sharing their breakthroughs and then playing one idea off of the other to create a better solution. Now that the Internet no longer limits researchers to geographic barriers, the rate of collaboration has gone up exponentially.

To close out this chapter, I would like to provide you with some examples of Crowdsourcing that can help you age with Freedom. Pick one or two and start experimenting with them. Worse case, you don't use them again. Best case, you just made your life easier and better.

o **Angie's List**—Listing, somewhat like the Better Business Bureau, but with real feedback from customers instantly. You can hire anything from a roofer to an electrician.

o **Task Rabbit**—Micro tasks that you need completed locally, could be trim the hedges or clean out the basement. You sign up through the app, list your task, and they'll match you up with a provider, then you choose the best one that fits your schedule, budget, and meets your rating. You pay through the app so you can avoid that "Where's my money?" awkwardness. You can also rate them similar to Angie's List.

o **Creative**
  - **99designs**—Graphic artists from around the world at your disposal for a fraction of the cost. Let's say you want a logo made up for your family reunion . . . done! Or you want to have unique Christmas cards made . . . done! They use a contest method so you'll get hundreds of entries for your agreed price, and you just pick the one you like the best.
  - **Fiverr**—This crowdsourcing app is a ton of fun! You can hire someone to

do about anything (legal) for five U.S. dollars and up. Leave a video message for someone in a famous voice . . . done! I made my audiobook through Fiverr and have also had handwritten thank you cards made. This is a very creative way to find unique crowd-sourcing opportunities.

o **Chauffeur Services**
  - **Uber**—Like a taxi, but there's no company. You log in to an app and tell them where you want to go, and they match you with a driver. You pay through the app and rate each other. They just partnered with GrandPad.
  - **Lyft**—Same concept as Uber. Also partnered with GrandPad. GrandPad is the smartest, simplest, and safest way to connect seniors with their loved ones so they never miss another memory.

o **Vitalitix**—They call it crowd-caring. The platform provides three-way communication between social angels (seniors, caregivers, and community). It also connects volunteers from other networks.

o **Honor Mobile App**—App helps you stay in touch, informed, and in control of your loved one's care.

o **Airbnb**—Homes and rooms in homes rented all over the world at much lower rates than a hotel. There are typically no services. It's more like staying at a condo on the beach (You have to clean up and make your bed.), but the experience of staying in incredible spots that are less commercial is wonderful. Like Uber and Lyft, you rate the renter, and they rate you. This helps the renters to improve and keeps jerks from trashing a home.

o **Home Delivery Services for Food**—Dominos Pizza, Donato's, and other fast food restaurants have been bringing food to our doors for years. However, utilizing the crowd and leveraging the Uber and Lyft drivers, you can now order food on various platforms (apps, websites, etc.) and have a variety of food delivered to your door.

▪ **Grubhub**—App where you can order food from various restaurants, and they'll use Uber or Lyft drivers to deliver it to you. All money is exchanged through the app. Think meals on wheels, but you can have anything you want from the best restaurants. All you have to do is order and pay.

- **Doordash**—Similar to Grubhub, but it may have different restaurants.
- **Uber Eats**—Uber's food delivery app
- **Cafe Courier**—Similar to Grubhub and Doordash
- **Skipthedishes**—Similar to Grubhub and Doordash
- **Bitesquad**—Similar to Grubhub and Doordash
- **ClusterTruck**—When you have family, office, or friends that want to order food but pay individually, ClusterTruck allows you to link the group. Then everyone goes into the website or app to order what they want, and they pay individually all through the platform. So there's no gathering up of money, or Bob realizes he doesn't have enough money (Who invited Bob anyway?) or the issue of dealing with five different credit cards and getting it all right before your delivered food is cold. It's a brilliant concept, and we use it all the time at work.
- **Seamless**—Similar to Grubhub and Doordash
- **Postmates**—Similar to Grubhub and Doordash

- **Delivery.com**—Similar to Grubhub and Doordash
- **EAT24**—Similar to Grubhub and Doordash
- **Foodler**—Similar to Grubhub and Doordash
- **Orderup**—Similar to Grubhub and Doordash
- **Munchery**—Locally sourced food that's prepared by chefs and can be ordered when you're ready to eat or in advance
- **Caviar**—Similar to Grubhub and Doordash
- **Meal Prep Food**—Another new category that's popped up that seems new but is just a reboot of Swanson's. These companies are providing food packages that have all the food prep completed and all the ingredients included, and you only have to cook them. You save time not going to the grocery store and get high quality recipes and fresh food.
  - **HelloFresh**—Not cooked.
  - **Blue Apron**—Not cooked.

- **Vital Choice**—Not cooked, seafood, organic fare, and supplements from wild fisheries and farms.
- **Plated**—Not cooked.

o **Aging Care Help** that may not be crowdsourcing, but they're worth a mention:

- **Molly Maids**—You're probably already aware of this, you can outsource your cleaning. Molly Maids provides the talent, and you provide the money and the dirt.
- **Home Care Assistance**—The only home care solution offering a balanced approach to longevity, emphasizing health, engagement, and purpose. They also just partnered with GrandPad.
- **Other Homecare Help:**
  - **Senior at Home Care**
  - **Senior Helpers**
  - **Visiting Angels**
  - **Right at Home**
  - **Comfort Keepers**
- **House Call Dentists**—Providing individualized dental care how, when, and where you choose
- **Silver Bills**—They take over the burden of paying bills.

# CHAPTER 6
## 3D PRINTING & ON DEMAND MANUFACTURING

Did you know that 3D printing has been around for quite some time? You may have seen it and not even noticed it. In 1999 (over 20 years ago), Align Technology changed the world of orthodontics with Invisalign and the technology of 3D printing. This opened up an entire market of adults who wanted braces but were embarrassed of the look. The clear orthodontic trays are manufactured by using 3D printed models representing the desired position your teeth will move. After a 3D scan is made of the wearer's teeth, a computer simulation creates a series of clear orthodontic appliances (retainers) to move the teeth over time.

While you may have been aware that Invisalign clear braces are custom manufactured using 3D printing, you'll be shocked to know companies are now printing organs, human tissue, leather, food, hearing aids, dentures, Barbie clothing, cars, drum kits, candy, and metal.

One of the most interesting aspects of 3D printing is that it is now possible to print multiple materials together. This allows for less assembly and faster printing.

Nanoprinting is also possible. The width of a human hair would be considered large in terms of Nano.

Nanoprinting is making it possible to not only make computers smaller and smaller, but the detail and microscopic scale allow scientists to nanoprint lattices that can grow living cells. What if organ transplant was a thing of the past, and you could grow what you needed from your DNA with no fear of your body rejecting it? Bad burns or the need for skin could be grown and then patched in like a scene from

Frankenstein except it would be all you and no one would ever know.

Another enormous implication is prototyping. It used to be that to take an idea to reality, you'd have to design it and hope it was perfect and then have a mold created or a die-cast. This could cost tens of thousands of dollars. If you needed to tweak it, you'd have to wait until you made your money on the first production run and then make another mold.

**3D Systems can create a geometric shape within a geometric shape within a geometric shape...well, you get the point. Not only the complexity but that nothing has to be punched out or assembled is amazing!**

As you can see, this kept a lot of great inventions from talented inventors from being able to compete with the big boys because the startup costs were large and risky. This was similar to computing power that we discussed in the previous chapter.

Now you can have an idea, create a computer model for it, print it out, and then tweak it hundreds of times before you have ever reached the cost of making a mold.

Dentures can also be 3D printed. I'm sure this will be hard to imagine, but humor me. Your dad loses his dentures, and instead of having to go to the dentist and go through the entire process again, you had a previous flash drive. You upload the prescription file to the cloud, and all you have to do is print the new set!

*Adidas is a trademark of the Adidas Group. Used with permission.*

Adidas (shown above) has 3D printed athletic shoes. Nike and Reebok also do. Reebok and Under Armour are hitting the ground running in combining sensors or what they're terming "wearables" with 3D printing. Some companies are printing shoes and shipping them to you after you custom-design them on a site, while others like United Nude are printing them right in the store.

Why is this relevant to Baby Boomers? Custom, Custom, Custom. Imagine going to a store where you're custom fitted for all your wearable tech—earbuds, hearing enhancers, perfect fit orthotics for your knees or feet issues, glasses, etc.—all produced while you whisk away to the nearest Starbucks for your double espresso latte.

For example, our ears continue to grow, and this leads to one of the major complaints about hearing enhancement devices—they aren't comfortable. This discomfort is usually due to our ears changing, and yet we wear a device that fit us two years prior. Imagine being a teenager and wearing the same clothes for several years during your growth spurt. I imagine Jethro from the TV show *Beverly Hillbillies* and his pants. For that matter, imagine wearing the same size shoe you did when you were 6. Up until now, due to the cost and the rigid materials needed to last 10 years in the production of hearing aids, you'd need to spend $4,000 every two years to get your hearing aids custom fitted so they would be comfortable due to the changes in your ears.[13]

What do 3D printing, Michelin Star chefs, and Baby Boomers have in common?

As we age, swallowing can be more difficult (dysphagia), especially for those with Alzheimer's/ Dementia. What's even more challenging is that the harder it is to swallow, the more pills it seems we need to take. While taking your pills with apple juice will help them go down easier than water, it can still be a huge issue.

From my experience, when I first started working in senior living, I was shocked to see that when a resident had difficulty swallowing, the standard method of operation was to take what the meal was for the day and throw it into a blender. Then the resident drank their hamburger. To me, it was much worse than baby food, as baby food usually sticks to veggies and fruits. From a dignity standpoint, it seemed like we could be doing much better.

My family also has issues swallowing, which I found out when my grandmother moved in with me. I started having issues and went to the doctor. Apparently, your throat can narrow as you age. My grandmother and some of her sisters even had theirs stretched—sounds pleasant and something to look forward to. I had no idea how common this was, but as with most things, when you're personally affected, you notice more and try to find solutions. Really, this is the purpose of the book: how my desire to change, how I age, and those I love can help others. It's that simple.

When I asked, what do 3D printing, Michelin Star chefs, and Baby Boomers living have in common, you may not have thought *food*. Molecular gastronomy and the foodie culture have merged these all together and allowed us to be creative in our cooking, reduce risks, increase independence, and have food prepared in a way that you only get in a 5-Star Michelin restaurant, all in our home. GE's 2025 Home of the Future positions the 3D food printer as being in everyone's kitchens in the same way as we have microwaves.

There are a couple of 3D food-printing companies in Europe making a huge impact by bringing this technology to our homes with a focus on aging in place.

Biozoon out of Germany isn't only focused on creating foods that look good and taste great but are also easy to swallow. They have lines that create molecular gastronomy and fancy cocktails. Molecular gastronomy is basically "food science"—a modern form of cooking that you'd see at a very fancy restaurant or on a TV show like *Iron Chef.* If you're still unfamiliar with what I'm referring to, it's things like oak moss vapor, liquid pea sphere, transparent raviolis, etc. This innovative cuisine has birthed new appliances to merge 3D printing and food into everyday cooking. It's really not that amazing when you think about it. If you have ever watched the Discovery Channel TV show *How It's Made,* you have seen all kinds of food being 3D printed, from Cheetos to the beloved Easter Peeps. This technology is now becoming available to our homes.

Molecular gastronomy is basically "food science"; it's a modern form of cooking that you'd see at a very fancy restaurant or on a TV show like *Iron Chef.* This image is of a liquid pea sphere offered at a high-end restaurant.

The ability to deconstruct food and then reconstruct it has been mastered with these machines, allowing chefs to reimagine what food should look and feel like.

It's not all Europeans who are on the cutting edge of 3D printed food. When I met Randi Zuckerberg (sister of Mark Zuckerberg of Facebook), she'd just started test kitchens to help kids get involved in technology. It's called Sue's Kitchen. It's basically a mashup of technology and food to teach kids and their families that tech is more than just staring at a screen. It can be interactive and fun. They can 3D print desserts or code with candy; not sure what that is, but I'm sure the kids get it. It's also not in N.Y.C. or L.A. as you might expect, it's in Chattanooga, Tennessee. When a Zuckerberg gets involved in a technology, I think it's safe to say it's here to stay and will only get bigger and better.

Another company out of Spain called Natural Machines has a 3D food printing machine called the Foodini that they want to be in everyone's home. They have created Foodini to be able to handle high-volume restaurants (professional kitchens) as well as a single user. The machine is still a bit pricey (around $4,000) but aims to be as popular as the microwave in the future.

While writing my first book, I was able to interview Lynette Kucsma, the CMO and co-founder of Natural Machines. The following is our conversation, and it should answer the majority of your questions regarding this new technology and how 3D food printing will be applicable.

Lynette explained how it all works:

> *Basically, the way Foodini works is there's room for up to five food capsules to put in the machine at one time. The size of the machine is about the same as a larger microwave. You can put in whatever food you want, whatever combination to accommodate for taste or for medical needs. It's all very fresh food. The texture of the food doesn't have to be all baby food formats, if you will. I'll use an example of a tomato sauce. It can't be too watery, but it cannot be overly chunky because then it's going to clog up the system, and it won't print. But you could have pieces of basil or seasoning at that spine.[14]*

I asked her if it has entertainment value or is fun to use. It reminded me of how much fun I had when I was little with my Easy Bake Oven.

Lynette responded:

> *Both. Let's say you want to print a spinach quiche in the shape of Batman. You can find a Batman logo from the Internet, pull it*

*down, and it makes the shape. I have two kids, a 4-year-old and a 6-year-old, and it's one of my ways to engage them in cooking because they know it's kind of like playing a game at the end where you're choosing your shapes and printing and then you have different shapes. And as you know, we use our eyes as much as our mouth in enjoying food.*

As you can see, 3D printing for dentures, hearing aids, clothing, prototypes, crafts, and now, food will revolutionize how everything is made. We're entering another industrial revolution, but it will be where we can print whatever we want, whenever we want. If you wear glasses, imagine printing out new frames and popping in your lenses if you want a new look or you broke the frames. Bill Gates imagined that every home would have a computer 40 years ago, and most of us would have said he was nuts. Then imagine a printer in your home. Remember when there were stores that developed photos? Now you either upload them to the cloud to be printed or print them yourself at home.

Everything is changing exponentially. They say if you want to see if a technology will be adopted quickly into the mass market, look at your kids and teens. If it weren't for teens, cell phones would have taken much longer to hit critical mass. Right now, little girls are printing their clothing and accessories for their Barbie dolls with their 3D printers. You can find files to download for free or purchase on many sites such as Pinterest.

Below are some 3D printers to look into:

- LulzBot Mini
- XYZprinting da Vinci Mini
- New Matter MOD-t
- Sindoh 3DWOX DP200 3D Printer
- FlashForge Finder
- ROBO 3D R1 +Plus
- Zeus All-In-One 3D
- MOD-t 3D
- MakerBot Replicator
- Ultimaker 3
- Formlabs Form 2
- Routine 3D printing

These printers range anywhere from $199.00 to thousands. Think of them like your desk jet printer you have in your house; the real cost is in the printing fiber, just like ink. Some use different types of materials to print with, and some have better prebuilt files you can download, modify, and have fun with.

Why does this matter to you? 45%[15] of Boomers consider themselves entrepreneurs—not just the traditional entrepreneur that does business consulting or owns the local pizza shop. Creating and crafting can improve your quality of life by connection, increased mind work, and learning new things.

Your imagination is now 3D, and unlike sculpting, you don't have to be a great artist—you can crowdsource that. Imagine you have a great idea for a new and improved gardening or cooking tool you'd like to have, but no one sells anything close to what you want.

You can sketch it up, crowdsource a person to build it in CAD (computer aided design—it's what I use in interior design) for under $25.00, then tweak it, and upload the file to have it printed for five bucks! Delivered to your doorstep is your new prototyped tool, ready for you to test and tweak, and if it's a hit with the neighbors and family, you might just be the next millionaire on *Shark Tank* or the *Home Shopping Network*.

# CHAPTER 7
## ROBOTS, EXOSKELETONS, & DRONES

## Robots

Technically, Alexa is a robot, but the robots I'm referring to here are more the physical kind of robot. We have two in our home, but we could have more. Right now, you can have your grass cut, pool cleaned, floors swept, and have a companion pet easily in your home with little tech knowledge. These are very *plug and play*, which basically means they're as simple as a vacuum cleaner or microwave to operate. You plug them in, and then you play, meaning you let them do their thing.

We use one of our robots, "the Dolphin," to clean the pool, and as a result, we've cut our pool service bills by 75%. Plus, the Dolphin always shows up on time, never complains, doesn't have the plumber's crack (The pool boy never looks the way he does in the movies.) and does a fantastic job. We also use a companion cat and dog to keep my grandmother company when we aren't in the room—she's 96 with dementia. I was a bit skeptical on companion pets at first, but she loves them and chats up a storm with the cat and dog. It's amazing that robots can provide comfort, connection, and safety for very little cost.

Robots range in everything from a Roomba vacuum introduced in 2002 that can vacuum your floors to those we see in manufacturing that have taken beer manufacturing facilities from hundreds of employees down to 10. Robotics is just another technology that depends on a multitude of other technologies. Robotics utilizes data mining, artificial intelligence, sensors, and infinite computing.

Whenever robots are brought up, ultimately, the discussion begins about the issue of unemployment when the robots take over all of our jobs. While it is true that robots are automating factories and taking on more mundane household tasks, people will need to retrain in more creative jobs that require human touch or complex problem solving. Let's be honest. Do you miss having to grow all your food and kill your meat? These processes have become automated first by other humans, then factories, and now robots. While most people today couldn't grow their food, this was not the case in the 1940s. There will always be purposeful work that needs to be done; it just may look differently. The great news is the tasks most of us dislike, like vacuuming the floor, cleaning the dishes, etc., will be taken over by robots leaving us more time to be creative and spend time with those we love.

Per Wikipedia:

> In 2012, the growth of robotic lawn mower sales was 15 times that of the traditional styles. With the emergence of smart phones

*some robotic mowers have integrated fea-*
*tures within custom apps to adjust settings*
*or scheduled mowing times and frequency,*
*as well as manually control the mower with*
*a digital joystick.*[16]

Jibo is touted as the "world's first family robot," which is a table-top robot that can be your phone, talk to you, help you find items on the Internet, remind you of your schedule, take family photos, act as a companion as it recognizes you and greets you, read you a story or the newspaper, etc.

Siri from iPhone has lessened our apprehension of talking to non-live beings to the point that we're comfortable with them materializing into an actual thing that we coexist with in our homes and work.

To understand how far these technologies have been developed, I'm going to take you to a place that may seem farfetched, but I can assure you it's real. At the 1939 World's Fair in New York, they had to show fairgoers a TV with a clear screen in the back so that folks could see the inner workings of the TV because they felt they were being tricked. In the same way, I'm going to pull back the curtain and show you what the world has been working on the last several decades. It is my hope that you'll recognize robots are here to stay, will be integrated into our lives in the very near future, and are here to help us vs. the ones from the sci-fi movies that we've seen where they come to kill us!

Darpa is the government's research and development (R&D) arm that helps to further along technologies that have real-world applications in the U.S. military. The robots that I'll be discussing through Darpa are public knowledge, and the implications are far-reaching. They basically host contests that are very specific to what they want to accomplish, and several companies will develop technologies to try to win the contract (Did you see the word "contests?"). That's correct. They use crowdsourcing—to accomplish what would either take too long to develop on their own or would be too expensive—through contests similar to the XPRIZE that we discussed in a previous chapter.

While I'm sure they have many top-secret technologies and contests, the ones that are public are incredible. A few of these awesome inventions follow. (I highly recommend you watch the YouTube videos on these; the links are provided in the resource section of the book.)

- Handle—A 2-legged robot with wheels as feet that can do backflips
- SpotMini—He kind of looks like a dog and a sock puppet merged. He can empty the dishwasher, open doors, go up and down steps, and is being researched as a robot that could replace your servants at home . . . okay, you're probably like me and don't have servants. But the point is that SpotMini could help get all the chores done at home and save you time, much like the vacuum cleaner did almost 100 years ago.
- Cheetah—A 4-legged robot that can run 29 miles per hour. Just fun to look up on Youtube.
- BigDog—A robot pack mule from Boston Dynamics (purchased by SoftBank Group in 2017)
- Petman and the later version, Atlas— Humanoid Robot that can perform search and rescue.
- SandFlea—Think of the remote-controlled cars you give as a kid's present. Now attach a camera and have it jump 30' straight up into the air.
- RHex—Similar to SandFlea, RHex is a 6-legged remote-controlled device the size of a toy car that's used to gain intel

safely. Some of these technologies are being used as in-home security guards for when your home or away, monitoring to make sure that no one breaks in and all is well.

These are just fun and real examples of robot technology that will open you up to where we're headed. Do I think I'll have a SpotMini in my home soon? Not likely, but in 10 years, it's a definite possibility that as I age, robots will be serving me.

These robots are created to save lives by accessing hostage situations, gaining intelligence, conducting search and rescue, and performing mission critical operations. While anyone could argue that the government could create an army of robots to use against us, we also understand that the term robot = mechanical or virtual artificial **agent** per Wikipedia and basically means that we're utilizing technology to perform tasks that are simple, repetitive, dangerous, or require immense strength. Imagine that your son or daughter (who is serving in the military) is able to deploy a robot that's operated by them from the safety of a base in the United States. They're able to perform a military action instead of being in "theatre," as it is called, when you're in the war zone. This is the intention of the technology: to keep our servicemen and women safe while they're protecting our freedom.

Manufacturing has been using robotics for decades. Now it is utilizing not only robots but also exoskeletons to reduce the impact on the human body when a process still requires the intelligence or nuance of a human to perform the task at the highest level. China is engaging in the use of exoskeletons for aging workers. As you can imagine, as you age, what was once easy is now harder and harder for the body, forcing some to retire earlier than they want, due to safety issues. Now factories will be able to maintain their more seasoned, experienced employees, by utilizing an exoskeleton to allow them to continue to do their jobs like they did when they were in their 20s.

Think of technology as the character Alfred (Batman's manservant), and you're Bruce Wayne, a.k.a. Batman. Alfred was a loyal servant who tended to Bruce's every need. He woke Bruce up, reminded him of the important things he had to do, and generally kept him on track in a busy double life. Alfred was always in the background, often unnoticed, but anticipated Bruce's needs and was ready to serve him whenever he was needed.

Technology should follow Alfred's lead. It should integrate so seamlessly that you barely notice that it's there unless you need it. It should help you with the day-to-day life obligations and provide connection and safety and save you time by doing things better and faster than you would on your own to allow you the best opportunity to be your best you! Whether you're jumping across rooftops as a crime fighting vigilante, needing more time to work on your passions, loving and caring for others and yourself, or just taking your medications, technology should make your life easier with minimal effort on your part. We all live multiple lives, whether it's a split between being a parent, a friend, an employee, an entrepreneur, etc. Incorporating technology into our lives can help us achieve our brightest goals.

Things change and improve, but there will always be work to do. Maybe not the same work, but someone has to design the robots, maintain them, and program them. Workers will have to up their skills to become masters of this new technology (machinery). A tailor would no more go back to hand-sewing a suit than an architect would go back to hand-drafting his design documents for your building. The benefits of technology are far too great not to embrace them.

One of the most exciting developments in robotic technology for factories is the flexibility of programming. Imagine that robotics currently are like the first-generation computers where you had to code what you wanted them to do just to create a simple contact list of all of your business associates (If you're under 40, this analogy will be lost on you.). Now, with the recent advances, you can literally teach your robotic friend via placing his hand where you want it to go, trace the series of actions you'd like him to do step by step, hit save, and voilà! The robot Baxter is programmed and then will fill in the blanks.

This has huge implications as we bring robots into our homes. We will now easily be able to program our robots by having them watch how we do it first. For instance, I was taught to fold towels in a German fold (three layers). They look great and take up less space than when you fold them in two layers. It's all in the details. If I have my home assistance robot folding my towels, I want them done my way and not what some scientific geek at Darpa thought was a good idea.

Another example would be how my grand-mother, who's now passed (the Italian one, Adelina, or "Della," who my daughter is named after), made her raviolis. I watched her make them numerous times and even asked her to teach me, which she did . . . kind of. I wrote down the recipe; I watched her several times, and she even had me participate. But you have to understand—she was a machine. She could make hundreds of ravioli in minutes; she'd have the dough made, the meat center made, and then roll out her dough on the kitchen coun-tertop with a broom handle or stick. Then in seconds, she'd literally have hundreds of meat plops in the exact size and the exact spacing. Then she'd lay another layer of dough on, cut, and fork each of them perfectly, again in sec-onds. It all happened so quickly you couldn't even catch the details. She was my robot. But what if I could have had a real robot watch her before she passed and learn how she did it? We'd still have her ravioli today. It's sad, but with college and working, I never have the time to *REALLY* learn how to make them, and now they're lost.

Per Moley, "The Moley robotic kitchen is a world-first: a fully integrated, automated kitchen designed for regular homes that cooks with the skill and flair of a human chef."[17] This robot is everything you think the future will be; it definitely stands up to the hype. The inventor of this kitchen robot believes it's a quality of life issue. "How can I have any delicious food at home that I want at any time? That's how I've invented the Moley robotic kitchen," says Mark Oleynik.

The Moley kitchen should hit the mass market by 2021 and cost in the range of $35,000.00. As an interior designer, this is an incredible price for what the robot does.

Not only is it performance cooking (Watching the videos is mesmerizing.), but it also can keep my grandmother's ravioli recipe alive. It uses two arms and sits behind glass, looking very much like a short-order cook. But it can produce way more than dinner food.

I'm planning on having one installed in the Limitless Living Airbnb style aging place showroom and center that I'm currently building and can't wait for everyone to be able to try this new technology. I can almost smell her sauce cooking for hours on the stove—the fresh pasta and pizza. Eating fresh vs. prepackaged and the incredible benefit to everyone's health.

For a small amount of money in the scheme of kitchen appliances, I can bring a little of my grandmother back and let generations to come experience the same flavors I did growing up, attending those monumental Sunday dinners with all the family.

As promised, I'm going to get to the really far-out, sci-fi robots that are, well—let's put it nicely—creepy. My intent is to expose you to where all this is headed so that you'll understand that robots are here to stay and getting more lifelike all the time. The next 10 years will be a wild ride. Think about it this way, do you remember when your phone was attached to the wall, you had to change the channel on your TV by getting off the couch, and there were no seatbelts? I can, and at those points in time, if someone told me about today's technology, I would have thought it outrageous, ridiculous, and unnecessary. But now I can't live without all of these things and wouldn't go back to the old ways unless forced. Being able to adopt new technologies in mind is half the battle. Below are some examples that will seem just as outrageous, ridiculous, and unnecessary.

Japan and Denmark have two of the top scientists in the world developing Geminoids. What are Geminoids? Essentially, they're a duplicate copy of a human in the robotic form but not a clone. The premise is that the Geminoid can interact for you even if you aren't able to be in the actual space. They're a teleoperated robot of an actual person. Similar to the Beam where your Skype-type image can move around on wheels, a Geminoid actually looks like the person and speaks. If you have ever been to Disney and witnessed Abraham Lincoln speaking and moving through the magic of Audio-Animatronics technology, it's essentially the same thing but on steroids.

Japan and Denmark have entered into a collaboration and recently hosted in Denmark the JST CREST / Patient@home SOSU Future Lab Workshop on portable androids and its applications in March of 2015. Per their website:

> *JST **CREST**'s (Core Research of Evolutional Science & Technology) research project, 'Studies on Cellphone-type Teleoperated Androids Transmitting Human Presence'*

*is going to finish its five-year research on teleoperated androids. The aim of this study is to develop cellphone-type teleoperated androids that enable us to transmit our presence, anywhere and anytime. A user transmits his or her presence to a remote place, and the partner in distant location can talk to him or her while feeling as if they are facing each other.*[18]

Denmark's Patient@home project is testing these robots for use in their healthcare.

You might be thinking, okay, now you're scaring me. What is a Telenoid, Geminoid, or Elfoid?

A Telenoid is a gender-neutral, age-neutral robot that's about the size of a 3-month-old baby. The arms and legs are truncated, looking like those dolls that were made of cloth before they sewed the plastic arms and legs on. They almost look alien. They transmit your presence, so if your child had one and you were traveling, you could light it up, and they would know you were thinking of them.

A Geminoid is a robot that looks like a person (your clone, but they'e a robot), and you could activate them to interact with others—for instance, at work or home. They're full scale and have incredible strength. They have AI, so they can carry on conversations and move around on their own. Erica is the latest version and can carry on a 10-minute conversation.

An Elfoid is a miniature Telenoid that's about 8" high. It contains a cell phone and has a camera that captures your emotions and then transmits them to the other Elfoid. You basically hold it in front of you. I would advise only using this with someone you really care about, or it may capture and project you rolling your eyes . . .

Of special interest during the JST conference was a session on seniors. The description of the session is as follows: "Portable androids for aged citizens: The study on the portable androids explores their applications in field experiments in which people interact with one another by their (the portable androids') mediation. With the focus on the social aspects of androids that may facilitate human communications, the Telenoid has been applied to dementia care."

A session was even dedicated to dementia: "Humanoid robots in dementia-care-inves tigating if Telenoid alleviates symptoms of dementia." What I see is that when family isn't near, could we use Telenoid to let them know we still think about them, love them, and therefore stay engaged more? As of this writing, the jury is still out on the benefits of telenoids and dementia.

Hiroshi Ishiguro from Japan has developed not only a Geminoid that looks just like him but has also developed a female copy of a woman.

Henrik Scharfe from Denmark has also produced a Geminoid that looks just like him and states that he has become attached to having him around. His Geminoid project made him one of *Time* magazine's 100 most influential people in 2012.[19]

It gets even creepier as they've found a way to get a microchip to merge with DNA and function as one—learning and mimicking. It's rumored that someone is looking to take his DNA and merge it with his Geminoid to create a robot clone of himself. Does anyone else think this was a plot in a recent movie? Others are working nonstop to have artificial intelligence (AI) in a Geminoid form and have successfully developed an AI that can think and have conversations. Phillip is an AI robot that can build a model of who he's talking to, complete with facial and speech recognition, and he learns every day. He seems to have a sense of humor, which is one of the most difficult things for an AI to accomplish. While the YouTube video is interesting, it's also unnerving. Experts remind us that AI is all around us—just think of your spam filter. While we can understand simple AI and Abraham Lincoln at Disney, it's hard to make the leap to having a copy of yourself in the closet, waiting to be booted up to talk to your kids while you're away on business. Or to pop in on mom to have dinner with her in Florida when you're in N.Y.C., or to have your late husband recreated so that you're not lonely.

Why, why, why would anyone want to do this, and what could be the potential benefits? As I've been told, the reasons are to help reduce pain and suffering in humanity and, get this . . . they specifically mention seniors as one of the target markets!

The first way they intend on using Geminoids to reduce pain and suffering in humanity is to provide them as an alternative to a live person for sexual use. Yes, I'm serious. They hope to alleviate sex trafficking. The thought is that they could substantially reduce the need for trafficking if these Geminoids were available without legal implications. If they could save even a handful of kids, I'm all for it.

Now on to a less controversial use of Geminoids. Say your husband dies after 50 years of marriage. You miss him greatly and also miss how he'd help you around the house. You could order up a version of your husband (could be younger or the same age as you), and he'd be your companion, help you carry out your daily routine, have the strength of Superman, and never leave the seat up! Sounds really bizarre, right? I'm not so sure; couples that have lived together for many years almost feel as though they've died when a spouse does. They're yin and yang, and when the other is gone, it's as if a piece of them is missing. You can see this taking hold in countries that are more accepting of technology and robots than America. But the point is, it could be accepted. It's similar to looking at pictures, watching a movie, or listening to a voice recording of a loved one that's passed. While you know they're no longer with you, the sounds and visual provide great comfort.

Don't think less of me, but it's my job to put myself in a future position and run through if I would actually use the technology or not. If, God forbid, my husband dies before me, and I can get a Geminoid, I'm thinking about getting two—one in the form of The Rock, Dwayne Johnson, with that beautiful smile and strength to help me while I age. The other would be Zac Efron because who doesn't need a gorgeous pool boy? As I think it through, there's no reason not to get a third. Hugh Jackman would be my bodyguard and also teach me how to dance. So if you're reading this, Greg (my husband), it will take three men to fill your shoes ☺. Saved that one!

Geminoids have been tested in hospitals to see how patients would react to them, and it seems that they are, in fact, creepy. People were uncomfortable with how lifelike they were, yet not human. It's a very similar dilemma that the computer-generated movie industry has experienced. We're completely okay with watching *Star Wars* and the creations that are imagined as well as *Toy Story* and the characters that aren't real. But as soon as we take this to a human form, it becomes a little too real, yet still apparent that it's not real, which creates the "creepy" factor.

Pepper by Softbank is a lot less creepy than some of the others. I've interacted with Pepper and always found him or her fun, pleasant, and helpful.

I'm seeing Pepper more and more at airports, banks, etc., and Pepper helps with all those questions that you'd normally ask at the information desk, hostess stand, etc. Pepper is mobile, approachable, and will make it much easier for us to accept a robot helper into our homes as we age.

Now that I've set the stage and you understand how far-reaching robots have become in our world, I'm going to review robotic technology that's being utilized now in homes.

## Personal Assistants

Hector is a robot that's available in Europe. He's used in both smart homes for Alzheimer's/ Dementia residents and as a companion robot for those who can still be on their own but need a little help. He reminds you of your appointments, classes, when to eat, and what to do. He can also Skype with other people, get your doctor, and play games with you. Hector moves the environment in a very similar fashion to the Beam device and utilizes yes-like movements to engage you (similar to Jibo, another robot personal assistant). But whereas Jibo looks more like a minion from the movie *Despicable Me*, Hector actually has a face that's more similar to a human.

Clearly, the lines are blurring. Robots interact with you and not only respond but have human features that blur the line between human and robot. They're no longer being perceived as a computer software program but very often as a real friend. What's so fascinating to me is that when we connect with them on a deeper level, amazing things can happen. Our emotions are triggered, and we're brought out of our shells; we can laugh, become competitive, appreciate and enjoy our quality of life on a much deeper level. In short, we come alive.

While not all robots were created for aging in place, some are showing great promise for Alzheimer's/Dementia. Milo is a robot with a child's face that's under 2' tall that's been used in therapy with great success with autistic children. Milo is now being tested with Alzheimer's/Dementia residents. Milo's benefits aren't only that his cost is substantially less than Paro (a Japanese baby seal, stuffed animal robot that costs $6,000), but Milo can carry on a conversation, ask a resident to exercise with them, and even tell stories. Milo doesn't get irritated when the same question is asked over and over again and speaks a bit slower than a person, so he's easier to understand. He does have a wild hairdo, but time will tell if this becomes an issue for older adults.

An even more engaging but less touchable technology is GeriJoy's dog and cat avatars. Essentially, through your tablet (iPad) or computer, the senior develops a relationship with their chosen cartoon dog or cat avatar on the screen that has a live person on the other end (women in the Philippines). Through previously loaded information such as photos, likes, dislikes, or needs, the avatar can carry on a real-time conversation! Because the avatar's voice is computerized, seniors can chat anytime they want and feel they're connected to their dog or cat (avatar) vs. being confused by an accent or different voice. The dog or cat can show them photos, check up on them if they haven't engaged in a while, remind them to drink water, or just talk—essentially, creating companionship virtually.

From JoyforAll comes a line of companion pets that employ AI, sensors, and robotics. They're similar to the Paro baby seal, but they're cats and dogs and cost around $99.00. These are the robots we have in our home that my 96-year-old grandmother with dementia uses to keep the agitation down and for companionship.

While the U.S. is certainly making strides in robotics and technology for seniors, the Japanese have been obsessed with robots, and this has culminated not only in the creation of the Geminoids that we discussed earlier but also in Honda's Asimo.

Asimo is by far the coolest, non-creepy robot around. He can dance, climb stairs, and now, even run! Honda has painstakingly made Asimo's look and stature in such a way that we don't fear him. He's smaller than a human and has a similar body structure but looks like he's in a spacesuit ready to land on the moon. His movements are so fluid that when he dances, you think he has to be human. He has rules built into him that make him step aside if he's crossing paths with a human. One of his most amazing feats of late is that he can run five and a half miles per hour. What's the big deal, you ask? Both of his feet have to leave the ground at the same time, and then he has to rebalance and land. This is something that a robot could never do previously. It's amazing how many things you and I can do that we think are simple, but to a computer, they're earth-shattering.

At Honda's headquarters, you can see multiple Asimos in the company cafeteria waiting on staff, taking their orders for coffee, making their coffee, and bringing it back to them. And no, I haven't heard of Asimo doing latte art yet, but I'm sure it's coming. Asimo has facial recognition that allows him to not only greet you by name and know your favorites but also remember who got what when he brings the orders back to the table. If you have seen the movie *I, Robot*, Asimo is very close to that reality.

I mentioned Pepper earlier but want to elaborate. Pepper is on a wheelbase vs. Asimo, who has legs, walks, and can go up steps. Pepper is basically a preprogrammed information desk; as long as you ask the right questions, Pepper will give you the right answers. Asimo is more about being autonomous and is still able to serve us.

The Japanese have unique reasons for developing their robotic technology, not only for manufacturing but for senior living and aging in place. They have the largest population of centurions, with a growing population of women entering the workforce and not marrying. Traditionally, the daughter would take care of the elder. The Chinese are starting to experience the same issues as the result of the one-child policy, which creates the perfect storm for not having enough young people to take care of the aged. Asian cultures have high respect for their senior population and are scrambling to figure out how to meet their needs with these new challenges.

A simpler version of Hector that's basically Skype on wheels is the Beam. It was created to answer the call of all the companies that cut travel when the economy experienced a dip yet still needed to interact with multiple teams and be there in person. The issue with Skype or GoToMeeting is that you're stagnant, only seeing what others want you to see, and not being fully immersed in the situation to be able to add value.

A Beam-like device was featured on the TV show *The Big Bang Theory* when Sheldon, the resident genius, decided it was too risky to expose himself to other humans. The wow factor of the Beam is that you can drive it where you're in control of who or what you're looking at. I currently have two: one I'm using at a senior living client's project that we designed to answer questions remotely without having to take a trip to the job site. The other I use to *beam* in when I travel, and I want to meet with the team to help with design projects.

Imagine if you could sign in to a Beam at your mom's nursing home or senior living facility.

You could literally be there, moving around, engaging with your loved one and the staff, and not feel the guilt of being on vacation or living so far away?

Families could sign out the Beam and go for a walk with their mother, say hi to her friends, and even go to dinner or therapy with her all while they're sitting at their laptop miles away. Gone would be the days of having to arrange a time to Skype (which is a pain for the staff and families), the staff getting Mom to the Skype room, and then just talking vs. engaging.

Beam also has a small version for the home that you can use for you and your loved ones. The most unique factor is that you drive the Beam—you move it at your will. When this happens, the lines get blurred between robot and human. Within minutes, people start treat the Beam as the person who is operating it. It's incredibly easy to use and can be turned off for privacy. The only issue is the steps.

Beams currently cost about $6,000 for a commercial model and are used in many businesses where travel is a cost or time issue. They've just started to ship a $1,500 model for the home.

While I know all of this information can become very daunting, the last thing I want you to be is overwhelmed. What I *do* want is for you to keep in mind: Even if you only adopt one technology in this book, you'll have a better life and live with more freedom and confidence than if you adopted none at all! It's not about how much you do; it's about choosing what'll serve you best.

I've put in an outline format some of the top robots available today. I'm sure by the time you read this, there will be more to add to the list, but just as Dorothy was advised in the *Wizard of Oz*, we too have to "start at the beginning."

- o **Servants**
  - ▪ **Outside**
    - • **Yard**
      - o Honda Miimo 3000
      - o Worx Landroid
      - o Husqvarna Automower 450X
      - o Robomow RS630 & RX12
      - o Denna L600
    - • **Pool**
      - o Dolphin
      - o Aquabot
      - o Hayward Tiger Shark
      - o Polaris

- o   Kreepy Krauly Prowler
- o   Solar Breeze
- o   SmartPool 7i
- **Security**
  - o   IPatrol   Riley—camera   on wheels
  - o   Aido
  - o   RoboteX Avatar III—infrared night vision, climbs stairs
  - o   Angee—non-moving, senses your presence. Motion sensors
  - o   Orbii   Monitoring—rolling camera ball, learns and gets smarter
- **Budgee** helps you carry things around the house or yard.
- **Inside**
  - **Vacuum Cleaner**
    - o   IROBOT Roomba 690 with Wi-Fi
    - o   Evovacs N79
    - o   Eventer Robins
    - o   Dyson 360 Eye
    - o   Samsung POWERbot R9350 Turbo
    - o   Neato Botvac Connected Wi-Fi
    - o   Eufy RoboVac 11
    - o   LG Hom-Bot
    - o   Koios 13

o  Shark ION 750
o  Mooka
- **Kitchen Bots**—now being deployed in fast food industry but available in our homes in the next five years.
  o  Café X
  o  Green Goddess—1000 salad combinations
  o  Zume Pizza robots—prepares all the dough, sauce, and oven work
  o  Noodle Duo—ramen making robots
  o  Burgermeister has a robot that can make 400 hamburgers in an hour
  o  Coffee makers
  o  Compact Naboo
  o  Moley launched 2020
- **Roboteam—Household Robot**
  o  Israeli robotics company, Roboteam, is planning to launch 10,000 consumer robots. Previously focused on military robots, Roboteam wants to create a new robot that helps people around the house. "Seven years ago, I went to visit

my dear grandma," says Yosi Wolf, cofounder of the company. "When I saw her trying to carry a cup of tea and cookies and she was shaking . . . I knew we could provide services to help elderly people."[20] According to Wolf, the robot will be 3' high with an interactive 10" display. It will be able to navigate around objects using 40 sensors, and it even has a tray to carry items.

- **Personal Assistants**
    - o Alexa—now can even remind you to take your medications
    - o Google Home
    - o Elli-Q
    - o Hector
    - o Sofihub
    - o Silver Mother—The hub plugs into your router and has sensor devices that attach to doors, refrigerator, pill boxes, bed, and more. Essentially, it will sense moisture in a bed or if the pill box has been opened. You can set it up to send notifications to yourself or your loved one if

they forgot to take their pills or eat. It has a data management tool to help you track your loved one without cameras and check-in when needed.

o Pepper—dances, give directions, recognize emotions
o Jibo—stationary family friendly interactive robot
o Kuri—mobile, Wi-Fi, Bluetooth camera, facial recognition, and takes pictures
o Asus Zenbo—smart mobile, companionship, entertainment, controls home devices, provides security, and reads stories
o Ubtech Lynx—humanoid that helps Alexa get mobile, play music, and home security
o LG Hub—Alexa-powered smart home assistant, facial recognition, share messages, and plays music
o Emotech Olly—smart hub and personal
o Robo Temi—video chat on wheels, music (Android system)
o Aido—family-friendly, plays with kids, provides reminders

for chores and keeps home connected

o Personal Robot by Robot Base—facial recognition, photos, wake up calls, and talks to smart home devices

o Buddy by Blue Frog Robotics—mobile, music, and a cute face

o Beam—mobile video chat device that puts you in the same room with those you love. BeamPro 2 can move the screen from seated to standing.

o OHMNI—mobile video chat robot, similar to the Beam

o Toyota's Human support robot—It's still a prototype but is designed to make independent living possible with assisting with day-to-day tasks.

- **Companion Devices**—Many of the above robots are considered to be companions also.

  o Hector
  o Paro
  o Joy for All Companion—Cat and dog robots with AI that will be your best friend but

never need to be taken out, fed, and won't destroy the furniture.

o GeriJoy—It's a mix of telemedicine and a companion device. A real person is on the other end but remotes in.

o Reminder Rosie—A reminder clock with different reminders for various times and reasons.

o ElliQ

o Grandpad—video calls, photos, etc.

o Claris Companion—It's a tablet, computer, digital photo frame, mobile phone, and remote monitoring system.

o **Mobility**
- **Autonomous (self-driving) Cars—** Technically a robot. 33 states have introduced autonomous legislation and 21 states have passed legislation regarding autonomous vehicles.
  - Manufacturer of autonomous vehicles
    o Mercedes
    o Tesla
    o Uber
    o Google
    o Navya

- o  Intel
- o  Nissan
- o  Apple
- o  BMW
- o  Volvo
- o  Rio Tinto
- o  Audi
- o  GM

Autonomous vehicles (or you can just call them mobility robots or freedom devices) will probably have some of the most life-changing implications as to how we age. Knowing we can get where we want, when we want, for as long as we want changes the game . . . changes *our* game.

Imagine your normal, yearly winter trip to Florida, Arizona, or California. Most Boomers I know drive because they want their car. But it's tiring (which can also mean it's dangerous) and gets more difficult every year. But you want your car! And you want it when you're there. Car = FREEDOM.

What if you could set the car and go? Once set, it would take care of the rest, and you could enjoy the ride, stopping where you want, and having your car when you arrive. This is a small example of how the future will change your life.

If you haven't had the chance to watch the Google Car video on YouTube, it's a must-see. Autonomous cars will be one of the largest game-changers in the U.S. in the next 15 years. What does all this mean for Baby Boomers? I know I wanted one of these autonomous vehicles for my teenager when she started driving. My dad could also use one as he now has macular degeneration and can't drive at night any longer, so everything is a timing issue. I've witnessed the tragedy of my 19-year-old nephew's passing due to falling asleep at the wheel. Imagine with an autonomous car, texting and sight issues would be a thing of the past. I think the roads would be a lot safer and the data substantiates this.

Per Scientific American:

> More than 90% of car crashes in the U.S. are thought to involve some form of driver error. Eliminating this error would, in two years, save as many people as the country lost in all of the Vietnam War.[21]

This isn't to say that autonomous vehicles will be 100% foolproof. We have already seen accidents being reported, but some studies show that you can get up to eight times more cars on the highway safely with autonomous vehicles. Just taking in to consideration insurance companies' thoughts, you can see why this is moving along so fast. And that's not to mention, as we grow as a country, the infrastructure would need to have a massive rework unless we can get more cars on the same roads safely.

The numbers work. Vehicle-to-Vehicle Communication Systems, or V2V, will change how we all drive. According to the U.S. National Highway Traffic Safety Administration, they predict that integrating V2V will reduce annual car accidents by 80%, with goals for mandatory manufacturer integration starting in 2020.[22]

Google knows this and has targeted seniors, people with disabilities, and those who need flexible transportation but could find better things to do with their time than drive.

When Google recorded their YouTube video on their autonomous car with first time riders, some of the responses were priceless and worth hearing. The video starts out with a designer who's explaining to the first test riders outside of Google that they're special. Of special note, among the first riders you have two female seniors, a senior married couple, a sight-impaired senior male, and a mother with her small child.[23]

The Google designer explains:

> *It was a big decision for us to go and start building our purpose-built vehicles. And really, they are prototype vehicles. This was a chance for us to explore what it really means to have a self-driving vehicle. But in the small amount of time we've been working on it, we have functional prototypes, and that's exciting.*

Here are a few quotes from some of the folks in the video, "A First Drive" on YouTube:[24]

**Senior Female:** "You sit, relax, you don't need to do nothing. It knows when it needs to stop, it knows when it needs to go. It actually rides better than my own car."

**Senior Male:** "The human feeling of it is very well-engineered and it is very smooth. There's nothing that makes you feel the least bit threatened. It's impressive! I'm totally in love with this whole concept. Our lives are made up of lots and lots of little things, and a lot of those little things for most people have to do with getting from place to place, in order to connect and do things, and be with people, go places that they need to go and do things. And so there's a big part of my life that's missing, and there's a big part of my life that a self-driving vehicle would bring back to me."

The impact on Baby Boomers is far-reaching. Imagine staying in your home longer with a Google Car or similar autonomous vehicle, as you can get to your doctors' appointments, card club, dinner with friends, and your grandchild's sporting events safely. Independence is maintained and safety for all involved is increased.

While it will take some time for other states to make it legal, we can anticipate that because California and Nevada have already legalized autonomous vehicles, Arizona would be next. 29 states have enacted legislation relating to autonomous vehicles already.

Honda has been at the forefront in personal mobility technology, developing devices using gyroscope technology. What's really neat about these transportation devices is that it's a blend between a Segway and a scooter that seniors use in the U.S.. While a Segway could be used by a senior, they would have to stand the entire time; these you sit on, so they're more appropriate for seniors than the Segway. Honda also has another version that's smaller and light enough to carry with you to use it when you need it.

Core strength would have to be improved if Boomers want to use this device, as slouching and couch-potato posture won't cut it. So you better get to the yoga studio now. If you have ever been on a Segway, you know they're incredibly intuitive; they're much easier to learn how to operate than a bike or a car. I anticipate that active independent living communities will be the first to adopt these devices, as well as seniors who are still living at home. Imagine Mom's knees give her trouble, but she'd love to go to the zoo with her grandkids, on a vacation, or a walk with her friends. She feels guilty about slowing them down or the hassle of trying to find a wheelchair when they get to their destination. With mobility devices such as Hondas, all of those worries are gone. Mom can come without any worries and, if need be, fit the device in the overhead compartment of the plane. Freedom and dignity all wrapped up in a nice little bow!

## Exoskeletons

While the merging of man and machine has entertained us for decades, one of my favorite TV shows in the '70s was called *The Six Million Dollar Man*. It programmed us to believe that man and machine would happen sooner rather than later. I can still remember hearing the sound they would play when Steve Austin *(The Six Million Dollar Man)* was slow-motion running! While it's taken quite a while to get to a real-life Steve Austin or his Bionic Woman counterpart, exoskeletons have arrived. Some exoskeletons are even controlled by thought!

Exoskeletons combine quite a few technologies to work, some of which are crowdsourcing, infinite computing, and sensors. The important thing to remember throughout this entire book regarding technology is that it rarely stands on its own; it's interconnected and typically requires multiple technologies to be successful. When thinking of adopting one of these technologies, it will be important to look at what other technologies are connected and how this will impact your execution strategy.

Man and machine have been merging since 1958 when the first pacemaker was implanted. Around the same time, cochlear implants were developed. Now, folks previously deaf can hear for the first time due to this merge between man and machine.

This topic is so large that at the opening ceremonies of the World Cup Soccer Tournament in Brazil 2014, the first ball of the opening ceremonies was kicked by a paralyzed individual named Juliano Pinto. Walk Again, the group that made it all possible, is an international collaboration with over 100 scientists. What's shocking about this? The exoskeleton is mind-controlled through a helmet that reads the wearer's electrical activity and translates this *intention* into action. In addition, to provide feedback to the user, they've created CellulARSkin that provides feedback to the wearer so they know when their foot touches the ground. While this is groundbreaking, it is only the beginning in mobility-assistive devices.

The U.S. military has long been a developer of the exoskeleton as well as U.S. firemen and emergency services. Imagine for a moment that you're tasked with rescuing a family from a burning building several flights up. You're in excellent physical shape and have trained to deal with all the potential issues. You know that you may need to carry out this family, who may be unconscious. Now let's add equipment that you need to wear not only to be safe but to be able to fight the fire: your fire suit (pants, jacket, boots, helmet), your air tank, hoses, and extra air. This adds approximately 100-130 lbs. of additional weight on your body that you'll have to take up the stairs. Then some of this will still have to be on you when you rescue the family coming down the stairs and out of the building via the fastest route possible.

The human skeleton was not meant to bear excessive weight on it to this degree. Muscles and ligaments are meant to take the pressure off of the skeleton so that it can move freely. "The HULC" (Human Universal Load Carrier) provides extra muscle that works by allowing all the extra weight to be transferred to the skeleton, bypassing the user, and transferring it to the ground. Providing the user with Hulk-like strength allows the mission of saving the family to be accomplished with less stress and more power and reduces the damage on the hero's body that would normally take place under this kind of wear and tear. Imagine that a caregiver or possibly even you could have one of these exoskeletons to help lift someone after a hip surgery. You become superhuman and don't hurt yourself while trying to help those you love.

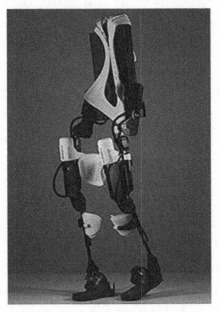

*Image Courtesy of 3D Systems*

Japan has had exoskeletons for rent for several years now. The intention was for the frail-bodied to be able to maintain their independence yet not be in a wheelchair. By far, you'll see that the Japanese have pushed harder on robotics than any other country to alleviate issues for their seniors. In comes HAL (Hybrid Assistive Limb), developed at Tsukuba University by engineering professor Yoshiyuki Sankai. The robot suit employs technology that reads your muscle impulses and delivers robotic assistance that can increase strength up to five times. The strength can be dialed up or down according to the needs of the user. HAL is now available to be rented monthly or weekly.

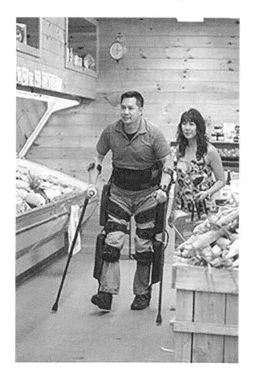

Recently, the FDA approved its first exoskeleton called The ReWalk for public use in the U.S.. The implications are earth-shattering to how we age. Can you imagine aging without a cane, walker, wheelchair, or scooter? How much more engaged would you stay? Besides the obvious benefits to physical independence for a Boomer with mobility issues, can you imagine still being able to walk the dog, go on vacation with the family and grandkids, and go up and down stairs easily?

Our minds and bodies weren't meant to sit still all day, and when they do, our energy is drained out of us and erodes our value. Everyone wants to be valued, and stopping the downward spiral that's created by being constrained to a wheel-chair allows you to engage in life, add value, and be valued.

The ReWalk not only allows the user to get up from a seated position, walk, and then sit back down, but it can help a user get up and down stairs!

Robert Woo is a 46-year-old who was para-lyzed from the waist down when seven tons of steel fell into his construction trailer. He has been able to walk again due to ReWalk, a robotic exoskeleton. Robert Woo stated in an interview with CBS News, "I didn't think I could be useful and I wanted to die. The worst thing is, I couldn't even pull the plug."[25]

Robert Woo put it perfectly. "To be able to stand up next to my wife and give her a hug for the first time, to be able to walk with my children to the park. These are things that we take for granted and I missed."

The cost could be the key: currently the ReWalk costs $70,000. Until the price point hits around $20,000, one could assume it won't be a mass-market item for seniors and those suffering from strokes. But as we saw with scooters, once the reimbursement was figured out, it was not that folks didn't want them; it was that they needed to be able to afford them.

Currently, falls could be eliminated with the new stabilization technology that's being employed by the Japanese Robot Asimo or with Segway's gyroscope.

While this technology is available today, it's a safe bet that it will move to the manufacturing sector first, emergency services, and then acute healthcare. At this point, the bugs should be worked out and the price point low enough that it will have a major impact on aging in place in five to 10 years. Move over Steve Austin, Iron Man has arrived and is no longer a fantasy . . .

People with peripheral neuropathy (balance, walking, and foot-health problems) in America come in around 20 million, and most are older adults.[26] WalkJoy believes they have a solution that will help those with peripheral neuropathy to walk normally. By placing a small device below the knee, it helps the person to walk better by stimulating nerves to send a signal to the brain that the person is walking. (Peripheral neuropathy reduces the feeling in your feet, which reduces the information the brain needs to walk properly.) The result: Falls are reduced, and the person has more confidence to walk, which not only engages them in life more, but gets them moving, which has numerous health benefits.

The data is in, and it's crystal clear; Boomers have no issues merging with machines to ensure they can maintain their freedom and lifestyle.

## Drones

Drones have been on the news constantly, typically flying over sporting events, providing unique views that were otherwise previously impossible unless you owned a Goodyear Blimp. They've filmed fireworks and live events. Farmers are using them to see their land without having to physically examine inch by inch, and the real estate industry is using them to get more up-to-date images than Google Earth can provide. They're being used for sports, crime control, firefighting, and delivering items through Amazon and even pizza by Dominos.

The impact of drones on aging is immense. One company out of San Francisco is delivering prescriptions through a drone system including pharmacy items for one $1.00 on top of the script. Because of this, you can stay in your home and have your medication delivered to you. You may drive, but when the weather is poor or you're sick, the last thing you want to do is drive to the pharmacy for your prescription.

Robots (A drone is just a flying robot.) have been around in some form or another for decades.

While robots have already replaced many manufacturing jobs, especially when the task is repetitive, robots are intended to move us up Maslow's hierarchy of needs, allowing us to focus on quality of life instead of survival. We can also pursue more meaningful jobs that require our talents and mind.

As we age, the robots will serve us, be our companions, caregivers, mobility devices, and safety and connection tools.

# CHAPTER 8
## WELL-BEING, MIND, BODY, & SPIRIT

This is probably the MOST important part of the book. But . . . it can only benefit you if you take action. It's a lot like a glass of water when you're thirsty—it won't do you any good unless you take action and drink it. Now, I know you're a person of action because you bought the book and started to read it, and you're all the way to Chapter 8 (unless you skipped ahead). This all gives me great hope for you and your future.

I've tried a lot of what I have in the book and can say from experience, even if you're consistently inconsistent (like me), something is better than nothing. I'm in much better health, mind, body, and spirit than I was 10 years ago, and I'm certainly not what you'd call a poster child of good health practices. My husband, on the other hand, works out six days a week, does his eye exercises, eats pretty healthy, and works reasonable hours. He's in better health than me, but the point is I'm getting better, little by little. You have to measure your *own* progress, not measure it by comparing where you are to others.

At the root of well-being is that this is *not* a discussion about healthcare. I've worked in healthcare for over a quarter of a century, and most healthcare is really sick care. There's little if any preventive care for the body being encouraged, and most of the time, the essentials are left off the list. Eyes . . . who needs to see? These are non-essential to our healthcare insurance system. Ears . . . who really needs to hear? Helen Keller did just fine without both; she's world renown. Teeth . . . who really needs them? Eating isn't a necessary part of being healthy . . . or is it? I'm being very sarcastic, but it's maddening. Throw in the fact that we're beings of not just body, but of mind and spirit; these aren't only ignored, but some experts cannot even agree that they exist. This is especially true when it comes to the spirit, soul, life spark, God within, or whatever you want to call it.

We are talking about a REVOLUTION here! The kind where you take back control of your life and your well-being. You live in the greatest time of all humanity where you can literally command (with some money as incentives) millions of people to do your bidding through crowdsourcing, where you can live like a king, and have access to technologies that allow you to think things like . . . what will I do with all my free time—watch *Game of Thrones*? Will I transport myself via Beam or through virtual reality to Rome for the weekend? Will I have my robot chef prepare the same meal that the Queen of England is having, or have my bum washed and blow-dried by my robotic toilet? With all of these luxuries, you need to pay attention to the most important ones, which are the ones that impact your mind, body, and spirit.

I'll do my best to keep this simple and actionable, but they're all interconnected just like technology is. Remember to ask yourself the three questions when evaluating what will be useful for you out of this section.

1. How are you going to be able to live your life with freedom and confidence?

2. Where will you be living your life?

3.  How are you going to care for your mind, body, and spirit?

By now, we know each other well enough that you know I love a good analogy. It helps me to understand the world and make a concept relatable. When it comes to new technology, I always follow the kids and what they're using. But when I think about Well Care, I follow the elite athletes and what they're using.

I've been blessed to have wonderful relationships with many professional and Olympic athletes. Most are older now and help others to be their best with what they've learned about keeping their mind, body, and spirit in optimum health.

This makes total sense, right? But wait, it gets better. Elite athletes (18-30 years old) intensely abuse their bodies, have knee, shoulder, and hip issues, and have memory issues. Somehow, they still show up every game day looking like a modern-day gladiator. Perfectly fit in mind, body, and spirit, ready for battle. How can they do this when they virtually have the bodies of an 80-year-old?

They apply the technologies that we will discuss in this chapter to *hack* their systems to recover quicker and to stay healthier longer. Most of which they do preemptively, but some are to fix the damage that's occurred and get them back in the game as quickly as possible.

As I write this, professional golfer, Tiger Woods (43 years old, born in 1975) is even making a comeback after struggling for the past several years with two back surgeries and other issues. This is even more impressive due to his age. It's extremely hard for an elite athlete to come back after surgery—especially the older they get. Maybe we should listen to what's going on and understand that the game is being rewritten and written in our favor.

At the Abundance 360 conference, I get to witness what earth-shattering new technologies are being created. This year it was all about longevity. The consensus was from all the experts—if you can survive the next 12 years, then you can decide how you want to live. Of course, there will be compromises, like, "Hey you can live healthy for another 50 years, but you have to give up sugar." Some of you might say, "I'd rather die in the next 20 years and keep my Cinnabons." It's all okay because it will be about freedom of choice. You'll have the choice to be sick or not sick.

Let's go to the crazy, not-so-far-off future for a moment. Dave Asprey, Dr. Craig Venter, Mark Allen, Bob Hariri, Keith Leonard, Osman Kibar, and Naveen Jain are the names you need to remember. These geniuses remind me of Edison, Tesla, Galileo, Da Vinci, and Einstein. They're utterly obsessed with their theories and will probably prove them and change the way we see the world today. I'm convinced they're going to change the way we view the length of our living space and how we age. In no order of importance, I'm going to run down what I've learned from these passionate, intelligent gentlemen that hopefully will provide you with a "future that's brighter than your past" to quote Dan Sullivan.

Dr. Craig Venter (one of the first persons to sequence the human genome) founder of the J. Craig Venter Institute stated that we're "moving towards where medicine becomes proactive, preventive, personalized, and predictive."[27] The data he presented was that one-third of the people who make it to 50, don't make it to 75 … This is the kind of data that makes you stop in your tracks and ask, "But I'm over 50, and I'm not 75, so where does this put me?" This risk is much higher as a male than female, and the major reasons are cardiovascular and cancer-related.

Because of this, the Human Longevity project combined with data from patient assessments, genome, AI, and data mining—they are finding information that's saving lives. Dr. David Karow of HLI says, "70% of all cancers caught early can be cured."[28]

In Alzheimer's disease, the Lancet commission states, "1/3 of the risk is due to modifiable risk factors"[29]—meaning you can change it if detected early enough. Check out more at humanlongevity.com.

Mark Allen, CEO at Elevian states that, "Regenerative capacity decreases with age."[30] He presented a study called Parabiosis, by Professor Amy Wagers. She took two mice, one old and one young, and sewed their circulatory systems together. The blood from the young mouse was flowing into the old mouse, and the blood from the old mouse was flowing into the young mouse. The result: The young mouse ended up prematurely aging, and the old mouse experienced regenerative properties of the blood from the young mouse. Basically, the old mouse got younger, and the younger mouse got older. What they found was there was a protein called GDF11. It was different in old and young mice, just as it was in humans. When they isolated this Protein and injected it in experiments, it repaired hearts, skeletal muscle, and stimulated new neurons to grow in the brain. What does this mean? GDF11 is reduced as humans age. You can inject it, and after nine days, it makes an impact. They also found a degenerative factor. Currently, they're working on animal studies in Coronary Artery disease, Sarcopenia (loss of muscle as a natural part of aging), Alzheimer's Disease, and Type II Diabetes.

Based upon what Human Longevity, Inc. says are the killers from ages 50-75, I'm interested in GDF11 and when it will be available in a couple of years. It's almost as if you'll get all the benefits of being a vampire without all the negative.

Bob Hariri discovered the concept of the placenta being the center of stem cell therapy and is a founder of Human Longevity, Inc. He's also part of Cellularity and the Applied Science & Performance Institute. The placenta stem cells can be used to create any cell, and your body won't reject it. It's also legal. A stem cell is the repository for the complete human genome. How does this relate to aging? As we age, our stem cells decline. Cellularity is looking at how to reboot our systems by injecting these placenta stem cells that were stored from birth back into your system as you age.

According to Happify.com, we're the happiest at 18 and don't get back to that happy point until 73, which increases until we're 85. What does this tell us? For me, the study says that we're happiest when we're free to be us. At 18, our lives are ahead of us, and we have endless possibilities. At 73, we've recently retired (if we're lucky), and we have the freedom to choose what we will do each day, who we want to be with, and where we want to live. We're no longer bound by the obligations of a job, and we can now pursue a *calling*. It may also be that between 50 and 75, we will see one-third of the people we know and love, die. Death has a way of creating clarity, allowing you to see what living life to the fullest really means for you.

It was once said that what gets measured, gets improved. I agree. When we have the data, we can correlate and correct.

Data = Knowledge = Wisdom to Take Action.

Keith Leonard with Unity BioTechnology has a mission to reshape human health span and longevity. The definition of health span per Keith is, "The period of one's life during which one is healthy and free of disease."[31]

Unity is focused on Cellular Senescent, Mitochondrial Dysfunction, and Loss of Circulating Factors.

Our cells divide up to 50 times from the time we're born, and then they stop dividing. This is when we start to age; they basically are dividing (living), dying or stopping (which is called senescent). As we age, we have more senescent cells.

During a study at the Mayo Clinic on senescent cells (SnCs), Unity genetically *removed* the *dying, aging, or stopping* cells, aka senescent cells, from one midlife aged mouse and *kept* the senescent cells in another genetically identical mouse from the same litter.

What they found was the mouse that had the senescent cells aged normally with all the problems of aging just like humans, but the mouse *without* the SnCs, while the same age, didn't have any of the aging issues. This is earth-shattering stuff. Basically, they're stopping the body from aging in terms of disease such as joint, sight, strength, and heart issues. The deleted SnCs mouse lived 35% longer without disease.[32]

Currently, they're in human clinical trials for Osteoarthritic knees. Overall, they're targeting 20 diseases and should have two more in trials in the next year or so. Imagine with an IV or a shot every year, you could remove (cure) macular degeneration, Osteoarthritis, Glaucoma, COPD, and other age-related diseases. While time will tell, this could be the fountain of youth—rejuvenating and restoring our tissue back to a state it was when we were young.

Dr. Joan Mannick from resTORbio is developing innovative medicines that target the human biology of aging to prevent age-related diseases. She's looking at TORC1, a protein that may have implications on how we age. During her presentation, she raised the questions, "Why do steamer clams live 28 years, but ocean quahog clams live 220 years, painted turtles live 11 years, yet a Galapagos land turtle lives to 193, and a mouse lives three years yet a genetically similar, naked mole rat lives to 28 years?"[33] Their research looks to unlock these secrets and apply them to extending our age and quality of life.

One thing to mention is that all this biohacking science compliments each other, and the scientists agree with one another's findings. If I were a financial planner, I would be restructuring my clients plans to live much longer than anticipated.

Dr. Osman Kibar from Samumed is developing drugs to restore the health of a particular tissue.

Progenitor stem cells—their job is to repair and replenish a tissue as needed. Samumed's particular research revolves around the Wnt Pathway. What they found was that Wnt is reduced in degenerative disease. This Wnt gene is identical across all animals, so it helps drug companies to know that it will work on humans.

The older we get, the Wnt Pathway goes off balance; Samumed has produced drugs to restore this balance. They currently are in human clinical trials in osteoarthritis (32.5 million Americans[34] have it), degenerative disc disease, tendons, psoriasis, colon cancer, alopecia (baldness), anti-wrinkle (L'oreal is marketing), and will be in human clinical trials this year for Alzheimer's/Dementia. Samumed has an injection that's regenerating cartilage in knees in about six months. They're also regrowing discs and growing tendons with a lotion. They're developing a pill that stops tumors from growing in some terminal cancer patients. They have a lotion that regrows hair, and the anti-wrinkle cream gets rid of 90% of the wrinkles in two weeks. One patient, in her 30s, with terminal pancreatic cancer was 70 lbs. She took their pill for a year and is now up to 110 lbs. and back to her normal life. She's now thriving after two and a half years being deemed terminal. To say these results are astounding would be an understatement. Once through all the clinical trials, which will still take several years, we could see cancer treatment dramatically change for the better. It gives me so much hope about the future.

The most exciting images were of Alzheimer's brains in lab animals. With a pill, they were able to completely reverse the disease. When I questioned Dr. Osman if the mice still had their memories, he said they seem to retain them, but until the human clinical trials start this year, there would be no way to know for sure. Imagine the amount of pain that will go away in mind, body, and spirit for those with these diseases and their families. While the drugs for you and me may not be available for a couple of years—have hope—help is on the way! We just have to stay alive long enough to be able to take advantage of all of this incredible science to turn back the clock. Imagine our bodies will be disease-free, and our minds will retain all of our knowledge and wisdom—this will be true freedom.

The goal, for companies like Samumed, is to not just stop the aging clock but to restore, rejuvenate, and de-age.

Naveen Jain, Founder of Viome, has a passion to put the drug companies out of business. He believes that fixing the gut will fix your health. If you meet him, he deeply stares into your eyes, sees, and hears you. You'd never guess he's worth billions. He's the kind of visionary that's on a mission and makes you believe that he'll walk through fire to accomplish that mission. His concept isn't new. As a matter of fact, Hippocrates, who was born in 460 BCE, said, "Let food be thy medicine and medicine be thy food" and "All disease begins in the gut."[35] Lucretius stated over 200 years ago,

"One man's food is another man's poison."[36] Naveen will often quote Hippocrates, and one has to wonder if he's not channeling him.

Naveen explains that the body is made up of more foreign cells than human cells—we have less than 1% that's human—we are a walking, talking ecosystem. What I've learned from my meetings with Naveen is that 90% of the serotonin that's produced in your body comes from your gut, and 70% of our immune system is in our gut lining. You know that burning in your gut when something goes wrong? That's your Vagus nerve transmitting messages from the brain to the gut. There's an actual physical connection. [37]

Most diseases are due to chronic inflammation. Naveen's company is trying to help identify where you have inflammation and how to lessen that inflammation so that you can get your ecosystem back in balance, vs. dis-ease or being out of balance (out of ease). Knowledge is power, and using this knowledge is wisdom.

While this may all seem a little *hippy* for you, mainstream medicine is even recognizing the microbiome. The Cleveland Clinic even recently released a study linking the microbiome with breast cancer. What's a microbiome? A microbiome identifies all the living organisms in your body, including bacteria. We actually have more bacteria in our bodies than we have human cells, and balancing our microbiome is critical to healthy living. When our microbiome is out of whack, you may experience anything from an upset stomach to fatigue or even disease.

While we're all similar, we're incredibly different. We need to eat what's right for us, but we also need to change it up based upon our ever-changing gut. I've been working on my microbiome health for the past two years, and I'm healthier for doing it. I would encourage everyone to get Viome tested.

Dave Asprey is a biohacker. If you want control of your body, then biohacking is for you. What changes will you make to live the life you want? *Head Strong*, Dave's latest book, talks about mitochondria. They make power for your body with food and light. If you're over 40, then you have mitochondrial dysfunction. Mitochondria are your body's batteries when they're working properly. Dave wants you to be able to make energy in your body like a young person and is producing products so you can.

Your circadian biology (what regulates sleep) is controlled by your mitochondria. The issue, as Dave explains it, is mitochondria are very old, meaning they're part of the oldest part of us being human. Because of this, they act like cavemen and simply put, they operate like cavemen in that they don't think in a complex way. They only know three things: 1) run from scary stuff, 2) eat everything so you don't starve to death, and 3) procreate. While this may have served us in the past, these cavemen aren't serving us now, yet they control much of what you do. So what can we do? We have to hack them, to make them do what we want vs. them making us do what they want.

Some of the fantastic products that Dave's company, Bulletproof Coffee, has created has helped me and my family greatly. He has a product called Unfair Advantage that helps your mitochondria to function better. My father was starting to forget things; we already have my grandmother with dementia in the house, so this new development was very worrisome. He'd leave to go to pick something up or pay a bill and would come back home having forgotten to do it—frustrated, embarrassed, and scared. This went on for a month or so, and then I encouraged him to take Unfair

Advantage because of how much better my thinking was when I took it. It was like I was firing on all cylinders again. He took it and went back to his full memory. It was like we dodged a bullet! Here we thought he was starting with Alzheimer's and really, it was mitochondrial dysfunction. He and I both notice a massive difference when we run out, so typically, we end up overnighting it. When you can't think straight, you're less confident, and you move through life with more caution.

As you can see, the tide is turning, futurist Ray Kurzweil has created a theory called the Longevity Escape Velocity—the point where you're living long enough that every year you're alive, science is extending your life for more than one year. He predicts that this will take place by 2030, which sounds like a date from Star Trek, but it's really right around the corner.

The relevance is that as we age and start showing symptoms of aging, it's rare that a brain scan is completed or labs are taken to determine if there's another cause for the muscle or memory loss. It's just assumed that it's part of getting older.

What if the loss could be reversed through supplements or medication, TMS (Transcranial magnetic stimulation), PBMT (Photobiomodulation/light therapy), psychological testing, neurofeedback, lifestyle changes, bioidentical hormone replacement therapy, oxygen therapy, hypnotherapy, IV nutrient therapy, prolotherapy, or platelet-rich plasma therapy. Not all of these therapies are for memory loss—some are for depression, anxiety, joint aches, etc.

Sound like anything you have? You have now been empowered to fight back and reclaim your vitality!

Reading this book is a great start. Research what works for you in the list above, and then talk to your doctor or find one that's up-to-speed on these biohacking technologies.

Currently, if you're in your 80s and you start to have memory loss, you're written off from really finding out what the issue is or if there's a possibility you could be restored to a higher level of cognitive function. SPECT scans that look at brain blood flow and activity patterns have been shown to change the treatment plan or diagnosis 78.9% of the time vs. just asking the patient for their symptoms.[38] This translates to almost 8 out of 10 treatment plans being wrong when not using the technology that we currently have at our disposal.

Studies show that older adults have fewer active brains, but we aren't stuck with this. Getting your brain back in shape helps you to think clearer and avoid the effects of mental aging. Dr. Amen has developed a system to get not only your brain fit but a holistic system for a diet that works with your brain type (He has a quiz.), and then brain training that helps to reduce the risk of Alzheimer's disease.

The 2018 Alzheimer's Disease Facts and Figures Report states:

> *An estimated 5.7 million Americans of all ages have Alzheimer's disease in 2018. This includes an estimated 5.5 million people age 65 and older. One in ten (10%) people age 65 and older has Alzheimer's disease. About one-third (32%) of people age 85 and older have Alzheimer's disease. Of those with Alzheimer's disease, the vast majority (81%) are age 75 or older.[39]*

With these numbers, developing a new strategy is critical as the drugs thus far developed for Alzheimer's disease have made little impact.

Why does this matter? The oldest Boomers reached 72 in 2018.[40] This creates more emphasis on why it's critical to manage our brain health as only 30% is determined by genetic issues.

What does this all mean? You can determine to a large extent how you age. This is awesome news!

Simple programs to engage the brain, provide proper brain nutrition, and utilize technology to identify issues and aid in early detection will be the key to solve this epidemic.

> *Anyone who stops learning is old, whether at twenty or eighty. Anyone who keeps learning stays young. The greatest thing in life is to keep your mind young.*[41]
> —Henry Ford

While these doctors, scientists, biohackers, and their companies are solving large age-related issues, you might be wondering if there are any small things that you can do now, without needles, tests, or waiting for FDA approval.

Small things you can do now:

- o **Mind and Body Health**
  - **Vasper**—An incredible machine that actually builds muscle mass in older adults (almost impossible to do) and increases testosterone in males. It is basically a reclining bike with arm extensions. You put cuffs (similar to blood pressure cuffs) that have cold liquid flowing through them on your arms and legs, and away you go. The cold tricks your muscles into thinking you have been working out for two hours, but really, you have only been working out 20 minutes. It's fast and brilliant. Several professional sports teams use the Vasper as well as the U.S. military. When I tried it, I was amazed at what a workout it was, and I thought I wouldn't be able to walk for days. Then I got off the machine and experienced the exact opposite; there was, actually, a burst of energy. So why doesn't everyone have one? The price. One machine is $50,000; that's right, $50,000. You're probably thinking who would pay that? I know one friend of mine that bought three!

When you think about reversing the aging clock and naturally increasing your testosterone, it might not be so pricey.

▪ **Z-Health**—While Dr. Eric Cobbs' primary business is training trainers of the most elite athletes in the world, he still offers some applicable products such as the Balance Gym and the Vision Gym to the general public. He has developed a system to get top performance out of the top performers in the world, so they have an edge on their competition. Synching of the vestibular (inner ear), vision, and core are key to keeping us safely moving. When all three are in sync, your body doesn't tense up, which can cause injury. As we age and still want to be active, we wonder why the weekly basketball game that used to be no issue now sends us to the ER for shoulder surgery. If we neuro-map prior to engaging in a sport, basically moving our body through a series of short exercises to make sure that our nerves are all *primed*, then when we yin, and we meant to yang, we're less apt to get injured. A better example might be a car accident (stay with me). The driver, who was drinking, rarely gets hurt, but the person in the car with them who was not drinking and tensed up gets hurt badly. Loose/ Connected = Less Injuries.

- **Amen Clinics**—Dr. Amen, the author of *Memory Rescue,* shows how a proper diet and blood flow can save your brain.

- **Hydrate IV Clinics**—Have you ever been sick or dehydrated, and the doctor gave you an IV in the hospital? Now you can get large doses of vitamins, hangover tonics, and much more at these IV clinics that are popping up all over. Typically, they cost less than a visit to the doctor. When I travel, I go to make sure I don't get run down (sometimes prior and sometimes after my trip—it depends on how I feel). You can also get B12 shots and other health items such as oxygen.

- **Electronic Stimulation Units**—The first time my knees gave out, the doctor prescribed one of these units for me. You hook a patch with a wire to your skin and attach it to the unit, then turn it on, and it stimulates your muscle without any potential damage to your body. Word to the wise: If you turn it up too high, you'll feel like one of those cartoons being electrocuted. Why would you use it? Some people are using them to tone flabby areas, but others like pro athletes, are using them to keep their muscles in shape with zero stress to their bodies, while watching their favorite TV show. These are $100.00 or so, but fancy units can get pretty expensive.

o **Apps**
  - **IMSHealth's Appscript**—Evaluates 40,000 healthcare apps.
  - **ElderCheck Now**—An Apple app for Apple Watch and iPhone that allows the caregiver to check in with seniors and access their GPS location.
  - **Skype**—While some people may consider Skype a useless app in a world of unlimited phone plans, it's important to remember these plans aren't universal. In fact, many seniors utilize the Lifeline program to access affordable cell service. Unfortunately, many of these plans offer limited minutes. With Skype, though, you can contact

your loved ones via a Wi-Fi connection. This means you'll save your limited minutes for when you're away from home and you really need them.

- **MindMate**—Just like Skype, MindMate is available on both Apple and Android phones. Unlike Skype, however, this app has features that actually fight against memory loss and dementia. The app's creators used real scientific research to decide what to provide in their offering. This research led to the app offering exercise workouts, nutrition advice, brain games, movies, and music, dating all the way back to the '40s. This means MindMate focuses on some of the most scientifically supported dementia-fighting activities out there.

- **Voice Dream Reader**—While you can set your phone with larger fonts and higher contrast, there's obviously a limit when these adjustments are no longer helpful, and this is where Voice Dream Reader helps. The simple app allows a phone to read anything aloud to its user. Whether it's an eBook, PDF, webpage, or a combination of other text, Voice Dream

Reader ensures no one is left without their desired content.

- **Android's Voice Aloud Reader**—has similar features as the Voice Dream Reader.

o **Personal Health Diagnostics**

- **Viome**—Gut Biome Kit (stool sample) that will help you understand what you need to be your best. Basically, it will tell you what you need (vitamins, etc.) and what you should avoid in foods so that you can tailor your diet to be your best you.

- **Freestyle Libre**—14-day blood sugar patch with readings as often as you like. This data allows you to make smart choices for your body vs. following what's *most likely* the best choice. Not everyone responds the same to carbs or a soft drink. Find out what causes your sugar to spike and then modify your diet without having to eliminate something that you love that may not be hurting you.

- **23 and Me**—DNA testing that helps you make smart choices about your health. For instance, my father has macular degeneration, and when I tested, I found out that I'm prone to get it also. So now, I'm taking eye supplements to help lower my risk.

- **Human Longevity Clinic**—Full body work up with MRI, DNA, and blood work. Data is knowledge—the more you know about your risks and what's not working, the more time you have to adjust your lifestyle and diet to improve your physical and mental health.

- **Kardia**—FDA approved EKG that's the size of a credit card and can help predict, five days in advance, if you're going to have a heart event. Kardia uses AI and data mining to create predictive analytics so that it *knows you* and when you aren't okay.

- **MyndYou**—Mobile platform to help maintain independence in early stage cognitive decline. Monitors cognitive, physical, and behavioral patterns and sends alerts so that steps can be taken.

- **Steps&**—Virtual smartphone assistant who guides and encourages physical therapy patients through home exercises. The interface, managed by the physical therapist includes: instructional videos, a motivation boost, goal-setting, prescheduling, and tracking features.

- **AbiliSense**—They are developing apps that essentially act as a seeing-eye dog would. These apps would constantly listen to all the sounds around the user then analyze them, and, if needed, send them to a smart device for an alert or call 911.

- **Mybitat**—A smart home product that's partnered with Samsung to data mine (take all the information it sees and hears in the home with sensors) and develop patterns for normal. When they're out of the normal range, the system alerts preselected contacts.

- **Easy to Connect (E2C)**—A Basic Smartphone (available in the United States and Israel) and a Basic Tablet (available in Israel) designed to help seniors easily access the latest communication technologies with large print, one-button navigation, and other streamlined processes. A Basic Smart TV and Basic Smartwatch are coming next, per their website. While you may think this isn't for you, you may be taking care of a parent or a spouse who may need this technology. Any tech that can reduce the stress of the Boomer (the primary at-home caregivers in the U.S.) is good tech to me and worth mentioning.

o **Mind Health**—A combination of exercises for the brain, proper nutrition for the brain, and learning to tune out the noise. (Our brains weren't built to handle all of the noise of the technological age. This causes excess fatigue and stress). A major change in the last 20 years is that doctors used to believe that our brains were hardwired and couldn't change, but now they know we have neuroplasticity. In another words, you *can* teach an old dog new tricks. We also now know that with the proper mitochondrial function, oxygen, blood flow, and vitamins in our brain, we can make our brain better! Not just slow the aging process, but we can get back what we thought may have been lost forever. This changes the game and puts us in the driver seat of our destiny.

▪ **Amen supplements**—Dr. Amen has excellent supplements to help your brain function the best. Please get some blood work done to see if you're deficient in vitamin D, Niacin, etc., then avoid sugar and start exercising.

- **Meditation**—Decluttering our mind from the noise of everything going on is critical to your brain health. Ten minutes a day in the morning can do wonders. I was against meditation at first as I thought it was a religion, then I discovered Headspace. This app guides you through ways of calming your brain and reducing your worries. If you're like me and thought, *I pray. I don't need to mediate.* But prayer is an active petition, and meditation is about not thinking about anything. Instead, it's about clearing the mind. They aren't in conflict, and meditation can help with depression and more mental clarity.

- **Brain Games**—Anything from playing cards, crossword puzzles, Words With Friends, to apps like Luminosity will help keep your brain firing and active. I like to think of it this way: in high school, I took four years of French. I was able to speak, understand, write, and read French at a decent level. Now I can barely say

Bonjour (Hi) or Oui (Yes). The point is, if you don't use it, you lose it.

- **Bullet Proof Coffee**—There are many items from mold-free coffee (mold is predominate in most coffees and causes inflammation) to Unfair Advantage, which happens to be my personal favorite. It helps me to get rid of my brain fog by increasing my mitochondrial function. As I mentioned, my grandmother, who has dementia, lives with us, so we're all very sensitive if someone else's memory seems to slip. My father was having trouble remembering, and we were all so worried that he may be going down the dementia path. He's in his late 70s and still works every day. I had him start taking Unfair Advantage and within a week or so, the memory issues were all gone! No kidding. We were all relieved, and he's now a raving fan. They have many more supplements that are excellent to keep your mind and body at its best performance levels.

- **Loop**—A portable display screen that can sit on a table or be passed around to family and friends. It instantly allows you to share pictures or videos safely. The size makes it easier to video chat. Loop is also a digital photo album and a great way to connect with family and friends.

o **Sleep Health**—Many experts would tell you that Americans have some of the worst sleep habits in the world and that most of us suffer from poor sleep health. This affects our body and mind health and our ability to heal. Going to bed at the same time each night is key (which I'm terrible at) as well as not looking at any screen device, TV, tablet, or cell phone for at least one hour before bed. Doing these two simple things can help you sleep better and become healthier, but if you're like me and lack the discipline, below are some items I've found very useful.

   ▪ **Bullet Proof Mat**—This is a mat the size of a bathroom floor mat with what looks to be plastic golf spikes sewn into it. If you have trouble sleeping, try laying on this for 10 minutes before you fall asleep. The premise is that most of the time you wake up (with the exception to go to the restroom) due to heat or discomfort.

But if you use acupressure to get the blood flowing through the entire back before sleeping, you'll have a much better shot at staying asleep. I use mine nightly. My mother, who's had five back surgeries, was having issues again, and I asked her to start using it and, yep, they went away—it was blood flow.

- **Noise**—Ensure that you have a noise machine if you're a light sleeper. White noise can help greatly to give your mind something to focus on so that it doesn't wake up at the furnace turning on. These are easy to find online or in any store.

- **Amber light vs. Blue light**—Make sure that your night-light is an amber color (orange/yellow) vs. a white/blue tinted light. The blue lights will tell your brain it's time to wake up, and it will be more difficult to not only get to sleep in the first place, but also more difficult to get back to sleep once you have gone to the restroom.

- **Human Charger**—One of my top recent finds! This device looks like an iPod with earbuds, but it doesn't play music. Scientists in Finland found through blind studies that you could introduce light into the brain not just through the eyes but through the skull. Your body's sleep cycle is controlled by your circadian rhythm, and this is controlled by sunshine. We spend 93% of our time indoors,[42] and if you live in a climate like I do, where three months out of the year there's no sun, then sleeping and even staying happy can be a struggle. The Human Charger has solved this issue by pumping sunshine (blue light) through your ears via the ear buds for 12 minutes when you wake up. It's magic! Seriously, in the studies of people with Seasonal Affective Disorder (SAD), 70% are feeling less depressed.[43] It also helps with jet lag and dementia. For me, it just changed me from a three-alarm girl to a one alarm girl, and now I wake up fresh and ready to go.

- **Vielight Neuro Alpha and Gamma**—A wearable light therapy device. This device stimulates the neurons in the brain to repair and heal themselves. It uses photomodulation, which is a form of light therapy. It improves mental clarity, enhances the immune system, improves energy, stimulates inner systems (such as improved circulation), and complements other existing wellness routines.

- **Wearable Technology**
  **Smart Watches and Activity Trackers—** Helps you to track your steps, heart rate, and other items. The idea is that when we're accountable to ourselves and others, we make better choices. There are way too many to mention, and they change daily, but here is a place to start. Remember, it's all about what's important to you, and don't forget the look and feel. I've bought many of these devices, only to stop using them because I didn't like them due to size or look. If the watch is a fitness or activity tracker, I've put those in a separate category.
  - **Bioguard**—Mayo Clinic device to remote monitor chronic or at-risk patients and scales and apps to update and track.
  - **Proof**—A unique and elegant solution to knowing if you have had too much alcohol to drive. It's a wearable wristband that can discreetly analyze

your blood alcohol content levels through your skin.

- **Fitbit**—Builds on this concept to engage us to get moving within a community of other Fitbitters.

  o **Alta**—Fits almost any wrist size, basic tracking—steps (no heart rate monitor or GPS).

  o **Zip**—Lets you track and compete with others and has a clock. Tracks distance, steps, and calories burned. No heart rate or GPS.

  o **Surge**—Tracks heart rate, GPS, steps, and has a clock.

  o **Charge 2**—Reminds you throughout the day to move. Tracks steps, heart rate, GPS, and has a clock.

- **Garmin Vivofit Fitness Band**—For under $100, this wearable tracks your activity level and then assigns you daily goals. It tracks sleep, steps, and calories, and can also hook up to a heart monitor.

- **Samsung Gear Fit 2**—A high-tech wearable with accelerometer, barometer, gyrometer, heart rate sensor, and

GPS. You can answer calls with it, and it has a touch screen.

- **Withings Go**—Simple display that switches between activity and clock. Doesn't have a heart rate or GPS.
- **Moov Now**—Has no screen and the tracker can last six months in between charges. Must use a smartphone to see data.
- **LETSCOM Fitness Tracker HR**—Activity tracker watch with heart rate monitor, waterproof smart fitness band with step counter, calorie counter, pedometer watch for kids, women, and men—for under $30.

o **Smart Rings**
  - **Oura**—Ring that monitors your pulse oxygen levels, heart rate, respiration, body temperature, and sleep. This is one of the smallest wellness devices available.
  - **Thim**—Ring that tracks and helps you to improve your sleep. It is only a sleep ring and not meant to be worn during the day.

o **Livio AI Hearing Aid**—Not just a hearing aid. This little, comfortable gadget is the newest wearable. It can easily monitor your body and brain health. It also translates 27 languages, has fall detection, is connected to your phone, and can even be found by GPS tracking when you can't remember where you left it!

o **Apple's AirPod**—Allows users to enable the operating system's Live Listen feature, which turns their phones into remote, directional microphones. They then may place their phones closer to a speaker to better hear the person's words.

o **Hearing Aid Apps**—A hearing aid app connects to your smartphone and allows you to use your hearing aid to make and receive calls and control volume.

o **Hapbee**—A feelings wearable device. It can be worn on your head or around your neck and connects to an app. You then select the feeling (happy, relaxed, alert, focused, sleepy, and calm) you desire. The patented electromagnetic frequency will deliver the desired feeling you choose all without chemicals going onto your body. It's basically a playlist for your mood.

Most of the current wearable tech is in its early stages for health management, but it's great for fitness management.

As listed above, Fitbit is one of the most popular name-brand, data-gathering bracelets that tracks your activities and encourages you through gamification (We will go into detail on gamification in a later chapter.). They capture the hearts of fitness enthusiasts that desire to get better results through tracking and tweaking. As the old saying goes, "What gets measured, gets improved."

Basis is a fitness and sleep tracker watch that was released in the past few years but claims to be the most comprehensive health watch on the market . . . and has now been discontinued. This is the issue with tech—you have to be flexible to change to the next thing.

I personally used this watch and loved the data but found it too large and clunky for my wrist, which meant it was hit or miss if I would wear it. Having said that, what the watch did was still outstanding. It gave me a push to get more active and develop better sleeping habits. The watch not only documented when I slept but also tracked my REM sleep, how many times I tossed and turned, or woke up. It employed gamification and also tracked my heart rate, steps, calories burned, perspiration, and body temperature.

I was mortified to find out that I burned almost the same amount of calories while I was sleeping as when I was awake! I guess sitting at your desk all day doesn't get the heart pumping. Just by learning this information, I've become more intentional about getting up and taking breaks, stretching, and taking the stairs instead of the elevator. By all accounts, I look fit, but my sleep score was terrible. The device woke me up, to say the least, to the benefits of sleep hygiene. I started darkening my windows, using the TV and phone less before sleeping, and created a consistent bedtime, which helped my score tremendously. The important thing is I feel better.

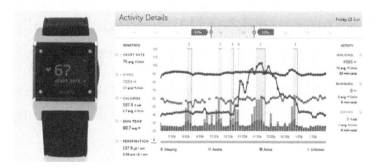

Many experts believe that Americans' terrible sleep habits are at the center of our health issues. The data you can see above is my personal data from the watch that gets synched with my computer and the MyBasis site. For less than $200 for the watch (no monthly fee), I had more health information reported 24/7 than my grandmother had when she was in short-term rehab. As we've discussed, it's not the event that we should all be concerned about but how to monitor the data we can easily obtain to reduce the risk of an event or put in place an action plan prior to the crisis happening.

Hearing aids are a wearable technology that's been around since the 17th century, with the first electronic hearing aide in 1898. Cochlear implants became revolutionary for those with extreme hearing loss but required surgery. Now, there's a hearing aid from Sonitus called Soundbite that's bone-conducted but requires no surgery and is FDA-approved. The really exciting part of this new technology is they're moving toward the ability to implant a hearing aide in a molar. Imagine a world where you're not having to look for the lost hearing aid anymore.

 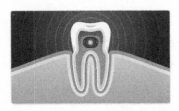

An assistive hearing device is the Nuheara IQbuds. They're wireless assistive hearing devices that work just like ear buds you use with your phone or tablet. As a matter of fact, they double duty as ear buds. They have various settings to control what you're hearing. This is important as louder isn't always better. The IQbuds hook directly to the TV so that others, three rooms over, don't have to hear what you're watching. Best of all, I can hit restaurant mode and hear what's being said at my table instead of all of the noise. While these don't replace a hearing aid, they're an excellent, cost-effective solution pricing at a tenth the cost of hearing aids.

Livio AI hearing aid is one of my favorite new technologies. Why would I get so excited about a hearing aid? Because it's not just a hearing aid. This little, comfortable gadget is the newest wearable. Forget the wrist to monitor your health; the ear is where it is at. Blood vessels are much closer to the device, so it can easily monitor your body and brain health. It also translates 27 languages, has fall detection, is connected to your phone, and can even be found by GPS tracking when you can't remember where you left it! I plan to get one and use it, not because I have a diagnosed hearing loss but for the monitoring benefits. I do have difficulty hearing in restaurants, but this isn't the primary reason. I want my health monitored, but I've never been a fan of smart watches. Plus, I can get rid of my Bluetooth earbuds. But the biggest win will be confidence when I travel. I'll be able to understand the waiter, taxi driver, and the hotel clerk.

We've discussed hearing, now it's time to move on to glasses. While Google Glass has been in the news over and over again, they've never taken off like Google thought they would. They have, however, inspired others to make glasses that are a combination between the sci-fi Oculus Rift virtual-reality gaming glasses and the glasses actor LeVar Burton wore on *Star Trek: The Next Generation*, which allowed him to see even though he was born blind.

What if they could make the blind see or, at the very least, help those who are sight-impaired with degenerative eye diseases see?

Professor Kohn of the University of California has developed such a device. He's using computers and math to correct the distortions seen by those with macular degeneration. He's working on both glasses and contact lenses that would be tailored toward the individual user.

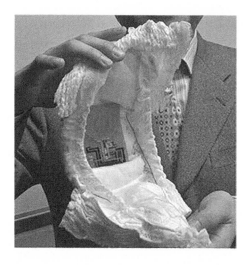

If you have an aging parent, this may be of interest to you. The Japanese have been using smart diaper technologies for babies, and these now have moved to the senior market. Adult smart disposable diapers are outselling baby smart diapers due to the rising age of seniors in Japan. The technology sends a wireless signal to the caregiver that lets them know if the diaper is wet. This is a tremendous advancement as it lets your elderly parents age with dignity. It's especially true if you're dealing with a parent who has Alzheimer's/Dementia; they no longer need to be undressed to check to see if there's an actual need for a change.

So far, the sensors that have been developed in Tokyo measure moisture, so you or a caregiver can know when to change someone. Pixie Scientific's diapers also alert you when the sensors detect a urinary tract infection, prolonged dehydration, or developing kidney problems.

I know with my grandmother's recent issues, these would have been a great help to our family at home. Quite often, the onset of dementia gets misdiagnosed, and it's actually a UTI (urinary tract infection). In older people, UTIs can cause confusion that mimics dementia. Left untreated, a UTI can cause serious health issues. Sensors of this type could not only help with correct diagnosis and getting Mom or Grandma back on her feet but also increase dignity.

Another great wearable tech that we've been trialing is the Freestyle Libre glucose monitor. My dad recently was diagnosed with "sugar," as he likes to call it, a.k.a. diabetes. He has high blood pressure and macular degeneration, so with the sugar diabetes diagnosis, it's a real concern. They impact each other negatively when not in the normal ranges. While at a business conference, I met a young man wearing a small disc arm patch about the size of a half dollar. I asked him if he was quitting smoking, and I congratulated him. He said, "no" and explained that from all his readings, he's learned that sugar controls how well we think and our health. He wanted to understand what foods and drinks impacted his sugar and then how to make changes so that he could be his best self.

A wearable device to compile data before you're sick that helps you to make wise choices; what is this world coming to? I asked him if they were expensive and to my surprise, they weren't. I asked him if I needed a doctor's prescription, and to my amazement, I didn't. So what did I do? I immediately ordered two of them and had them shipped to our home.

I mentioned before that I live in a social experiment. I experiment, within our family, the best ways to live our best future by using design ideas, health devices, and anything that might be called "smart home tech." Well, this was a perfect opportunity to try another experiment. I introduced the idea to my mother and father, and they were excited. I think that in the past, we've had so much success that they now look forward to the next new tech I bring home to make their lives better. So far, we *have* had pretty good success.

A little backstory, my father loves bread, Arnold Palmer sweet iced tea, and desserts in general.

When he came to live with us, he was a huge Pepsi drinker, and we asked that he stop drinking pop as it was so bad for him. Out of respect for us, he did but then found Arnold Palmer sweet iced tea as a replacement. To me, it was like mainlining sugar; this seemed to be our weekly battle.

Until, that is, the Freestyle Libre Glucose Monitor Patch entered our lives. The idea for the patch is if you could know immediately what made your sugar go up or down without the pain of constant daily pricking, you could then adjust your diet and exercise to how your body reacts to foods vs. what a doctor thinks it would do. This could mean that my father could keep some of his favorite foods and drinks. Or he'd have factual data that the iced tea was killing him. The thought that he could have a patch on his arm with a hair-sized needle that would stay on for 14 days and then read his blood glucose levels at any time was very appealing.

As you can see, sensors are just starting to surface in everything, from reading the blood glucose levels in our tears and on our arm patches to how we take our medicine, when to change a diaper, knowing how long we slept—including how many times we tossed and turned and what our sleep quality was—to sensing the electrical impulses in our brain and allowing us to move paralyzed body parts.

Athletes and the military are at the forefront of sensor technology but make no mistake—it is weaving into all of our everyday lives.

Soccer shoes have been equipped with sensors to discover speed and how many miles a player runs in an average game. The results are staggering: A pro soccer player runs seven miles during a 90-minute match.[44] Basketballs, soccer balls, and tennis racquets are now equipped with sensor technology to help you understand how to strike the ball better or how often you're hitting the sweet spot with your racquet.

Our children and grandchildren will never argue with the TV over whether or not the ball went in the goal and the referee made a bad call because the ball and the goal plane will both have sensors and automatically signal a goal.

Fabrics are currently being released that have sensors woven into them. A quick search on the Internet reveals new categories of wearable tech every day, and health management is looking to be the largest sector. Baby Boomers not only need to integrate home IoT (Internet of Things) and safety sensor technology but also follow health monitoring that allows, with ease, the monitoring of your heart rate and sleep and your loved ones. The game is certainly changing.

Anyone involved in healthcare or dealing with an elderly loved one knows that medication compliance is difficult. Besides toileting issues, help with medication seems to be a huge driver to getting Mom into assisted living after she forgot to take her pills or took too many, sending her to the hospital. While senior living has done a great job at managing medications, it is still unclear if they're working properly for the individual. What if we could know that Mom not only took her medications, but they're working? Protus Digital Health has a solution for this, which, when taken to the next level, could also be used for mom to stay in her home longer as data will be immediately sent to the doctor or caregiver via Bluetooth if she's missed her dose or taken too much.

Protus Digital Health has created the first FDA-approved ingestible sensor (the size of a grain of sand) for medication compliance and feedback. The sensor reacts with the stomach acid and creates a type of potato battery with its small amounts of magnesium and copper. This allows data to be sent out to a smartphone or other device. The device passes out through the normal process.

Currently, Helius (Protus Digital Health's name for the pill) is being utilized for heart failure and hypertension but looks to add other chronic disease management. This is the first step in ingestible sensors that will be coming down the pike for all of us, giving us better feedback loops. If we know what's actually working immediately, we potentially could take fewer pills, with better results.

## Induction Looping Technology

Almost one in two people over 65 have some form of hearing loss. Those with moderate hearing loss have triple the risk of cognitive decline and dementia, per AARP.[45] Hearing can cause not only issues for the person not hearing but also for the loved ones, coworkers, and friends who constantly have to repeat themselves, are misunderstood, and plain frustrated all around with the situation. When communication becomes difficult, folks become paranoid and disconnected. Of course, we've had hearing aids for years, but this only helps with part of the issue. While induction looping technology has been around for years, it isn't well known. The basic premise is that if you're hearing-impaired, even with a hearing aid, it is difficult to hear in a large setting such as at church, sporting events, airports, concerts, activities, dances, etc. Basically, it's tough to hear with a hearing aid anywhere a microphone or speaker system is used. Induction looping allows those with a

hearing aid to hear directly from the microphone without all the background noise. Louder
doesn't always mean easier to understand.

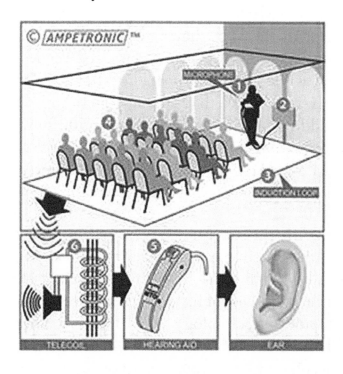

How it works is a loop of wire is installed in the
space that can be small or has large events and
uses a speaker system; this can be anywhere
from a living room to a stadium, bingo hall, or
church. The wire transmits a magnetic signal to
a telecoil, which is found in most hearing aids.
The hearing aid can then directly hear what's
coming out of the microphone, TV, or speakers
without all the background noise. Europe has

been using this technology for years, but the U.S. has been slow to adopt. There are some 48 million people with hearing loss in the United States.[46] Michigan has been the largest initiator in the U.S., having installed induction looping systems in several hundred venues as well as the Detroit airport and Michigan State University's basketball stadium. New York City is adding hearing loops in almost 500 subway information booths,[47] and for all future taxis—they'll be equipped with looping technology and have been branded the "Taxi of Tomorrow."

As with most great technology, the looping solution is simple and elegant. You might be thinking why can't Bluetooth solve this issue without the cost of installing a looping system? Bluetooth technology sucks battery power, while the telecoil requires zero. This gives the telecoil a major advantage. Another advantage is that looping can be utilized in both large and small areas while other wireless technologies (such as Bluetooth) can only be used in small areas. Finally, hearing aids all have different proprietary wireless technology depending on the manufacturer. The telecoil is the only universal wireless receiver.

**Key Benefits to looping system**:

- **Universal**—compatible with any manu-facturer's hearing aid
- **Affordable**—very low-cost technology per space
- **Energy Efficient**—zero drain on the battery
- **Flexible**—can be used in large and small spaces
- **Scalable**—start with one space, add on over time
- **Easy**—simple to operate, both for the resident and the staff, reduced listening effort
- **Independent and Convenient**—if looping technology is available, the hearing-impaired person is completely independent of the need to ask for a por-table assistive device, then having to plan to pick it up and remember to return it
- **Dignity**—no need to ask for earphones or to be moved closer

Interviews that have occurred after installing the technology will bring you to tears. Those enjoying the technology speak about how they were able to enjoy the event, hear the sermon for the first time in years, or just simply be part of the moment with everyone else, laughing at the joke that was told. In the *Hearing Journal,* Dr. Linda Remensnyder tells of other denominations attending services at St. Mary's of the Annunciation Catholic Church because they have a hearing loop. We all want to engage in life, and hearing is one of the most important senses that allows us to do so. Being alive means being able to communicate. Something as simple as being able to hear the joke, TV show, sermon, or your favorite song connects us and feeds our soul.

Positive statements from the study were as follows:[48]

- "I didn't have to work so hard to hear the speaker."
- "In a loop, I don't need to read the captions."
- "No more need to read lips."
- **"Freeing."**
- "Feels like I have normal hearing."
- "The clarity in a loop is **amazing.**"
- "I could hear things my wife couldn't hear."
- **"So much better, I cried."**

- "I would not attend (meetings, church services, etc.) if they didn't have a loop."
- "It is awesome to be able to understand, not just hear. I don't think folks with normal hearing can appreciate just how awesome it is!"

Imagine, with this one simple technology, how your life or that of a loved one could improve by the simple fact that you, or they, could hear what was being said. TVs could be turned down. Engagement in conversations would exponentially increase, creating more energy and a higher quality of life for all. The ripple effect will be enormous for everyone involved.

For more information on how you can have this technology implemented into your home, please see their website: (**hearingloop.org/ vendors.htm).**

## Telemedicine

Remember back to ancient times? Those days of yore when you actually had to go to the doctor for a pregnancy test? Okay, maybe you don't remember, but it used to happen. Now? You go to any drug store and buy a kit. This kind of instant testing tool has created enormous flexibility in our lives. Now, imagine it in much broader terms, and you've got telemedicine.

Telemedicine is about technology giving you the ability to take your doctor with you. You're no longer going to be anchored, or some might say *imprisoned,* to whatever your support system is—i.e., your doctor or your health records. Telemedicine is real-time, real data. With Telemedicine, you'll never have to make an appointment to go to the doctor again unless you want to.

Telemedicine will allow you to take your doctor with you wherever you might be: Scottsdale, Rome, a cruise, and your home. Telemedicine can range from a phone call to a video chat. Insurance companies are finally starting to see the light that most office visits could have been handled with a video call, and they're paving the way to making telemedicine billable in several states. Add in any health data device, such as Kardia, Freestyle Libre, or iPhone health devices, and the doctor can read your vitals while you're in two different places. No more having to go to a clinic when you're out of town and give a random doctor your 60-year medical history!

## Fitness

Let me start by defining what I think *fitness* is all about. To me, it encompasses physical, emotional, and spiritual well-being. I really believe that without all three, you're not *fit*. And technology is here for you in this part of your life, too, providing a lot of tools that can help you take back control of your body, mind, and spirit.

There's yoga, the memory diet, the balance gym, and the vision gym—just to name a few. Think of these tools as helping your body, which maybe has been asleep for a little bit, wake back up.

The more you sit, the more you disconnect. And anytime you start disconnecting, you start degrading, then you start atrophying in body, mind, and your spirit too.

Maybe you're finding yourself sleeping more, not engaging in conversation, or reading or growing in any number of ways. By making the choice to physically reconnect, you start to plug back in. And I do see this very much like physically plugging an electrical cord back into a socket that's been disconnected—it brings you back to life.

Fitness is about reconnecting your body, mind, and spirit so they can work the way they all should to power you up fully. The action of plugging back in and making the connection is proactive. You can start by taking a walk around the neighborhood, volunteering, reconnecting with old school mates on Facebook, going to church, temple, mosque, or wherever your religious preferences take you. You can join a club, start taking supplements, meditate, or whatever you desire. Start with one and then add on when you feel you can. In a year from now, I promise you'll be glad you did. If you thought today you had another 50 years to live, guaranteed, and the only thing you could do is decide if you wanted to live them sick or healthy, which would you choose? What actions would you be willing to take today to know that in five years, you could live free from sickness, assuming that was your choice?

To me, this is all about what lifts your spirit. For some, it's meditation. For others, it's movies. While some might find it in a religious community, others feel it in nature. And then others use yoga to connect to their spirit, and still others connect through music, dance, or laughter.

So this is really all about remembering what you need to do or what you need to experience to feed your spirit. Think of this as your new prescription, tailoring something so specifically to you because you know who you want to continue being as you age.

My point is that most of us live with a mentality that the future is dimmer than our past—both mentally and physically. With all the technology coming down the pike that will help us to be our best, and what you'll learn in the upcoming chapters, we have to consider that we're in control of our destiny, and that means we have to make wiser choices. Left to our own devices, we *will* binge-watch TV, we *will* eat all the Thin Mints, potato chips, ice cream (Pick your poison!), and we *will* choose to disengage from something that we used to do and liked because we're tired and don't want to put in the effort.

While I'm far from retirement, I used to think of it as not having to show up anymore. What a profound statement—let it sink in. I used to think retirement meant *I'd stopped showing up for life.* I would no longer have to show up for anyone anymore. I wouldn't have to look nice or be accountable. Then I realized that I don't want to live out my days looking like a hot mess, not adding value. So I've decided that, for me, *retirement* will be choosing where I can add value. It will be all of me showing up, with less stress, but with the freedom and confidence to do what I want, when and where I want. So when you're changing to that season of your life, the question is: *How do you balance being a human being who's doing what you want to do and also one who's making wise choices for your long term health and well-being? What happens when you lose community?*

Remember, it's up to you. What's the *prescription* you need to write for your life to be the best it can be?

# CHAPTER 9

## CANNABIS & AGING

Full disclosure, while in high school, I was pretty intense. I had friends in all different social groups and was even president of the entire high school. My mother was also the high school head cook. This created two problems for me. First, if I got busted drinking, I would have been kicked off of the student council, and second, my mom heard about every party in the lunch line. I needed to maintain my good kid status but be able to decompress a bit. For me, the answer was smoking pot. I didn't do it every day but enough that I knew what I was doing. Pot reduced my intensity and made it easier for others to be around me and me around others. It took the edge off.

When I went off to college, I worked three jobs to make ends meet, so paying for anything recreational was out of the question. And then I got married and had kids. My days of smoking pot were a high school memory. As I got older, a lot of my highly successful friends would mention they smoked.

Then the laws started passing in Colorado, California, and other states. CBD oil and the benefits for seizures and other health issues surfaced, including the positives of pot with cancer and dementia.

Yet my industry of senior living was still ignoring the subject, even though every conference was focused on how to attract Baby Boomers to senior living. My first thought was: *Heck yeah, the spaces we design are awesome, but my friends would never come unless they could have their freedom and still use marijuana or cannabis.*

So I decided to break the silence and conduct an anonymous survey of Boomers and cannabis use that I could use to start a healthy dialog. What I found opened my eyes. When I presented the data online, I was even challenged that it was overstated—I can tell you that this isn't the case. We had over 15,000 respondents from all

50 states and eliminated 4,000 responses that felt illegitimate (possibly generated from a bot).

It's an important conversation to explore. The stigma of using cannabis is fading, and now with Canada making it legal for both medicinal and recreational use, I believe we will see a huge shift in the U.S. moving towards federal legalization.

## Cannabis for Boomers: An Emerging Market

For many Baby Boomers, the word marijuana conjures up nothing more than, perhaps, some recreational memories of the 1960s. But a significant number of seniors have displayed an increasing interest in the potential benefits of marijuana, also known as cannabis, as a modern-day option for improving their quality of life. Both medical and non-medical cannabis products hold potential benefits for this aging segment of the population.

As more states have legalized its use, there's a lot more to know about the applications of marijuana. Let's examine this phenomenon to see how legal cannabis has become big business, how marijuana might help Boomers with certain conditions, and what forms of this substance have become available for purchase.

## The Need for Real Data

As a senior living designer for over 25 years, I'm often shocked at how our industry talks out both sides of its mouth. My clients say they want younger, healthier residents in their senior living homes but do little to meet them where they are. Let's be honest, if you have ever visited someone in an assisted living, memory care neighborhood, or short-term rehab (a facility for recovering from knee and hip replacement), then you know that even in senior living homes that charge anywhere from $45,000 a year after taxes up to $150,000 a year, you're getting a beautiful environment with lots of services and amenities, but you aren't buying freedom.

This is the rub for Boomer friends who don't just want freedom; they consider it oxygen to their soul. Let's factor in that recreational drugs were a definer for their generation, and quite a few have never stopped, at least when it comes to marijuana.

When attending functions within the senior living industry, discussing the need to allow senior living residents to partake in cannabis for medical or recreational reasons is like showing up to church in your underwear. I'm not talking about a housecoat. I'm talking about full-on Tyra Banks Victoria Secret undies and maybe even the wings! You're looked at like you're the antichrist, to put it kindly.

I didn't even realize how polarizing the subject was until I was on the construction site of one of our projects (a brand-new senior living facility, which is incredible) for my client. I streamed Facebook Live with the property in the background (I did *not* mention it by name.) and asked everyone to take my marijuana survey. By the time I left the site and my plane landed back home, I had 20 messages telling me to take the post down ASAP. The client wanted in no way to be associated with marijuana. I apologized and immediately took the post down. But this was exactly why I decided to do the survey—someone needed to. Everyone was running around scared to death of the marijuana monster in the closet. Yet they didn't even know how their customers felt about the subject. We need real data to start the conversation.

I felt so strongly about the need for the data that I postponed the release of this book, which was completed in March 2018, to be able to include this chapter and the results.

## The Survey

Let's clear the air—I'm not pro marijuana or against. I just wanted to have a discussion with my clients about the subject with real facts. My personal mission is to help seniors and Boomers embrace living and to help move from fear to freedom, and this subject seemed to evoke a lot of fear.

The survey consisted of 12 simple questions:

1) Do you live in a state that's legalized marijuana?

2) What state do you live in?

3) If you currently use marijuana, why?

4) If you don't use any form of marijuana, why?

5) If you use marijuana, in what form?

6) How often do you partake?

7) Why do you use marijuana?

8) In what social setting do you use marijuana, if you do?

9) Do you grow marijuana?

10) Do you use CBD oil?

11) If you use CBD, for what reason?

12) Your Age

I opted to use a third-party quiz software called Leadquizzes to ensure the anonymity of those taking the survey. This means, other than the answers to the questions above, I have no data and no emails, nothing. In hindsight, I wish I would have asked if they were male or female and possibly their economic bracket, which I think would have been very useful.

I posted the survey on LinkedIn, Instagram, and Facebook and ran ads, posted videos, and begged my coworkers, vendors, family, and friends to not only take the survey but to pass it along. It took around a month to get around 15,000 takers and over 67% completed the survey, which translated to over 10,000 legitimate survey results!

The results, frankly, shocked me. I believe they'll create a great dialog for senior living, our nation on aging and aging in place, and what it means to have the freedom to be your best you.

## The Rise of Medical and Non-Medical Cannabis

Times have changed since the U.S. universally condemned all forms of cannabis as illegal

substances. In recent years, laws broadly le-
galizing medical use have been enacted in
Arizona, Hawaii, Montana, North Dakota,
Minnesota, Michigan, Illinois, Arkansas,
Louisiana (except for smokable forms), Ohio,
West Virginia (but only for cannabis-infused
products), Pennsylvania, Maryland, Delaware,
New York, Connecticut, Rhode Island, and
New Hampshire. Additionally, recreational
marijuana has been legalized in Alaska,
California, Oregon, Colorado, Massachusetts,
Maine, Nevada, Vermont, and the District of
Columbia. These changes have brought a ma-
jor new industry into being. It's estimated that
the total CBD market will be worth some $2.1
billion by 2020.[49]

There's nothing new about the use of cannabis.
Cannabis has been administered both recreationally and as a medicine for thousands of
years. The ancient Chinese used it to treat everything from gout and rheumatism to memory
problems and malaria. Ancient India found it
helpful for digestive issues and also brewed a
relaxing tea with it. Medieval Europeans in-
corporated cannabis into folk medicine, and
as early as the 1700s, American and English
doctors were studying marijuana's potential
medical benefits.

## States Not Legal in Any Form

## States Legal Recreationally

## A Variety of Benefits

Today's society has access to many different forms of cannabis, some of which produce altered states of consciousness and some of which don't. The difference is the presence or absence of THC, the compound that actually makes people *high*. Recreational marijuana depends on THC to create its relaxant effects. Cannabis products created for medical use focus on another ingredient instead—CBD, or cannabidiol. CBD oil and related CBD products don't have psychoactive effects. They do, however, offer many promising medical benefits, especially for seniors and Boomers troubled by age-related complaints. These include:

- **Alzheimer's disease**—In the laboratory, the THC in recreational marijuana has demonstrated the ability to slow the progression of beta-amyloids, the abnormal protein accumulations associated with Alzheimer's/Dementia.
- **Cancer and chemotherapy symptoms**—Elevated cancer risk is a sad fact of aging. Cancer patients often experience nausea and vomiting, whether they're receiving chemotherapy or palliative care. Smoking marijuana appears to ease these symptoms, along with neurological damage related to their cancer treatment.
- **Chronic pain**—Seniors often struggle with chronic pain conditions such as arthritis. Studies indicate that CBD products can help relieve arthritis symptoms and other forms of chronic pain. The THC in recreational marijuana also appears effective for easing chronic pain symptoms.
- **Mood disorders**—Depression, anxiety, and other mood disorders can afflict empty-nesters and seniors dealing with various health problems. CBD products can help manage these potentially dangerous conditions by increasing the amount of serotonin in their system.

- **Loss of appetite**—As taste buds age and sedentary habits take over, many seniors lose interest in food, leading to malnutrition. Medical marijuana can re-activate the <u>insula</u>, an area of the brain that encourages appetite.
- **Glaucoma**—Pressures inside the eye can destroy the optic nerve. This condition, known as glaucoma, becomes more prevalent after age 60. Medical marijuana has demonstrated the ability to <u>lower high eye pressure</u>, potentially preventing blindness.

## The Many Faces of Cannabis-Based Products

Cannabis comes in a wide range of <u>delivery methods</u>, of which smoking marijuana is only one. While smokable marijuana is indeed available in a variety of strains and brands, CBD oil (the key ingredient in many CBD products) can also be found in:

- **Tinctures**—Tinctures contain CBD oil in a fluid base. In its more highly concentrated forms, you only need to put a couple of drops under your tongue.

- **Capsules**—You can take CBD capsules just as you might take any nutritional supplement.
- **Topical products**—CBD creams and lotions can be applied directly to the skin. This can be an effective method for treating chronic joint pain and inflammatory disorders.
- **Sprays**—CBD sprays are meant to be sprayed into the mouth or throat. While the concentration tends to be weaker than that of other delivery methods, sprays are quick and convenient for travelers.
- **Vapes**—It's possible to take CBD oil in vape form. But this delivery method, like the spray method, provides relatively small dosages.
- **Edibles**—There are a variety of CBD candies, gums, and other edible products on the market today (at least for residents of states in which such purchases are currently legal).

## The Results

Percentage of participants by age group

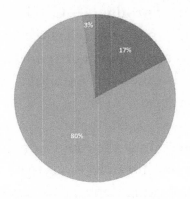

■ Borderline Boomer 50-53    ■ Boomer 54-72    ■ Silent Generation 73-93

**Who took the survey?** 80% of those that took the survey were Baby Boomers, with 17% being a borderline Boomer, ages 50-53, and 3% over 72 years of age.

While I'm very pleased to see such a large sample from the Boomers, I wonder if we'd have had higher results on those age 73 and up had we conducted a house to house or mail survey. I believe the channels in which dispersed the survey possibly hampered them to respond.

**Where do they live?** The biggest shocker was that 37% of the respondents live in a state where marijuana isn't legal for medical or recreational use! This gives even more validity to the survey as this isn't the result: *It's legal here, so of course, we do it.* I have to be honest, I thought the majority of the respondents would have been in California, Colorado, and Nevada since *everything is legal* there; however, Florida, Ohio, California, Texas, Michigan, Pennsylvania, Oklahoma, Indiana, and Illinois had the top respondents in terms of number of people who participated in the survey.

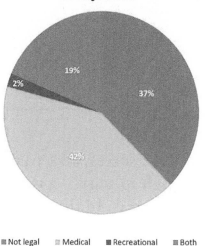

**Do you live in a state that has legalized marijuana?**

■ Not legal    ▨ Medical    ■ Recreational    ▨ Both

Certain states that are technically legal for medical marijuana, like Ohio, may still be perceived by the general public as illegal, hence why the 37% of respondents stated they lived in a state where it was not legal.

## How often do you partake?

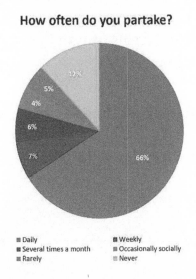

**How often do you partake?**

- Daily
- Weekly
- Several times a month
- Occasionally socially
- Rarely
- Never

According to the survey, 66% partake daily. If this isn't enough to start a conversation, then I don't know what is. In the survey, 12% have never used, and 5% do so rarely. This leaves 83% who partake often with the vast majority doing it as much as they brush their teeth. Keep in mind that 80% of the folks taking the survey were Boomers. These numbers could be even higher if we took out the Silent Generation and the Gen Xers.

## Why do you use marijuana?

While 17% don't use at all (This ties into the 5% + 12% = 17% above.), almost 50% partake both for recreational and medical reasons.

**If you currently use marijuana, why?**

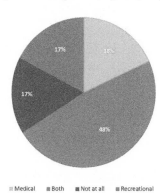

⬛ Medical    ⬛ Both    ⬛ Not at all    ⬛ Recreational

Then there's almost a 50/50 split for those surveyed who partake either medically or recreationally.

## Do you grow marijuana?

**Do you grow marijuana?**

YES, 15%

NO, 85%

☐ NO  ☐ YES

Survey says, No, at least 85% of the respondents don't. This means in those 41 states where recreational marijuana isn't legal, Boomers are getting it, somehow.

## If you use marijuana, do you use CBD oil? And why?

62% of respondents use CBD oil, and the vast majority—59%—use it for aches and pains.

## If You Use Marijuana do Use CBD Oil?

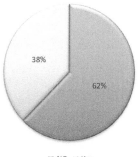

NO ⊔ Yes

A shocking note on the results was that very few sited glaucoma for their use of CBD, which may be due to the fact that they're using marijuana instead.

Other than general aches and pains, the highest percentages of use were for anxiety at 11%, arthritis at 7%, insomnia at 7%, cancer at 3%, and back pain at 3% were the other top reasons for using CBD oil.

While the numbers were too small to chart, there were several respondents who were using CBD for their pets.

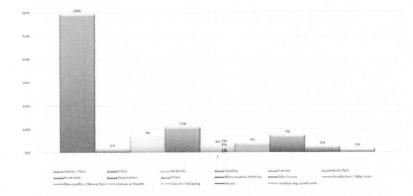

As you can see, there's a great deal more to marijuana than just getting high, especially for seniors battling health and comfort challenges.

My hope is that, cannabis, just as any other biohack, gets used responsibly to improve our quality of life as we age. And if you're wondering, I don't partake at the moment, but the thought isn't out of the question for the future.

# CHAPTER 10
## SMART HOUSE

Let's start by explaining what a smart house is. The typical definition of a smart house is a house where your appliances, lighting, heating and cooling, water temperature, TVs, phones, music devices, cameras, and security devices are all connected. They talk through Bluetooth or Wi-Fi from a hub and can be accessed by you, your phone, or your computer. They learn your patterns of life and can save you money by shutting items off when they know you don't normally use them. They can alert the police, wake you up, make your family room a disco, and turn off the stove if you leave it on too long.

It all sounds fantastic right? Sign me up right now . . . here's the glitch. Smart homes are a lot like fixing your own car; I'm sure it will get simpler in the future, but they currently make me feel like I'm 16 again.

On one of those days I remember thinking, *I was always pretty good at fixing my bicycle, so how hard could it be fixing a couple items on my car?* With all of the confidence that a teenager has, I went to one of those auto parts stores like Pep Boys or AutoZone. All I remember is how it felt like I was in a factory that built cars rather than my local—very easy to use—department store. All I needed was some oil and a couple of windshield wipers. When I got to the counter, I found out that even those required that I know the make and model of my car. The clerk asked the make and model, and I answered . . . "Red." (It's the same answer I give politely to the clerk when I check in to the hotel and I'm asked the same question about my rental car; thankfully, they take pity on me.) Apparently "red" wouldn't do, so I went back out to the parking lot and obtained the needed info. Then I made my way back up to the counter with the make and model as requested. They opened up this huge blue book, found my car, what oil it took, and the model number of wiper blades, and then I was off to the races. Or so I thought, until I had to install them and add the oil. It all worked out, but it made me realize that it was a bit more difficult than I anticipated.

Creating smart homes is a lot like getting oil and wipers for your car; if you know the make and model and are willing to put some elbow grease in, then you can probably do it like I have on a fairly small scale. Granted it's just my Google Home hooked up to my Phillips Hue lights, but I'm able to turn the lights on and off, play music from my phone through Google Home, ask Google a joke, the news, or the weather, but she still won't sync right with my calendar. I've yet mustered the courage to try and connect the Nest thermostat and camera to the Google Home as they're working fine right now, and who knows, I might screw it up and leave us without heat in the middle of winter.

Now if you're the Iron Man type or some sort of tech genius, then God love you, you probably shouldn't even be reading this chapter. This is for those of us just trying to figure this thing out and understand how it can improve our lives. To put it simply, we want technology to serve us and not the other way around. I don't want hooking up my smart house components and keeping them all connected and functioning properly to become a full-time hobby or worse, a job. I just want to live like *The Jetsons* did with my 3D printed food, Rosie the robot cleaning everything, flying cars, and maybe get my figure back to what I looked like in high school. That's not too much to ask, right?

Now that I've scared you, don't worry too much because chances are good you already have a smart home. Do you have a thermostat that automatically tells the furnace to come on and off based upon your settings? If you have a garage, do you have a garage door opener? Maybe one even mounted on the inside of your house? Do you have a device or contraption that alerts you when someone is at the front door (hint: it's also called the doorbell)? I know I'm being funny, but these are smart home features. Does your car connect with the garage door and open it without another remote in the car? Can you auto set your coffee pot to come on in the morning, so that hot cup of joe is waiting for you on command? Then I bet you already have a smart home . . . oh, my gosh, I just realized I sound like Jeff Foxworthy when he does his shtick. Sorry about that, I must have been channeling a redneck.

It does make sense that it all should be able to be connected together in a plug and play model similar to our phone or our computers. When it's done right, it's very similar to how your phone works. Your phone is the basis of where all the apps sit; they work together to help you take a photo, post it to Facebook, or email it to a friend. You can put reminders on your phone to have it start playing music to wake you up at a certain time and so on. It's all a beautiful ballet. Now think about your phone having more apps; this time, they control your thermostat, lights, TV, and more.

How cool can this be? You're driving back from visiting your mother's for the weekend, and before you left, you set the thermostat to 65 degrees Fahrenheit. It's zero degrees out now, and you should be home in an hour. You log in to your Nest app, which is on your phone, and turn the temperature up to 72 degrees. (I realize some of you just thought I was nuts going above 70 degrees. Don't judge me; I have a low core body temperature.) Voila! When you walk in your door, it's nice and cozy as it can be.

Or let's try another scenario. You're at the airport getting ready to take off for vacation, and you realize you left the stove on . . . have no fear; an app is here! Just log on and turn it off. No worries, no panicking phone calls to neighbors, friends, and family all the while trying to figure out how to get them the keys. Just use your finger and swipe, and it's done. Smart home technology can provide immense peace of mind, energy savings, and the conveniences that we will discuss in the many products that are on the market to help make your life more enjoyable.

If you're thinking this is a fad, it's not. Smart homes were actually created in Scotland in 1975. This *fad* is similar to indoor plumbing. Smart Home technology is already here. The problem is, I would never even think about trying to plumb my house or install a new hot water tank, yet the commercials and big box stores make us think it's as easy to install as plugging in a radio and turning the knob to our favorite station. My advice after I've struggled is this—hire an expert just like you'd hire an electrician or plumber. You'll have none of the pain, leaks, or fires and all of the benefits of the technology.

One thing to know is that it all works with a strong Wi-Fi. You need to get this installed in your home first and make sure that it's boosted to the whole house. I ended up having to purchase an Orbi system after I'd purchased another system and wasted my money. The reason the first system didn't work was that it took my Wi-Fi system and split it. So the signal was degraded—the more people we had on it, the slower it became, and depending on how far away you were from the *home hub*, you could end up being in a dead spot. With the Orbi system, somehow, it doesn't split the signal but *clones* it instead (best way I can describe it). Not only are there no dead spots, but it was also incredibly easy to set up. It also works with Google Home and Amazon Alexa (We have both.), but similar to the Nest; I'm not ready to work through getting these all connected yet.

Once you have great Wi-Fi, you can decide what's most important to you and your family. Do you want to stream Hulu, Netflix, Amazon Prime, YouTube, or others to your TV? If you don't know what these are—no worries—I'll explain. Remember, things are changing so fast that you NEVER need to feel dumb about technology. I'm at conferences with the most brilliant minds in the world, and when someone presents a new technology, we all look at each other like they must have looked at Galileo when he first described the world was round instead of flat. Eventually, we all get it. Just remember you don't have to understand the physics behind how a car works or how to fix it to be able to enjoy driving it.

If you're not familiar with names I've listed above, these services are basically like cable TV (on demand for you). Instead of waiting for a show to air, you search for it on your TV, phone, computer, or tablet, and watch away. Typically, these services come with a monthly fee. Sometimes, Amazon Prime comes with basic movies and TV, but if you want to watch a new release that still may be in the theatre, you pay an extra fee on top of the monthly. The really cool thing about having a smart TV is you can get a stick to plug in to it that provides access to these services that you already use on your phone, computer, or tablet.

Amazon has the Firestick, Apple has Apple TV, Google has Chromecast, and there's also Roku. You only need one. If you're an Apple user, then Apple TV is probably your best bet. If you're not an Apple user (I'm not.), then you can pick any of the others. I went with Firestick. It was easy to install, and I even got one for my mother. She stated she "felt like a queen." While I'm not exactly sure what she meant by that, I know that she loves the wide range of movies, shows, etc., that she has access to through our Netflix, Hulu, and Amazon accounts. It is possible to get rid of cable when you have a stick and the accounts. I may try that, but I need to make sure I don't lose *Oak Island* first. ☺

What this means to you is that all your entertainment will now be linked to all your devices. And if you have an Amazon account, you can even hook up Alexa to your TV and order items online. It's like the Home Shopping Network taken to the next level.

You may be wondering, what if all my stuff in my smart house that's now connected to the Wi-Fi loses power? I highly recommend getting a generator if you live outside the city. We have one, even though we live in the city because we live in a four-generational household. When I moved my parents and grandmother in with us, it seemed too big of a risk not to have one, and now I'm even more glad we did get one. I'm not sure which would be worse— freezing to death or the Hallmark channel going out (Please know I'm kidding! This is just a little four generational household humor.).

We've discussed the general concepts of a smart home and many of the pros and the cons, but how does it work? And further, besides being really cool, how can it help me age in place?

A smart home can be set up to sensors for motion, temperature, heat, etc., and this could trigger certain actions that you want. The way this happens is by using a site called **IFTTT** (If Then, Then That). Basically, you decide what you want to happen, what needs to trigger that to happen, and then it will work like clockwork.

For example, I could set up a scenario that **IF** the motion sensor picks up movement from my grandma's room after midnight, I **THEN** get an alert to my phone or from Google Home. Or it could be as simple as **IF** the pizza guy is on his way from Dominos, and the app is linked to my smart home, it could **THEN** turn the front porch light on as he's driving down the street, helping to signal the house to him. You can also use it for things not related to your smart house but mostly on the Internet. Let's say, I set a trigger that **IF** a birthday notification comes up in my Facebook feed, **THEN** it would automatically respond to that person with a "Happy Birthday!" Now I don't do this, but I could, and so could you. This logic is pretty simple but may require an expert to help set up. Let's try one for fun: **IF** the smoke detector goes off in the kitchen, **THEN** the _____ shuts off. I'm sure you got that—it was the stove that needed to shut off. Pretty simple, like I said, but pretty helpful. One more to get the hang of **IFTTT**: **IF** you're speeding on the highway and you see a police officer, **THEN** you_____.

While there's no way for me to go into all the details of smart homes, I believe that a smart home isn't just what we spoke about above; it's also the intangible things that are *smart* in a home. I call it creating Soul Space—you know, that place where your soul just feels at ease. It may be that perfect chair or the sunshine coming in the breakfast nook in the morning. Whatever it is, when you can create it, your house **THEN** becomes your home. I also believe you can employ smart design strategies to help you age in place with ease in your home. I've developed The LOVE design method as an easily adoptable design guide to improve your confidence and freedom as you age in place.

But before we discuss the LOVE design method in Chapter 11, I want to introduce you to some wonderful smart technology for your home. This isn't a complete list, and typically,

I don't list them alphabetically or in order of preference.

In an effort to expose more people to technology and how it can increase your freedom and improve your quality of life, I've purchased a 1914 French Opera Style Manor House that I'll be converting to a Limitless Living Airbnb Style Home.

The goal of the renovation is to create a unique and flexible space where anyone can experience the latest technologies in home living while also creating a community space for people to come together and connect, stimulating the imagination about what the future could hold as we age.

This renovation will showcase the technology we discuss in this book and be updated periodically to ensure the best limitless living tech available. I think of the space as a living showroom for aging in place technology, from furniture, fabrics, flooring, toilets, baths, sinks, lighting, Wi-Fi, sound, maximized closets, TV, kitchen, and much more. A spa will be integrated into the space with the latest aging biohack technologies available.

This won't be a senior center; it's designed to be a true community space to bring all generations together. It will be a place for community events, meetings, and classes as well as a space that will be designed with technology intended for Boomers to be able to age in place and continue to contribute to the community.

I want the renovations to create *Soul Space* for everyone to enjoy and come together with everyone engaging in the same space, feeling great about being there, and able to connect on a deeper level with one another.

Boomers will find a space that showcases the possibilities of technology assisting them as they age. The technology will be integrated directly into the renovation. The best aging in place designers will partner with highly touted vendors such as Shaw Flooring, Delta, Kohler, and Toto to redesign various rooms and demonstrate the reality of limitless living.

As you can see, writing this book has more than inspired me; it's created a whole new living laboratory that everyone can be part of—moving us from fear to freedom! Now let's continue with the smart home tech.

## Comfort and Energy Savings

Comfort is a difficult subject; everyone feels temperature differently, and the actual temperature can be felt differently by the same person, depending on what material it is coming from. As we age, it becomes even more of an issue when we take into consideration the loss of fat in our bodies (Fat insulates and holds our core temperature, hence the flabby skin.), blood pressure, and less mobility. Depending on where you live, keeping cool could be your issue or keeping warm. Whichever the case, when we're comfortable, we're at ease.

One of my favorite smart features in our home for comfort is the radiant flooring (heated floor) for my bathroom tile floor. It may not seem like something you want to invest in, but it is incredibly comfortable to visit the bathroom and touch a warm, comfortable floor instead of a cold tile floor that sends shock waves up your spine. I know this because sometimes it resets and turns off—typically on a cold winter night—and it seems to be reminding me of how awesome it is and not to take it for granted.

While the radiant flooring may be my favorite, the Nest thermostat has a close second in my heart. Our master bedroom was an addition from the previous owner and is situated over the family room. You guessed it, if I want to change the temperature in the bedroom prior to installing the Nest, I would have to truck downstairs to the family room to do so. Now I just open my app and adjust as needed.

Nest is one of the largest players in the smart home thermostat market place and also has cameras, smoke, and CO (Carbon Monoxide) detectors, doorbells, and alarm systems. It can be controlled from anywhere, will turn itself down when you're away, and will save energy. Nest is owned by Google and ties into Google Home but also ties into the Amazon Alexa. Currently, Amazon and Google are in a battle over the smart home, and Nest is right in the middle. We will have to wait and see how this all plays out. Some of the other manufacturers for you to look at are Ecobee4, Honeywell Lyric T5, and the Lux TX500U.

Besides comfort and ease, these smart thermostats can learn when you're home and when you're not and save you energy by turning down when not needed. They also can be changed remotely to get the chill out of the house before coming home from work.

Smart plugs are interesting items. We've changed most of our outlets to have a USB charger (this can charge your tablet or phone) in each. It's fairly inexpensive and ensures that you can charge whatever you need to in the house. The smart plugs take this to the next level. Basically, it's a plug on your outlet that you then plug your appliances into. These smart plugs can turn the item on and off, but mostly, they monitor energy consumption. Fibaro, Wemo, and TP-Link are smart plugs that tie into a larger smart home system. The plugs range from $30–$60. While they say they'll help you to save energy, at $60.00 per plug, plus the cost of command center, that's quite a bit of energy they'll have to save to give you the value for your investment. However, it would be awesome to know what's using the most energy and then having the tools to manage it.

## Safety and Security

Safety and security are interesting categories. People often confuse the two, but in reality, they're quite different.

Security keeps you free from danger or threat, while safety is when a product is designed to prevent damage or injury.

One is responding to an outside force, and the other is preventing damage or injury by design. Still confused? I feel the same way. For example, a shower grab bar to help you steady yourself and keep you from falling is an item that falls under safety. A lock on your front door is a security item. If you don't lock the front door, you won't injure yourself, but you could be injured or harmed by someone that wants to enter your home to rob you.

You don't need to worry about which is which. It really doesn't matter. What matters is these products provide peace of mind and freedom—two of the most valuable items on this earth.

## Security

When it comes to security, I'm certainly not an expert. I do lock my car and the house at night, but I've yet to install cameras and smart locks on the doors. Our family has been way more safety-oriented—probably due to the fact that there's always someone home and very rarely is anyone ever alone.

**Ring** is a doorbell camera system for your exterior doors that allows you to see who's there before opening the door or even getting out of bed. Their camera systems are stylish, can have a spotlight, floodlights, alarms, and motion sensors. They can also have cameras in the home, if desired, and it's all connected to live security folks when you need them. Your neighbors can even be notified, so they can be on alert if you choose to be connected. It's the next level of a neighborhood watch. A unique feature is that you can install it yourself. They can also integrate in with a smart lock system so that you can lock or unlock your doors from home which can be convenient if you forgot to lock the door or need to unlock it for your dog sitter. Compatible lock systems are: LockState, Kisi, and Lockitron.

The family of **Nest** products includes indoor and outdoor cameras, thermostats, doorbells, alarm systems, smoke, and CO (carbon Monoxide) alarms. Nest works with other products like light bulbs, the washer and dryer, and door locks. An example they give of a smart connected home with Nest: Your smoke and CO alarm detects carbon monoxide. The Nest system would then contact your furnace and shut it down as this may likely be the cause. They also do the traditional security sensors on windows and doors to keep you safe.

**Schlage Connect** is door hardware that connects to Amazon Alexa via SmartThings, Wink, Iris, or Nexia. It is a great exterior door lock system, and when you connect it to your Alexa or other device, you can lock it or unlock it whenever you want to or need to. No more leaving keys for people, or if you're halfway to the movies and can't remember if you locked it or not, just lock it from your phone. It will even send an alert or an alarm if it's being tampered with.

**Iris** is unique in the security system arena as they focused not only on a connected home but helping latch key kids and seniors live safer. They have the cameras (indoor and out), the sensors, smart plugs, thermostats (Honeywell and Nest), but they also have an Iris Care Pendant and a Smart Fob. The Smart Fob is actually pretty smart. It has four customizable buttons that can turn on lights, lock the doors when you're not home, and even send a text to Mom that you got home safely. Think of it like a remote control for your house, only preprogramed. The Iris Care Pendant can be paired with sensors, so you can track if Mom is okay, or it can even send you alerts if she's left the house. I know we could have used this the other day with my grandma. She had never gone out the front door and wandered off, but she did last week, and it was a very cold morning. She said she was waiting for the school bus.

Things change daily when you're living with Alzheimer's/Dementia, and now we have to lock the front door even when we're home. We may be looking at getting the Iris sooner rather than later. While it doesn't have all the bells and whistles of the other motion sensor alarm pendants, having the system connected to the smart home devices is a win. Lowe's has also done a fantastic job with its senior-friendly bathroom products, and I encourage you to check them out. Falls in the bathroom can mean surgery and a trip to the short-term rehab. At my age, anything I can do to preemptively avoid having this happen and give me confidence as I age is a *must* do. Don't wait until you have an accident to install these safety products.

**ADT** has been around forever. We even had them at one point, but then we got rid of our landline, and they weren't able to work without it. It was quite the ordeal to get out of the contract, but from my latest interview with them, things have changed. They've become very flexible, which is great news for you and me. They have the locks, sensors, key fobs, cameras, app, and personal support. Like Iris at Lowe's, they have added a senior and health addition. They now have a medical alert system with fall detection and GPS. It's definitely not the prettiest, but when did pretty mean good? Okay, Apple proved me wrong, but you get what I mean.

**Frontpoint** is a DIY (do-it-yourself) security company with great customer service. They have cameras and sensors (These can also be on cabinets and drawers.). They work with Schlage for the smart locks and also offer flood sensors. Best of all, the system is portable so that it can move with you.

**Vinint** has a camera doorbell, cameras for inside and out, sensors, 24/7 video recording and monitoring, thermostats that help with energy management, and garage door control. They also have live video, and it works with Amazon Alexa.

**Protect America** integrates with Amazon Dot so you can use it hands free. They have the standard sensors, cameras, motion detectors, and smoke detection. They provide 24/7 monitoring and have a smartphone app. They are a security company.

**LiveWatch** is 10x faster in an emergency with their response times per their website. They have a Plug & Protect system that can serve up to 40 security and smart home devices such as smart locks cameras, thermostats, sensors, detectors, etc. Their basic system comes with door sensors, motion sensors, and 24/7 monitoring.

**SimpliSafe** looks like a smart home security system. It is well-designed and could be confused for an aromatherapy diffuser or Google Home. They have various package sizes, which can include anything from the base kit with a keypad and sensors to motion sensors, panic buttons, freeze sensors, water sensors, smoke detectors, and cameras. It can detect intruders and not confuse them with your pets. It has 24/7 support and is ready right out of the box.

As you can see, not all products do all things. You have to go back to the questions below that we discussed in the previous chapters to help you make the wisest decision for yourself.

## 1. HOW ARE YOU GOING TO BE ABLE TO LIVE YOUR LIFE WITH FREEDOM AND CONFIDENCE?

In other words, how much technology will you let into your life? Everyone has some sort of line in the sand that they draw; what's yours? Cameras inside or no cameras? GPS tracking devices on your keys and your phone so that you can find them easily? Weigh the pros and the cons. You probably do already in all aspects of your life today. I'm willing to get patted down at the airport so that I can travel. 30 years ago, I would have said, NO WAY! That would have been an invasion of my privacy and not worth it, but now, I'm like a cow going to a milking station—they tell me where to go, what to take off, they have sniffing devices that go through everything in my suitcase in front of everyone, then they pat me down like I'm a prison inmate. And that all comes after I've been x-rayed! It's all relative—what you'll give up if you think what you're getting is better than what you're giving up. Technology and security are no different.

## 2. WHERE WILL YOU BE LIVING YOUR LIFE?

Will you be home a lot or traveling quite a bit? This could influence the type of system you have. If you have another house, I would invest in the same system for both properties so that you only have to deal with one app where you can have it all connected and monitored. If you spend part of the year in a sunshine state, are the freeze warnings and energy efficiency important to you?

## 3. HOW ARE YOU GOING TO CARE FOR YOUR MIND, BODY, AND SPIRIT?

Answering this question requires that you think really long, hard, and carefully about future flexibility. You don't want to get locked into a system that can't grow with you as you age. On the other hand, you may want everything portable and not connected so that you can change what isn't working well or if conditions change. Know your personality. If change is hard for you, then select a system that will be around in the future, can grow with you, and fits your level of learning new things.

## Safety

On the subject of "Help, I've Fallen, and I Can't Get Up" devices, there are so many devices out there with great information to help you stay connected if you or a loved one would need a safety device such as these. I believe, in the not too distant future, these features will be integrated into the basic consumer wearables such as Fitbit, Garmin, or Jawbone. As we saw with the new hearing aids, fall detection is part of the device. Wearables are currently starting to track more than your steps, heartbeat, and sleep patterns. Look for them to track your oxygen and sugar levels. Add in the AI for fall alert, and we all will be wearing a device that provides constant feedback, alerts to help us to make better choices, and gets help when we can't ask for it.

While most have a range of pendants you wear around your neck, quite a few are moving to the watch model. It certainly is a better fashion statement and doesn't scream that I can't take care of myself. It's interesting to me why these devices are so popular, but then I have to remember that if my parents and grandmother didn't live with me, I would worry, and this would be a great solution. When my grandmother fell and broke her wrist and hip, my mother was right there, eliminating worries about her laying there for hours by herself like other horror stories I'd heard from my family and friends. However, I did notice the cloud of doom and gloom from so many. "Oh, she broke her hip—that's the number one cause of death in seniors over 65." Really, is it? NO, it's not!

According to the CDC in 2017, heart disease, cancer, and chronic lower respiratory disease are the leading cause of death by a mile. At almost two million deaths per year in adults 65 and older, only 2% are from unintentional injuries, where Alzheimer's disease accounts for 5.5%.[50] However, the CDC also reports conflicting information and states, "Falls are the leading cause of injury and death in older Americans."[51] Did you catch it? They've lumped death and injury together. In reality, their data doesn't conflict; they've just sensationalized it. It still stands that 2% of deaths may have been the result of falls. I'm not trying to belittle the issue, but the CDC has scared Americans to death—making seniors afraid to move for fear of falling when the exact opposite is true—we need to keep active to not fall. I wish I could issue a cease and desist for the CDC. Most studies agree that being overly tired, over medicated, or blood pressure dropping when we stand up are the most common reasons for falling. It's not the steps or being active.

My advice would be to take normal precautions. When it's icy, turn the lights on when you're walking around at night. Don't let magazines lay on the floor as they create a trip hazard, and make sure cords are tied up. Doing these simple things will reduce the likelihood of a fall. But it's soft drinks, potato chips, and being a couch potato that are more of a danger to your health. Don't be afraid to be active.

Having preached for the last paragraph, I still recognize that these devices help with freedom and peace of mind, so let's do a quick rundown of some of the brands you may come across.

**Medical Guardian** has lots of options from pendants and watches to an all-in-one system. It can detect a fall, has GPS to pinpoint your location, and has sensors in the home that can help keep the family aware and involved with alerts that are triggered. **GreatCall** wireless and medical alert system is the backbone behind the Jitterbug cell phone designed for seniors with a smart screen, senior-focused apps, medical help, GPS, and a 5Star urgent response MobileHelp. Others are: **LifeStation, Helpbutton, Lifefone, Alert 1, Life Alert, Philips Lifeline,** and **BeClose Senior Safety. Mynotifi** is a simple wristband with a one-time payment that notifies loved ones through an app on their phone when you fall. The app also has mobility exercises to help keep you active. You can also ask for help by touching the band, or it uses AI algorithms to detect if you have fallen and will notify others. Best of all, it's waterproof.

You may be thinking, *I thought this book was for me, a Boomer?* This sounds like a bunch of stuff for old people or my parents. Well, according to the National Institute on Aging, one in three people fall over the of age 65.[52] Of the 77 million Boomers in the U.S., (according to AARP) seven Baby Boomers are turning 65 every minute.[53] So my bet is some of you will find this helpful, and if not for you, maybe a parent.

I try very hard to make sure that I place my phone, glasses, and keys in the same place every night. This helps me not to lose them. When I get lazy and don't follow my ritual, it can be a day or so before I find something, which is very frustrating. It just happened to me with my winter gloves. I thought they must have fallen out of the car because I was sure I searched everywhere for them, and they had disappeared. I've done this often enough that I no longer blame others as I know I probably misplaced them. Where did I find my gloves? In a bag in the trunk of my car, right where I put them. Apparently, other people also have my issue, and there are plenty of companies that want to help us out. They call these trackers, and they basically hook (think of a keychain attached to your keys) to the item that you deem important enough, and then when you can't find it, these trackers will help you locate it through GPS or by making a sound.

I actually bought them for my parents, and then we tied it into the Amazon Alexa. When my mom can't find her phone, she can say to Alexa, "Please ring my phone," and Alexa does it. It's a pretty neat feature. The GPS locations aren't sophisticated enough to pinpoint the exact location, but you can see if you left it at work, a friend's house, in the car, or in the house. Just don't expect it to tell you which room.

## The Kitchen

The kitchen can be one of the most creative, fulfilling, drudgery, or heart-of-the-home spaces depending on one thing: you. Love it or hate it, it's a necessary part of every house just like the bathroom. If you're a gadget geek or foodie, you're going to love some of the latest technology for the kitchen. I've also got some products to discuss to make it safer. On a side note, make sure you have a smoke and CO detector.

Let's start on the safety side—making sure the house doesn't burn down is always a good thing. Even if your memory is fine, we're so distracted and used to doing 10 things at once. I know that when I'm cooking, I'll start other things like the wash while I'm also looking at my phone or watching something on my tablet. I walk in and out of the kitchen, and next thing I know, there's something burning. Recently, I had water on the stove in a big pot to help add moisture to the air. I apparently forgot to fill it up before going to bed, and yes, I could have burned down the house. A product like **Fire Advert or Intelligent Stove Safety** is what saves the day (or night) in these kinds of instances. They hook to your stove, and either by a timer or the smoke detector going off, they will shut the stove off. Think of the peace of mind, especially if you live by yourself.

**Cool Tech and Foodie Products for the Kitchen (just a few):**

**Pantelligent** is a smart frying pan, which helps teach you how to cook. The pan tracks temperatures and adjusts cooking time automatically. It will send you a notification via an app to let you know when it's time to flip your meat over. It will even keep you from burning food.

**Drop** is a smart scale; it allows you to do several helpful things. It will weigh ingredients as you add them. If you're low on an ingredient, the app will adjust the recipe for you. It can also help you to make the perfect cocktail. This changes how we will shop. We won't buy more than we need, and we will be able to use more of what we have without having to see food go bad. Based upon this alone, it's a very smart technology. If you have downsized, you may not have the storage in your kitchen you used to, and the Drop will help you eliminate the need for that extra bag of flour.

**Paragon** is a portable induction cooktop that can cook almost anything. Of course, it comes with a mobile app that allows you to set the temperature. It can steam cook, fry, and basically do anything you need. One of the really neat features is that it can hold your food at the right temperature until you're ready to serve it. Induction cooktops are like what the electric stove was; they'll be the future as they're portable, safe, and free up your counter space. The only drawback is that they require new connected cookware.

**June** is an intelligent oven that can toast, bake, broil, and roast. It has a built-in camera and can give your phone updates. It's the size of a microwave and has a temperature probe to make sure meat is done perfectly.

**Samsung Family Hub** is a computer, personal assistant, and refrigerator, all in one! The hub allows you to see what's in your fridge from your phone, set expiration dates for groceries, get notifications, create shopping lists, have a family schedule, write notes to the family with a whiteboard function, listen to music, or watch movies. But the best part is it can order groceries from Instacart and works with the Alexa. With its three built-in cameras that snap a photo every time you close the door, it allows you to look at the phone app when you can't remember what you had in the fridge while you're grocery shopping.

**Egg Minde**r is a simple egg tray that holds 14 eggs and tracks how many are in it. LED lights next to each egg will tell you which ones are the oldest so you can use them first. You can look at—you guessed it—the app when you're shopping to see how many eggs you might need for that recipe. This product is from Quirky GE—products invented by real people (another example of crowdsourcing).

**Orange Chef Prep Pad** is a smart food scale with nutritional balance, based upon weight, to make better eating choices—yes, it has an app. Not sure what I would do with this, but I'm sure you foodies get it.

**Smart Thermometer** by Williams Sonoma is an oven tech probe that can be used alone or with an app so you're not tied to the kitchen while you're cooking. It also helps you to make sure the meal is perfectly timed and cooked. I have to admit I don't think I've ever used a thermometer while cooking, but it sounds like a great idea.

**HaPIfork** helps you to eat slowly. Think of a sonic toothbrush but in a fork. The smart fork reminds you to slow down and eat mindfully by vibrating or lighting up if you're eating too fast. And yes, it comes with an app and gamification. It can even go in the dishwasher.

**HestanCue** has smart cookware with induction cooktops, recipes, and videos all in the app. It's perfect for parties or everyday cooking. Mobile induction cooktops, like this one, allow you to carry your kitchen with you, wherever you're living. IKEA even has one for camping.

**Panasonic Smart Kitchen** is a future item for the U.S. but already available in Japan and Canada. Maybe it's a metric thing? They have some of the coolest storage items for a kitchen that I've ever seen, doubling your storage capacity. You'll have items you use all the time in high cabinets that easily open and drop to arms reach. I'm certainly trying to get them to come to the U.S., so stay tuned.

**Kessbohmer** has some similar products to the Panasonic Smart Kitchen called iMove. iMove is a shelving system that eliminates the need to use a stool to reach the upper cabinets. It has a bar inside the upper cabinet that you can pull down, and it lowers all the upper shelves to within reach.

**Legrand The Adorne Collection** is an incredible, well-designed, smart under cabinet lighting system that's way more than just lighting. Imagine all those ugly outlets—that are in your beautiful tile or granite between your upper kitchen cabinets and countertop—can now be gone! Besides the fact that the one outlet you have means the coffee pot has to be in the wrong place and moved every time you cook dinner. Legrand has solved these issues putting all the lighting and electricity on a bar under the upper cabinets. The electrical outlets can be moved around as needed, so in case your countertop appliances change, you don't have to have cords strung all over—just relocate the plug. The other great aspect to this bar is that you can get accessories to hold your iPad, tablet, smartphone, etc., and it is easier to clean, more beautiful to look at, and can also be moved easily. Now your countertop is flexible and free and clear from clutter.

**Future Kitchen Tech Soon to Release:**

**Frigondas** sounds like a dinosaur or something from a Godzilla movie. But it's really more like the movie *Transformers*. Just like in the movie where the cars seem like they're only cars but then turn into these huge alien robot things (They are good huge alien robot things.), the Frigondas looks like and acts like a microwave, until you find out it can cool and freeze food in minutes. This is a great appliance if you're downsizing.

## The Bathroom

Bathroom technology revolves around three main things: comfort, safety, and independence, all while trying to make sure you don't feel vulnerable.

Let's look at comfort first, as you may be familiar with the comfort items found in most master baths of multi-million-dollar homes. But as we age, these become less luxuries and more desired necessities. Take, for example, a heated floor. As we age, we get up more often in the middle of the night. That's a shock to our system as our feet hit the cold tile and it chills our whole body. A heated floor can help to ease the transition from bed to the bathroom. A towel warmer and a heat lamp are both wonderful to have and help you keep your body temperature warm as you get out of the shower. As you age, you lose body fat, which helps to keep you warm (insulated). And so when you get out of the shower, your core temp will drop, and it's much harder to get it back to normal. These simple little things do make a huge impact on our comfort as our bodies age.

Consider mounting an amber LED strip (on a sensor) on the bathroom door to easily see it in the night and orient yourself. This will help to reduce falls as you won't be looking down at a night-light. You can also use the light in the Bidet as a night-light.

If you want to get a fan and motion light together, ISO Humidity Activated Fan and Exhaust Light is a great product that's ultra-silent, has a bright overhead light, and a motion sensor activated night-light made by Quirky GE.

What else should you do? Definitely add an anti-scald device to your showerhead and faucet. These typically won't let the temperature get over 117 degrees and help to keep the body safe due to less fat to protect us from water that's too cold or too hot.

Also, add USB outlets so that you can charge your phone or tablet when you're in the shower or watching the news while you're getting ready. These can cost as little as $10.00. If you go with a smart plug, you're looking at $25.00.

Replace your toilet paper holder with a Grabcessories. It's basically a grab bar built into the toilet paper holder with great grips on the back. It's perfect for helping you to further steady yourself right where you need it: your center of gravity. They also carry a variety of other items.

Living with your parents sometimes means you see things you can't unsee. One morning, I was running late, and by the time I left for work, my father was up (typically he's not). When I came out of my bedroom suite, apparently he thought he was alone and forgot to close his bathroom door because there he was in all his glory standing at the Bidet toilet seat with his hands on the wall to steady himself going to the bathroom. While I never will be able to shake that image, it got me thinking and researching fast! That's how I found a great product by Grabcessories. It's a grab bar shelf mounted over the toilet for gentlemen to steady themselves while they're going to the bathroom. It helps them, and it keeps their wives from complaining about the handprints on the wall. This is what we call a real win-win.

36.5 million rolls of toilet paper—that's how much Americans use each year. The cost to the environment to create this toilet paper is huge and accounts for 15 million trees. If you have ever used a Bidet, as they do in Japan, Europe, and other countries, you feel like you're stuck in the dark ages when you come back home to the method of *cleaning* Americans use; TP or toilet paper—paper, paper, paper— there's no water involved, just dry tree pulp.

The best way I can explain my feeling for the Bidet goes back to a story I told in my earlier book *HIVE* in a chapter called, *Royal Flush*. In 2007, I had a chance to travel to Japan for an Entrepreneurs Organization (EO) conference. Typically, I don't bring my family on business trips, but EO is different; they support the whole entrepreneur and encourage spouses to come along—sometimes even kids. Since family trips *Cini Style* also mean taking my parents along, I mentioned to everyone that, "Japan would be an awesome trip for us all to go on." Immediately, Grandma, then 86, piped up with an enthusiastic, "I've always wanted to go to Japan!" Frankly, I didn't even have her on the guest list, but it seemed like a once-in-a-lifetime event that I couldn't possibly deny. And so the entire family—Grandma, my parents, my husband, and kids (ages 10 and 13)—flew off to Japan for what proved to be "an awesome trip," and all of us treasure the memories of it to this day.

Now what does this have to do with toilets?

Well, a lot, actually. While there, every toilet we experienced, even the public ones, had Bidet seats on them that provided great comfort, greater cleanliness, and had a remarkably wide range of options. Among the options: a heated seat, a hidden wand that, at a touch of a button, would spray you off, and when you pressed another button, your bum would be blow-dried. In simple terms, these toilets were frickin' awesome, and we were frickin' impressed.

Arriving back home, I did some research, and guess what Santa (me) bought Greg for our master bathroom that Christmas?

Now back to the Christmas season, I was waiting and waiting for weeks for the Bidet. And nothing. I waited more and still nothing. Then I tracked the package and saw that a neighbor had signed for it.

A little background information: Not long before our Japan trip, we'd moved into a National Historic residential neighborhood. The kind that was gated and you have to be voted in. If you don't get my drift, think of it like this: Most of the neighbors weren't baking pies and showing up to say, "Howdy, folks, welcome to the neighborhood." But they were signing for my Bidet.

Great, now their first impression of me was going to be the kook who came ringing their doorbell to ask if they'd signed for and forgotten to give me my toilet seat from Japan. And well, yes, that's exactly what their first impression was, because that's exactly what I did. And yes, they had it, and yes, it was as awkward as you can imagine. Not that it mattered, because when Christmas came and we installed the seat, Greg loved it.

And then the weirdness came. That's right; what you read above was not weird. Pretty soon, every single friend of my kids who came over to the house—when they had to use the bathroom—traipsed upstairs, walked into my bedroom, and yep, you got it, beelined into my master bathroom and used our toilet. It didn't end there. Whenever we had a party, which we often did, we noticed the same exact phenomenon happening. Did I mention that we have three other common bathrooms? Yet everyone felt completely comfortable entering our master bedroom to get to the master bathroom toilet. When I happened to mention this to my friends, I was surprised at their reaction—they knew all about it. Turns out the "Cini toilet" was the talk of the town.

A few years later, we decided to sell that home and begin our new multi-generational lifestyle. And while we didn't know a lot of the details regarding what was going to happen, we did know one thing: The 4Gen Experiment would include many Bidet toilet seats that could wash and blow-dry. But I have to admit, it was not just because I loved my Bidet toilet seat and all its neighborhood acclaim. There was a different reason, too, which was lying in the answer to this question: How can I avoid having to wipe my parents' bum if they have surgery or something happens to them? It's not as strangely hypothetical as it might sound. When my mother-in-law had surgery, my sisters-in-law had to help her go to the bathroom, which also meant helping clean her—embarrassing for my mother-in-law and tough on Greg's sisters. So when I thought about not having that happen to me, my next thought was about the Bidet toilet seat. At around $400 per toilet, it seemed like a small price to pay for their dignity and my sanity. And not just mine, but for my mom's, too, who was to be the primary caregiver for my grandmother.

After she settled in from the big move, our social experiment was up and running. One day I asked Grandma if my mother had shown her how it worked and how she liked it. I don't know why, but I was shocked to hear that she loved it! I didn't remember that Grandma was completely able to understand it and use it all by herself. I'd forgotten that she was no virgin to technology and that she'd seen more changes in technology than any of us: the development of new-fangled things such as the car, indoor plumbing, radio, TV, phone, cell phone, electricity, and the Internet. When you think about it like that, really, would a toilet that could wash and dry you be such a big deal?

And she had a reason to like it too—it let her take care of herself without being a burden on my mother. With her shower, she needed help, but the toilet seat allowed her to (basically) take a sitz bath. My age group doesn't quite get this concept, but for folks her age, this is what they grew up doing: Water was either collected in a rain barrel or from a well, or sometimes, if you had the luxury, the city got water to you. Regardless, water was not something you could waste. Women would often use a sitz bath for personal hygiene, so this wildly new contraption (in our minds) was, in a sense, incredibly familiar to her.

The Bidet has fans and other options, too. I remember with absolute clarity (and delight), the first time my father, a combination of Robert De Niro and Archie Bunker, used his Bidet seat. Since he didn't exactly read the manual from cover to cover, he went in, and a moment later came out screaming that he had a "G.D. tornado up his A." After some quick coaching on the settings, he turned his down from high and very soon he, too, came to love the Bidet toilet seat. Grandma didn't have the same model as my father. We were testing out different manufacturers on each toilet to see our likes and dislikes. I can honestly say I'm not sure why the setting *Vortex* should ever be on one of these Bidet toilet seats, but my father was the lucky one to try it out.

My daughter's graduation party speaks to the Bidet's widespread appeal. Since we had several hundred guests, we rented Porta potties. Guess what happened anyway? I had parents coming to me, asking if they could use the toilets inside because they had heard so much about them. It's a weird conversation to be sure, but it also goes to show how amazing they are.

Since our social experiment started, we've finally been able to convince some of our senior living clients to put them in their apartments! The lesson here is that with a small dollar investment, you can increase the dignity and independence of your loved one and reduce your burden.

The positives end up being for everyone, which is a huge win-win. Update: I would also highly recommend getting the Squatty Potty. It's like a step stool for going #2 which helps you to avoid straining yourself and getting hemorrhoids. Yes, it's official, I'm an adult. I've talked about all of the bodily functions without even one giggle. I know this all may sound crass, but denial isn't wisdom. When we can arm ourselves with strategies that are proactive, we can age with confidence and freedom.

## Lighting

Candles were a main source of lighting during non-daylight hours for centuries. Oil, gas, and kerosene lamps created a more stable source of light but still needed maintenance and could be very dangerous. It was not until the 1930s when the incandescent light bulb became a mainstay in American homes in major cities, but in rural areas, only about 10% of homes had electricity. By 1939, 25% of rural homes had electricity.[54] Even with the low percentage in the rural areas, incandescent light bulb technology changed forever the way we worked and lived. We were no longer dependent on the sun; our work days could be longer, and factories could add second and third shifts instead of building more factories.

In 1939, my grandfather left Canton, Ohio, to work at the World's Fair in New York City. He'd tell us stories of all of the movie stars and famous people he saw when they came through his "guess your weight" stand while at the fair. It was the place to be. It was branded as "Dawn of a New Day" and had an exposition of *The World of Tomorrow.* TVs were introduced there as well as nylon, color photography, air-conditioning, and fluorescent lamps.

GE held the patent to the first electric bulb. In the next three years, electric bulbs were being produced by many companies and were installed in many manufacturing facilities and open office plans. Not until 1980 did compact fluorescent lights (CFLs) become available to retrofit into the same socket as an incandescent light.

While enough lighting is crucial to see, aging eyes require up to 70% more light to see than those of a 20 year-old.[55] If you have ever been to a restaurant with your friends and everyone pulled out their cellphones and turned on their flashlight apps to be able to read the menu, you know what I'm talking about. The details are just as important: color, temperature, not having bright spots or shadows, reducing the amount of fluorescents due to the eye strain caused by flickering (You may not be able to see it, but the eye still has to adjust.), and consistency. Lowering the light levels can make it more difficult to see steps, chair seats, and handrails, which causes more stress and fear in you.

When you factor in that every individual sees differently with colors and light levels and then factor in, for good measure, issues with sight such as yellowing of the cornea, macular degeneration, nearsightedness, and farsightedness, you can see why good lighting is so critical as you age.

## LED Lighting

LED lighting technology has moved faster than expected, with GE and Phillips both moving at the speed of light to develop this technology and bring the price structure down.

The exciting news on LEDs is that they're now cost-effective enough to use in homes. LED lights have been integrated into handrails in showers, door casings, and crown molding and can change colors to help simulate sunrise, daylight, and sunset to help those with cognitive difficulties.

When LED uplighting is utilized in crown molding in your home, it can be used to simulate the natural light changes from day to night. The lighting is controlled by a computer connection that will sequence sunrise, daytime, sunset, and then go off at night. This simulation can help with your circadian rhythm, increasing the melatonin production to reduce sundowners, especially for those with SAD and Alzheimer's/Dementia.

It was suggested to me by a doctor to add blackout window treatments in the bedroom to ensure that not too much light can seep into the room at night for the best possible night's sleep. I've also found my personal experience substantiates a better night's rest when the room is dark. If you live in the country with very little city lights pouring in at night, this isn't much of an issue except for full moons. Please take into consideration that when you do blackout your room, you'll definitely need amber nightlights so you don't kill yourself making your way to the bathroom in the middle of the night.

LEDs, integrated into flooring, handrails, stairs, and door casings, help reduce tripping and falling. These integrated lights can double as night-lights and should be colored amber to avoid keeping you up at night, as mentioned above. Elio's LED handrail system shown in the image cannot only bear the weight of you and be easy to find when your eyes are full of water but also provide a night-light for the bathroom.

Imagine this scenario that the rooms in your house automatically light up when you enter because they're tied to motion sensors. The up lighting in the crown molding around your room is the same color temperature as the hour of the day, and therefore, it will change throughout a 24-hour period. The door casing (amber-colored) is lit to help orient you and navigate at night to minimize the risk of falling, creating a holistic lighting solution that allows your smart home technology to give you confidence and be as free as possible. Kohler introduced many integrated lighting solutions in their bathroom products just this year.

An LED light over the toilet comes on when you approach it and gets brighter as you get closer. Like me, you may also have a night-light in your Bidet toilet. I have to say I didn't think it would really help, but it does, and I would insist on having them if I ever moved. Inside the shower and beside the toilet are integrated

 LED light handrails that make it easy for you to see, especially when your eyes may have water or shampoo in them.

For getting out of the shower, a water-resistant LED light strip helps to define where the flooring change is, to avoid trips and falls. Then back to the bed, where the sensors lower the light levels back down until you're safely in bed and off to restful sleep.

In the morning, the LED cove lighting gently awakens you with the warm colors of a sunrise. The theory is that provided this cuing, the body's circadian cycle will be properly set, and poor sleep and sundowner's syndrome could be diminished, if not avoided.

Great smart lighting that isn't only bright but even and flexible with color and dimming capabilities all connected to sensors and your smart home technology lets you create mood and improve quality of life. Who doesn't like a sunny day vs. a cloudy one?

## OLED Lighting

OLEDs (organic light-emitting diodes) are different than LEDs (light emitting diodes). The major difference that matters is OLEDs can be extremely bendable, thin, and even translucent. They're also better in color, which translates to not only better lighting but better, thinner, curved TVs, phone displays, and computer screens.

There are numerous simple ways that OLED smart lighting can be applied to your home. A few examples are under cabinet lighting, closet

lighting, bathroom mirrors with built-in lighting, stair tread lights, toilet seats with built-in lighting, vanity mirrors, cove lighting, ceiling panels, and hanger lights.

OLEDs will be as great a transformation as the light bulb was to the candle.

Some high-end restaurants have clued in to aging eyes to ensure their guests keep coming. I experienced this myself in a fancy restaurant in Germany. They used OLED technology behind the menu, which backlights the menu, so it was easy to see, and it only came on when you opened the menu. It was incredible—no struggling, no almost catching the menu on fire because I came too close to the table candle.

If you have cataracts, then it is difficult to see in bright light, and you should avoid glare. You can see the dilemma, right? One spouse needs the lights bright, and the other needs them not too bright. This is the exact reason you should use smart home lighting. You can set them to your preferences just like you do in your car for the seat adjustments. I'm 4'11", and my seat and steering wheel are set very differently than my husband's (he is 5'10"). It used to irritate me to no end when we had a car that didn't have these programed positions. I would have it perfectly set for me, and then he'd change it. Then it seemed like I could never get it back to where I had it perfect again. Smart home technology is a lot like a luxury vehicle that adjusts to your preferences, helps to protect you with airbags, sensors, locks, and alarms, guides you with GPS (It may even parallel park for you.), creates the perfect comfort level for you in temperature, and allows you to easily communicate with whoever you want, all while doing its primary function of providing you the freedom to go where you want when you want.

When you're buying your smart lights from **Lifx, Phillips, GE,** etc., look for a CRI (color rendering index) of 80 or higher. The range is from 1–100, and the higher the number, the more accurate the colors you'll see. The better the colors, the better you, your food, and your environment look.

## Protect Yourself

When everything is connected, everything is connected . . . just like you protect your car, diamonds, and money, you need to protect your system from hackers (They are basically like Internet bad guys.). There are many ways to keep the hackers away, but they're each tailored to what system you have in place and if you want to hook something up yourself or hire a professional.

Password protection is key, but it's not enough. When you're connected via Wi-Fi, having passwords that are easy to guess can leave you vulnerable.

## WELL Building

Here's an interesting concept that's gathering steam—so much so that it's really becoming a movement now. It's called WELL Building, and it's moving past the Green movement and LEED certified buildings. *Back in the day,* which was not that far back, the concept of Green or a LEED certified building was to help protect the environment and reduce energy consumption. It did this by sourcing local materials and utilizing the position of the building relevant to the sun to reduce the heating and cooling system costs, avoiding a fight against nature. Mother Nature always wins, so it's better to work with her than against. You also need to use local plants that require less maintenance, irrigation, and so on.

The WELL Building Standard considers the environment, but it focuses on those of us living in that environment as well . . . neat concept, right? What if the air quality, light, and water in your home or workplace actually made you healthier and allowed you to live a better, more engaged life? With 90% of our time spent indoors, the WELL Living Lab, in collaboration with the Mayo Clinic, is researching just how to do this and how our environments may assist in our well-being.

When asking President Phil Williams of Delos Commercial—the company that created the WELL Building Standard—what's at the heart of having a WELL building? He stated, "Right or wrong, every generation is spending over 90% of our time inside buildings."[56] The places where we now live must and can move from "Do no harm to great." This applies to the physical place, the cultural place, and our personal place.

## Universal Design

In senior living, the U.S. government makes designers like myself comply with the ADA (Americans with Disability Act) when designing our large, purpose-built senior living facilities. The problem is that while they're well-intentioned just like the CDC, they're actually, in some cases, making it more difficult for aging adults to thrive. Unfortunately, this has found its way into our aging in place environments as well. To understand the issue, you need to know how ADA came about; it was not for the aging adults. It came out of the Vietnam veterans coming home with limb loss and great upper body strength—most were males between 18-21—so I'm told. So it made perfect sense to design a grab bar that was similar to what the Olympic gymnast use—think of it, the still rings, parallel bars, pommel horse, and the high bar. All of these revolve around gripping a bar and then swinging your body around by the strength of your hands, arms, and upper body. What's the issue? We're not 18-21-years-olds, and most of us don't have great upper body strength. Throw in arthritis, which makes it difficult to grab something in the shape of a tube. This is why a round door knob is more difficult to turn when you have arthritis than a lever door handle.

So what can we do? Intro, please . . . meet Universal Design. It's similar to WELL in that it looks at the whole picture and figures out the best options vs. being prescriptive for one group or another. Universal Design works for everyone, not just those in a wheelchair, although it works for that too. If you're aging in place, downsizing, or designing a new house, look for Universal Design elements—you'll be glad you did.

There are seven principals in Universal Design, but what it really comes down to is common sense. Can you make an environment simple and intuitive, able to be used with low physical effort, and have it accommodate people of all sizes and abilities?

As you may have figured out by now, in order to know what really works for me or not, I'd really rather be living in my environment than figuring it out by being book smart. When I wrote *HIVE, The Simple Guide to Multi-generational Living*, I was able to help others because we were living in our social experiment, and that meant that some of what I thought of as brilliant ideas at the time just plain old flopped. When I wrote about these, I followed my mentor Dan Sullivan's advice to "focus on progress, not perfection."

While I had employed some Universal Design aspects to our home, I found that the better source for my information (and inspiration) happened to be right here in my town, living in her own living laboratory of Universal Design. Her name is Rosemarie Rossetti, now age 65. Her life changed on June 13, 1998—that was the day that a three-and-a-half-ton tree came crashing down on her. She became paralyzed from the waist down at age 44. In her interview with me, she told me that when she returned home from the hospital, she quickly realized that her home was working against her, not for her.

She's an incredible, smart woman, so let's start there. Some would say she's taken lemons and turned them into lemonade, but really, she made lemonade for the world. She told me it's really about having a resiliency mindset. And she's on a mission to help others "make their life easier." She looks at everything and asks what she calls the *four mores:*

- What will make my life more convenient?
- What will make my life more safe?
- What will make my life more independent?
- What will give me more peace of mind?

While I won't be able to go through everything she stands for and advocates for within this book, please look her up on the Internet and see all the great data, tools, and resources she has. She, with the help of her husband, Mark, and lots of wonderful vendors, built an environment where Rosemarie tests products similarly to what we did in *HIVE*. And so Rosemarie really spoke from the heart about what worked and what didn't. She's part of the inspiration behind the Limitless Living Manor House.

If you're a younger Boomer, born around 1964, you may not think this applies to you, but hear me out. If you're planning on aging in place, which 90% of you are, then figuring out how to renovate the home you're in, downsizing to a new house or condo, or even buying a new house should have you thinking about what can you do to allow the environment to work for you, not against you, as you age. The time a crisis happens isn't the time to be figuring this all out. Plan now. Ensure your future freedom.

Now we will return back to your previously scheduled HGTV show, LOL (laugh out loud). One of the first things you'll notice is that the space is more open than a normal house, doorways especially. Pocket doors and barn doors are used wherever possible so that the floor space isn't taken up by the door, and the opening is as wide as possible. When you use a normal 30" door, let's say, due to the hinges and the actual thickness of the door, you lose a couple inches, and this means you may really only get a 27-28" opening. For someone in a wheelchair or walker, this can mean the difference between fighting through every door opening and not.

Next, you'd notice that the house isn't built just for someone in a wheelchair. What? Shouldn't everyone have to accommodate the person with needs, even if it means they're less comfortable? Not necessarily. A great living space means having a great living space for everyone in the home. Rosemarie is 5'1" standing and 4'2" in a wheelchair. Mark is 6' tall. Her kitchen is the perfect display of Universal Design. The island has three heights to it, 34" high for the workspace for Rosemarie vs. normal 36" high cabinets and 30" table space for everyone, including Rosemarie and others who might be sharing cooking duties in there.

All of the kitchen cabinets are 34" high; Kraftmaid makes them standard at this height. Some unique features are that the upper cabinets are 14" above the countertop vs. the standard 18". This helps her to access them from a seated position. The oven is below 34" and has a side door like a microwave, so it's easier for her to get her food in and out of because she's not blocked by the door.

I fell in love with the whole kitchen due to my height. At 4'11" and over 50 years old, it's getting more and more difficult to vault up on the counter, precariously stand to open the cabinet doors, and then jump to get down. I used to do it with ease, but now, when I'm getting up and down, I look like a gymnast doing the balance beam, and I'm very aware of the great pressure that comes from needing to *stick my landing* so I don't end up in a cast.

One of the unique features that I think we all can appreciate and use as we age is Rosemarie's built-in steamer and drainer. She has this right next to her burners and beside a pot filling faucet. A better explanation is it's very difficult for her to fill a pot with water then transfer it to the cooktop, then after the pasta is cooked, transfer the scalding water and pasta back to the sink to then pour the water into a strainer. There are lots of opportunities to end up with a huge mess on the floor, or worse yet, a burn unit. With the layout of the steamer and boiler and drain well, she fills the pasta cooker utilizing the swinging faucet, then turns it on, puts in the pasta, and then when it's done, hits the drain button! The pasta cooker looks very much like a sink, but it actually cooks pasta and steams.

You can see how this smart appliance technology helps her with all of her *four mores*: What will make my life more convenient? What will make my life safer? What will make my life more independent? What will give me peace of mind?

Her unique bathroom pocket door isn't a door at all; it's a privacy divider that goes into the wall. When pulled out, it hides her on the toilet. Should she ever need help in the future with transferring when she goes to the restroom, the pocket door can be slid into the wall, opening up the floor space for someone to have room to help her.

## Future Planning

Future planning is the process of proactively designing your home environment with elements that aren't fully built out but make it easier to install in the future. It also gives you the confidence that if you need to install support items for aging in the future, adding them will be easy, but until then, you don't have to compromise your interior design aesthetic.

Imagine this: You want to be able to age in place, but you're not ready to have grab bars in the bathroom yet. Future planning would be adding the blocking into the walls behind drywall or tile. Blocking provides stability to the wall so that heavy items don't pull out or loosen. When you install grab bars into normal drywall or tile, there's little to hold them past the half-inch of material, and with the amount of weight being placed on them, they can loosen or even fall out of the wall, which can cause serious injury. If you add blocking to the walls of your bathroom, staircases, and even bedroom and bathroom ceilings before you need to add the grab bars, this will future-proof your home, and you won't have to rip out all the walls to add blocking when you're ready to add grab bars. Grabcessories has solved this to a certain extent with their patented toggle bolt, but it's still wise to have blocking.

Other things you can consider when future planning besides blocking are: handrails at all stairs, outlets by the bedside, night-lights, electricity by the toilet if you want a Bidet toilet seat in the future, heat lamp, and lower counters if you're renovating.

While these may all seem insignificant, they can make an enormous difference in your freedom and quality of life, with much less cost and disruption when you decide to make the physical changes to your environment that will allow you to age in place.

Rosemarie also has future planned many items and hasn't compromised her design aesthetic in any fashion. She's a living example of how fantastic, supportive interior design can still be beautiful and tasteful.

## Biophilia

Biophilic Design encourages the connection between the inside and the outside. Research has found that we're happier, require less pain medication, sleep better, and heal faster when we're connected to nature. When we're inside, this can happen through windows and artwork. Spending 90% of our time inside, it's no wonder we desire to be connected to nature. That 2-week vacation to the beach just won't cut it.

Besides views of nature, biophilic design also encourages the dynamic use of sunlight, being able to hear and see water (a fountain, stream, lake, ocean), natural ventilation, and the introduction of natural forms and materials into the interior home. This design technology fits perfectly with the WELL Building Standard and Universal Design.

When all of these smart house options are pulled together, you can be confident that you can have an environment that will support your needs, not only now, but in the future. The key is future flexibility and understanding what's important to you and then tailoring your home's solutions toward these goals.

# CHAPTER 11
## THE "LOVE" DESIGN METHOD

If, by chance, you read my book *HIVE, The Simple Guide to Multigenerational Living*, first let me say, THANK YOU! Second, you'll notice that this section comes from that book with some updates and tweaks. My first book, *The Future is Here, Senior Living Reimagined, How Technology Will Change the Face of Senior Living in the Next Five Years* has also been borrowed from and updated for this book. It's basically a mashup of the past five years with lots of great new stuff. Now back to the LOVE design method.

As I've previously mentioned, my folks and my 96-year-old grandmother with dementia moved in with us several years ago. This social experiment forced me to think deeper on how I would execute memory care design in my own home without making the whole house institutional for the rest of us. What I discovered was that great design works for everyone.

While you may not know someone with memory issues, the LOVE design method works for anyone. If you do have someone you love that suffers from memory decline, then please dig in. I know there's something that will help make your life and their life easier, and isn't that what love is all about?

When it came time for me to sit down and design Grandma's apartment, I hit on an easy-to-remember design philosophy, which is remarkably similar to a life philosophy "LOVE": Light, Optimize, Visual, and Ease.

If you design with "LOVE," you increase independence and dignity. Designing with LOVE means you're allowing the persons suffering from Alzheimer's/Dementia to be their best selves at that moment in time. And designing with LOVE gives you the flexibility to adapt to their ever-changing needs. That all sounds so positive and enlightened, but oddly enough, the

LOVE design method caused a very non-loving response between all of my family. The LOVE design method caused me to argue with my siblings and parents about how to best design the environment for my grandmother. Today, four and a half years since the renovation took place and three and half years of living in this social experiment, I can say that the **LOVE design method** works.

Some of what I implemented for Grandma was different than what I would do in an assisted living home design that we'd create at my company, Mosaic Design Studio. Here, in my own home, I was able to experiment with what I felt would work best vs. what code requires when designing a commercial space for seniors. And Grandma's bedroom was one such place, where the minimum square footage requirements in senior living are much larger than the space I had to work with at our home.

Grandma's suite was designed to have a living room, bedroom, bathroom, and outdoor entry. We added large French sliding doors to any outside wall possible. If there was a wall that was not connected to the inside of the house— this meant that, if it could have a window or door placed in it to the outside to bring in natural light—then we put them in. We were employing the first letter of the LOVE design method, **L = LIGHT**. We put integral blinds into the French doors so that she wouldn't get them all gibber jawed by playing with them. Integral blinds mean that the mini blinds are sandwiched in between the panes of glass. They can still be opened, closed, and raised up or down at any height. They're safe and don't need to be cleaned. We also placed a window in Grandma's bedroom. Since the brain's alarm clock is kicked off by light, which produces melatonin, the benefit of all this natural light was to help Grandma sleep normal instead of having her waking up at all hours of the night. Natural light would also help cue her to the time of day. This would be a big help to early stage Alzheimer/Dementia folks, helping them to recognize the difference between breakfast and dinner and the appropriate time to go to bed.

Tip: Make sure to close all the blinds and drapes at night so no outside light sneaks in. Actually, this tip is for everyone, it will greatly help you sleep and regulate your circadian rhythm.

Now here's one I know might be hard but . . . NO watching TV, tablets, or looking at smartphones or screen devices one hour prior to going to sleep. The light emitted from these devices actually tells your brain to stay awake and screws up your circadian rhythm. TVs are worse than phones and tablets, and if you use those, use the night time lighting. Also, get a Human Charger and use it every morning. If there's one gadget besides the Bidet toilet seat that's high on my list for everyone to improve their quality of life, this is it.

Light sensors are great. Definitely use them when you need them. As I've talked about, Grandma definitely needed them; she had five stairs off her living room, so to keep her safe, we put a light sensor on them. It comes on automatically when it senses movement, which is great because we didn't have to worry about her remembering to turn on the light when she moved around. We also have a railing on one side of the steps and wanted to be sure she used it, which meant being sure she saw it. (It's not rocket science; most times it's just common sense.) So rather than it being the same color as the wall and blending into the wall, we stained it so that it would contrast with the wall color. This makes the railing *pop,* and she never missed seeing it!

Lighting has to be great in the bathroom—that's obvious—but my decision on *to dim or not to dim* was less obvious. Ultimately, I didn't put the bathroom on a dimmer. I didn't want there to be one more thing for her to have to mess with and didn't think she needed yet another gadget to cause her confusion: a light switch that isn't quite a light switch? Or wait, is it? See how easy it could be to get confused? So I opted to use the amber-colored night-light to draw her into the bathroom, rather than a dimmer on the main bathroom light. Once inside, she sees a light switch, and she hits it, and it turns on, then she hits it and turns off. It's clear to her. Sometimes the simplest is the best.

**O = OPTIMIZE** in the LOVE design method. The bathroom space is optimized by only having what Grandma needed and nothing that she didn't. As in her bedroom, which had a bed, nightstand, dresser, and bench—this was done to reduce her confusion, stress, and frustration. In the bathroom, our lack of space and need to remove obstructions caused us to use pocket doors (Universal Design feature) between her bedroom and bathroom. Having the pocket door to the bathroom open makes it easy to get in, and when open, creates the largest clear floor space for maneuverability and visual cuing. Not only does a normal door take up floor space, but it's also one more thing for Grandma to manipulate around on the way to and from the bathroom.

An easy example of how to optimize is by combining multiple features into one item to save on space, cost, and function. In the bathroom, we have this in a combination: light, heat lamp, and fan fixture, which doesn't come on automatically. It's located near the shower, and she had to turn it on, but usually, it was my mother who did this for her because Grandma was less independent and needed help showering. This is another place where you can take it up to the next step by adding a temperature control setting to make sure the water won't scald anyone. This is great whether you're coming in to check on your loved one once a day or once a week.

We also added another optimized item which is a combo grab bar and toilet paper holder. The problem with most grab bars is that they place your hands so far back that your center of gravity is off. While it's okay to help you steady yourself, it's actually difficult when it comes to helping you get on and off the toilet unless you have great arm strength (Most women have poor upper body strength). The location is perfect because it lets your center of gravity be in the right location, so you can easily get up and down with the least amount of effort. It's also smaller and looks better, and what kind of interior designer would I be if all I cared about was function?

It's funny what you think of as bells or whistles when you're younger and how they become essentials when you're older, or at least designing for someone older. That was the case with something as simple as a heat lamp in the shower. As I mentioned earlier, getting older means losing about 70% of our body fat (This is why our skin starts to sag.), and that fat is what's helping us maintain our body temperature, and it's also helping us *get the chill off.* Coming out of her shower, Grandma would go from hot water to cold air relatively fast with very little insulation. The small addition of a heat lamp (This is the combo fixture.) in the shower helped warm up the air for her and let her step out to a warmer space. For the folks who don't want to take a shower anymore, making the bathroom a warmer, nicer environment is a little thing you can do to make it more enticing. While Grandma's bathroom didn't have this, my bathroom has heated floors and a heated towel bar. I often get up in the middle of the night with no slippers or socks, which she'd never do, and these little items are a great comfort during our cold, midwestern winters. These aren't essential, but they sure do make the bathroom experience more pleasant.

Grandma's shower had a curtain, not a glass door. Like most of the decisions I made for her, this, too, had specific reasons behind it. A glass door would make it difficult for her to get in and out. Also, since my mom was there helping Grandma shower, the glass door would restrict my mom's movements, making it harder for her to help. And then there was my biggest concern—what if she fell? The glass door could possibly shatter, and they could both be hurt. A curtain made a lot more sense. We were able to optimize the space to be large and less restrictive for my mother, helping my grandmother by using a curtain vs. a glass door.

The third letter in the LOVE design method is **V = VISUAL**. Visual isn't just about seeing better but also about visual cues, which are the brain's highway signs to let you know that you're on the right path. The key idea here was separating the spaces as much as possible. I wanted Grandma to understand the reasons for the spaces—for their design to be apparent.

Doing this would help her be less confused by her environment, or so I hoped. When she walked into her apartment, I wanted it to be easy for her to understand the purpose of each space and to know what to expect. If she did, it would help her be less agitated, again, or so I hoped. Easily understood spaces would allow Grandma to have a higher level of independence; she'd be able to enjoy moving from one area to another for specific reasons that would engage her, and the way they were designed reinforced their purpose. The key thought behind designing for someone with memory issues is this—when dealing with people who are already confused, don't confuse them further by the interior design. Taking this to heart meant, for me, having Grandma's apartment work with her, not against her.

Even the things that seemed like mindless decisions need more thought than you'd think. Take towels, for instance. Standard white, right? Easy and done. Except, think again. Grandma was old, her eyes were bad, and without her glasses, her world was a blur. Giving her towels that have color provided a contrast to her off-white painted walls. She was able to see her green towels easily without her glasses.

A simple and helpful idea for wall color is to paint the wet wall (the one the toilet is attached to) a brighter color, or accent color. This makes the toilet clearly visible and so much easier for someone to see. And for men, it's even more important because they're standing up and aiming. Placing a grab bar behind the toilet at shoulder height allows a man to steady himself while urinating (In my family, we say, "peeing."). Putting an amber-colored night-light directly over the top of the toilet is another thing that helps them aim. In many bathrooms, handrails beside the toilet are a good idea. We didn't need it because the sink is so close to the toilet that Grandma uses it to steady herself. My husband, Greg, still added a handrail on the left-hand side of the toilet.

Bathrooms are tricky places for the memory impaired; in the same way, they're tricky places for small kids. Lots of things there could be misinterpreted. The liquids don't look lethal but could be. Powdery things that seem harmless could be unless they're consumed. Then there are creams, the ointments, the lotions, and the colorful little pills—how do you design for all their needs and still keep them safe, yet as independent as possible?

If you're waiting for me to talk about the medicine cabinet in Grandma's bathroom, the wait will be a long one—there wasn't one. There was a mirror, but not a medicine cabinet. Every day, my mom came into Grandma's apartment with a little basket that had Grandma's meds. She gave them to her, eliminating the chance of any medicine cabinet mix-ups, toss-outs, or flush-downs. Things happen as the memory goes. As her symptoms increased, Grandma became more argumentative and a bit more paranoid. Some days, she thought she already took her meds and that maybe she was being poisoned. In her heart, she knew she took them, and she was right; she did—but at another time. Soon, we started seeing her hiding them, and soon after that, my mother started becoming more stern with Grandma to take them. Rather than getting into an argument and saying, "No, you didn't," Grandma would respond with all the attitude fit for a teenager, "Yes, I did." My mother would snap back, and it would go from there. Eventually, we just said, "Yes, you did, but this is a new one." This is part of positive manipulation, which was needed to get her to take medicine; it's telling her a different story.

The same goes for what you'd normally have under your bathroom sink cabinet. I have an easy rule: *If you don't want them to take it by themselves, don't have it in there.* So cleaning supplies? They're not going to be in there where Grandma could possibly mistake it for something to drink. Medicine? Not going to be there. Mouthwash? If you drink it, it could be dangerous in excess, but toothpaste is fine. We only had pump soap for her to use for washing; bar soap can get slippery and flip out of her hands, and then she could have slipped on it. Sometimes employing the **V = VISUAL** in the LOVE design method is as much about making sure you don't see certain things as it is to help a person be more independent and safe.

Visual cueing can also mean having items that are familiar. Grandma's bedroom had been familiar to her since back to move-in day, a day that was hard for all of us but especially hard for her with her strong reliance on visual cueing and familiarity. The thing we did here to help her was bring her own bed and furniture; it helped her then and continues to do so to this day. She knew her items, her bed, her nightstand, and her bedspread. They not only helped her to remember but also helped provide her with the great comfort that familiarity brings. We all know that people have relationships to blankets and pillows. This starts early on in our childhood and never seems to leave us. You might be tempted to freshen up with a new look for your loved one's bedding, but I would advise against this. Keep as much as possible familiar (even if it's a decorator's nightmare). Trust me; if I can do it, you can too.

And then there's her faucet: a one-handled one for Grandma. The pros outweighed any cons. It's a safety thing. With a faucet that has separate cold and hot levers or knobs that you have to turn on each and then blend the water to the right temperature, there's a risk. This goes against the fourth letter of the LOVE design method: **E = EASE**. It's not easy to blend or even to remember the need to do so. The consequences could range from simple discomfort of the water being too cold to scalding herself with the hot water only turned on. With a one-handed faucet, there's a much smaller risk of her turning on the wrong one and scalding herself. There's one con to take into consideration—if someone has never used a one-handed faucet, they might be confused. You can add to the faucet a temperature controller to ensure that water that's too hot doesn't come out.

At the top of Grandma's stairs, we made another purposeful, **E = EASE** design decision:

We moved the door out to give her a 3' landing. And so whenever she was getting ready to open the door to go to the rest of the house, we didn't worry about her teetering on the top step before going in or out. She'd get to her landing, pause, get her footing, get her balance, and then move to where she needed to be. It's just a simple landing before opening the door, but it made a huge difference for her. In fact, just these few little things for her stairs—light, handrail contrast, the landing—made the steps so much easier for her to use. If we'd made it difficult for her to use, she wouldn't have come into the rest of the house as much, and that's the opposite of what we wanted for her. This is a great example of the **E = EASE** in the LOVE design method. We wanted her to be all around the house, engaging with us, not cooped up in her apartment all day. And so far, to a pretty great extent, we've succeeded.

What helped me wrap my head around the LOVE design method was something I noticed about myself. I travel three to four days a week, and I noticed something: I often can't remember the layout of the hotel room when I'm trying to find the bathroom in the middle of the night. I get up, disoriented, and sometimes, I'm the thing that goes bump in the night. And yes, in more extreme cases, I'm the thing that goes bump and falls in the night. Though I don't have Alzheimer's/Dementia, I do have difficulty when in a new environment and just waking up. So I reasoned that my grandmother, who may not remember her bedroom layout, may be just as disoriented as I get in various hotel rooms, perhaps even more. In nursing homes, it is common, when someone is a fall risk, to place their twin bed up against a wall. This would help them to not get trapped on the inside wall if they rolled out of bed. It also helped to create muscle memory, so we tried the same concept of only allowing her one option to enter and exit her bed. The intention of the design was to create **E = EASE** for my grandmother, reducing choices and creating muscle memory.

We also designed the bathroom space to have a shower with a seat, a sink, and a toilet with a Bidet seat. It sprays, blow dries, and the seat is heated. Some models even have night-lights, which is something to consider too. The Bidet let Grandma clean herself, or if my mother was helping her in this department, it really helped reduce her efforts, and that was a nice plus for her. Once, after grandma came home from a short-term rehab following surgery, I helped with her toileting, and I can assure you, the Bidet toilet seat is now my best friend and worth every penny. As I mentioned before, sometimes the things we may consider the bells and whistles become necessities not only for a loved one's dignity but also for your sanity.

When I was in college in Dallas, Texas, it was a world of difference from my small town of Canton, Ohio, where I'd grown up. Driving on the Dallas super highways created a combination of fear, confusion, and frustration daily. What I found looking back was this was mostly due to the fact I was unfamiliar with where I was going, the system, and needing to make fast choices.

There was no GPS back then, so trying to figure out on a six lane highway, with exits to the right and to the left and signs all over, which lane I should be in when, which exit was mine, and trying to get off in time caused that burning feeling in my stomach. If I couldn't figure it out quickly, then I would become paralyzed, unable to make a decision, so then I would just drive along, and soon I'd have to pull off to get my bearings.

Eventually, I figured out the system, but it got me thinking. My grandmother's life was a lot like being on a Dallas super highway. Except she NEVER figured out the system. So how could we make her life have less panic, frustration, confusion, and fear? I remembered driving on the highways in Canton, two lanes generally, with exits only on the right. Clear exit signs ahead told you where to get off. When you see the exit you need, you get off at that exit. No fear, confusion, or frustration. Then it hit me! **When you limit choices, you increase independence and confidence.**

One thing I didn't design in her bedroom was a closet. In part, it was due to space, but there was something else at work here too. Every day, my mother would lay out Grandma's clothes for her on her bed. This was another way of providing **E= EASE** in her decisions and another way of helping her to be more independent. Dressing herself was a big part of Grandma's independence, and since we wanted that to happen for a long time, we did things like this to help encourage it to happen. By my mother laying out her clothes every day, Grandma had one exit sign to use. She didn't have to view a closet full of choices, deciding if pajamas should be worn for lunch or a dress for bedtime. She saw the clothes on the bed (one outfit) and my mother said, "Get dressed, Mother" (Get off at this exit), and my grandma could successfully get dressed with no stress.

There's another reason for limiting Grandma's choices. Let's look at her bed again. There it is against the wall. Grandma was not making a choice in how she's going to get up; she's just going one way. So not only did this help her get up without a hassle; it also helped her start building muscle memory, which she could build vs. mental memory, which she couldn't build anymore and lost daily. No matter what our age, our body can build muscle memory, and it happens simply by doing the same thing every day in a way that becomes almost automatic. Ever sat down on a toilet at a restaurant or airport and felt yourself drop? It's because your derriere is trained to a certain height, most likely the height of the toilet in your home, and you've built muscle memory that tells you how high and where to sit. I was always looking to improve Grandma's muscle memory, and making her daily choices repetitive and automatic helped accomplish that. Building muscle memory for getting in and out of bed is a great example of the "E" in the **LOVE** design method.

This let Grandma get up to less confusion, which reduced some of her stress around decision-making. It's stress that comes from her wading through her life and wondering, *What do I do here? I don't understand.* Without a lot of decisions required of her, she was able to be more independent, less frustrated, less anxious, and less agitated.

So though we didn't add all the bells and whistles, partly because we wanted the space to be able to grow with her as her needs changed and partly because we were on a budget, what we feel we did do was create a manageable *home* within our home for Grandma to live with as much independence and ease as possible.

Finally, the toilet. I actually have a whole chapter on this in *HIVE,* so be sure to read it for all the details. I may have mentioned that I wanted to test some theories for those with Alzheimer's/Dementia that I haven't been able to with my clients. The Bidet toilet seat was one of those items. It's a seat that goes onto a conventional toilet and costs about $400. You need to have an outlet, which most bathrooms do. The toilet seat makes the seat height correct for a senior and is antibacterial and antimicrobial. It is warm, can come with a night-light, and has a sprayer that can be positioned for various private parts, but it only sprays if someone is sitting on the seat. It is, by far, the largest success story of this whole 4-Gen social experiment. I was concerned that Grandma wouldn't understand it. I asked her what she thought of it, and she said, at first, she didn't know that it was anything special. However, after my mother showed her what it did, she loved it. She felt it was wonderful to be able to give herself a sitz bath and reduce the burden on my mother. My mom let me know on several occasions that if it were to ever break, it would be the first thing to be fixed. Even if Grandma could no longer remember to operate it properly, my mom's effort would have been substantially reduced compared to a regular toilet. I believe it is so successful because it engages all four of the four design philosophies in the **LOVE design method: Light, Optimize, Visual, and Ease.**

If you know someone over the age of 85, then there's a 50/50 chance they're suffering from dementia. Empathy is one of our greatest human traits and gifts. If you can't quite understand how difficult it is for someone with Alzheimer's/Dementia on a daily basis, I would ask that you do these three exercises and then write down how you felt. Understanding where they are helps you meet them where they are and reduce stress for everyone. Emotional understanding is just as—if not more important—than a physically supportive space. When you have both, it's a winning combination for everyone.

**Exercise 1:**

Take a piece of paper and write your name and birth date with your *non-dominant* hand.

Now write how this made you feel.

Everyday, a person with Alzheimer's/Dementia feels this way. They know they were better, yet somehow now slower, disconnected, and frustrated, and sometimes, it's difficult to even get your brain around how to form the letters. It takes extreme effort and concentration, and yet you've been doing this for years! Imagine 80 years. You know your name and when you were born, but trying to get it on paper legibly and fast is a task. The brain takes 20% of the oxygen needed in your body, which is why mental work is so exhausting.[57]

**Exercise 2:**

Take out a piece of paper and write down all you did in 30-minute increments two days ago—from the time you got up until when you went to sleep. Most people don't get very far. Write down how this makes you feel. Now remember how we snicker when Grandma can't remember if she took her pills today or ate breakfast. The more someone sleeps, the more difficult remembering becomes.

**Exercise 3:**

Place your index finger pointed at the sky above your nose (with your head looking up). Now, turn your finger slowly clockwise, while slowly moving it down (yet close to your body) till it's at your nose. Then lower it, continuing to turn it clockwise. Now your head should be looking down at your finger, and what do you notice? If you have done the exercise correctly, your finger has switched to counterclockwise. Magic? Confused? I bet you are; Most people will do this 2-3 times before they believe it.

I created a video that may help you understand this exercise a little better that you can view on YouTube. (http://bit.ly/3c4LTUa)

Write down how this made you feel.

What happened? Your perspective changed. My grandmother experiences the world differently than I do because her perspective is different due to the dementia. All the explaining to her in the world can't make her understand my finger was going clockwise if she's looking down on the finger and I'm looking up at the finger.

What if every day, hour, or minute your perspective changed and disoriented you to understanding your reality? Seems pretty cruel, and then you have people who you thought you were safe with and who loved arguing with you, and you know you're right, but they tell you you're not. So you become a bit untrusting and paranoid; they're crazy, not you, right? This happens with my grandma taking her pills. She believes that she's taken them, and her perspective says she's 100% right. So why would someone force her to take more unless they were trying to hurt her?

This simple exercise can help caregivers, spouses, and family members to understand the change in perspective of someone like my grandmother with Alzheimer's/Dementia. It can help them to adapt to using positive manipulation techniques to get through the normal functions of life vs. arguing with their loved one.

**Exercise 4:**

This exercise comes from Z-Health. You'll need two people for this exercise and a cell phone to video.

Blindfold yourself and have the other person video you. If possible, place earbuds or ear protection in your ears to help reduce sound.

Now march in place for a minute.

Take off the blindfold and take out the earbuds (if you had them) and see where you're standing now. What happened? When we take away our sight and lose some of our hearing, it is often more difficult than one would expect to understand where we are in this world and that we're moving, even when we think we're staying in one place.

Recognize that aging adults have lost a substantial amount of their senses, from sight to hearing, touch, and so on.

The largest lesson from these exercises is to have empathy so that we can meet them where they are. When we come from a place of understanding others and their challenges, communication and connection are increased, which is in direct correlation to having a wonderful quality of life.

Looking back at all I've written, I realize I probably come across as some kind of a worst-case scenario extremist who has a bunker in her backyard filled to the gills with supplies for an inevitable demise of the human race, but that's not me at all. I'm an optimist at heart, and I think that heart can relax, open up, and give Grandma so much more love when my brain's not worrying about what might happen next. The key is to make the space easy for her to use, which means the rest of the family doesn't need to worry with all the *what if* scenarios.

## The Bathroom Dos and Don'ts

### Dos

- Have the toilet in view of the bed.
- Have an amber night-light over the toilet or by the toilet, if possible.

- Have a pocket door to the bathroom to allow the entry to be as wide as possible and ensure the door is left open at night so they can see into the bathroom.
- Have a walk-in shower with seat that's easy to use.
- Have a heat lamp. Core body temperatures of seniors are lower, so when they get out of the shower, it's harder for them to get the chill off without the heat lamp.
- Have contrasting color towels so they can be seen easily. A different color than the wall works well.
- Have basic needs such as toothpaste and a toothbrush out and accessible. Use the safety latches on cabinets to secure what you want kept safe.
- Provide a trash can in an easy to see and reach space.
- Have a Bidet toilet seat for ease in personal cleaning.
- Have a contrasting toilet seat for visual cuing.

## Don'ts

- Don't have items available that could cause an issue such as cleaning supplies, mouthwash, etc.

- Don't have medications easily accessible.
- Don't have trip hazards such as rugs.
- Don't have sharp edges, if at all possible.
- Don't have a faucet with two blades for water (They may only use the hot or the cold.).
- Don't have carpet as it is difficult to clean if there's an accident, which is more likely closer to the toilet.
- Don't have slippery floors.
- If you have hard floors—avoid tile if possible (Vinyl is fine.). Grout is difficult to clean, and tile is harder if there's a fall, and so it can cause more damage to the body.
- Don't have curling irons, hair dryers, etc., accessible.
- Don't have an open drain—change it out so that jewelry, etc., doesn't fall in and get lost.
- Don't use a glass cup for water. Use plastic or small disposables.

# CHAPTER 12
## UNIQUE HOUSING OPTIONS FOR BOOMERS

As we age, our needs change. Kids move out and then maybe back in again and then hopefully out again. Many of us go from an apartment to small houses as we start in life, to bigger and bigger homes, and then we do it all in reverse and downsize. 25 years ago, there were few options as we aged. You could downsize to a smaller home or apartment, move to a sunshine state, move in with your family, or move into senior living.

Now there are so many choices it has become overwhelming and hard to sift through the options, costs, and what might work best for us.

To help us decide, we need to go back to the foundational questions:

1. How are you going to be able to live your life with freedom and confidence?

2. Where will you be living your life?

3. How are you going to care for your mind, body, and spirit?

Sifting through all the different options is difficult, but these questions will help you to make smart choices that will offer you freedom, flexibility, and confidence.

To be clear, there's no *Right* or *Wrong* solution. The right solution for you may be the wrong solution for me.

There are options for all different types of unique housing situations, but to be clear, I love senior living; heck, it's my life's work! Whenever my husband, my kids, and I would tour a new senior living home that my team and I'd just designed, we all agreed that we'd love to move in. What's not to love? The apartment would be cleaned for us, the laundry done, food prepared for us whenever we wanted, a workout center, and the kids would be safe and sound with 100 grandparents around whenever I traveled. It seemed to me, for a working, traveling mother, that senior living was the perfect fit; but the rub was I just was not old enough . . . then.

So why shouldn't everyone choose to age in a private-pay (resort-style) senior living?

Stick with me on this . . . because private-pay senior living is a lot like sushi (raw fish)!

So that we're on the same page, I'm defining private-pay as homes and facilities that don't take Medicaid. Basically, it's out-of-pocket or paid for by your long-term care insurance policy. Now that we've gotten this out of the way, sushi is one of those foods that you either love or hate. Sushi is expensive, no matter if it's good or great.

If you don't like sushi then don't try to make yourself like it. Just eat a hamburger (or veggie burger) and do what works for you. No matter the cost, if you don't like sushi, it's not going to start tasting better to you. If on the other hand, you like sushi, then go all in. You can try all the variations of how it's made and different types of fish.

I find this analogy to hold true with so many of the beautiful resort-style senior living homes we design at Mosaic. Some residents thrive and come back to life when they move into senior living. They love having a community, activities, help, and the safety of the environment. Senior living has reconnected them to life.

On the other hand, my parents want to be in their home, and they want to be by their kids, close, really close (Remember, they live with us.)—connection isn't an issue for them. So to move them into a senior living facility would actually cause them disconnection, not greater connection.

It's a matter of taste. Do you like sushi or not? As my Italian grandmother would say, "To each his own." In other words, your sushi is fine for you but not for me.

If you don't have kids or they're grown and you're tired of tending to the yard and doing constant home upkeep, why not look at some interesting alternative ways to live? For instance, did you know that you can actually live aboard a cruise ship and that the cost is comparable to an assisted living facility? How about getting a place together with several of your friends and having a girls' night every night? Have you considered life as an expatriate in a tropical paradise? You'll be surprised to find out how affordable and stress-free that type of life can be! Do your homework and keep your mind open to possibilities that you've never considered before. As the young folks say, you only live once!

While there are so many options, I'll do my best to introduce these concepts to you in a simple, concise format. It's up to you to decide what piques your interest and then dive in and learn more, applying the three foundational questions to help you decide what's best for you.

While traveling to Israel this past summer, I was exposed to something called a Kibbutz concept. It's a community centered around a common goal like agriculture where folks all live together and share resources and duties. Some would say Israel wouldn't be where it is today if not for these communities. In their Kibbutz living, they've found a unique housing solution that's worked for over 100 years and is still working. Now, Baby Boomers in the U.S. are applying some of these principles to help improve their quality of life as they age and live on their own terms.

## Co-Housing

Similar to the Israeli Kibbutz housing, but you have your "owned" private spaces, and you come together in shared community spaces such as large dining and gathering spaces. It's similar to assisted living without any services. Neighbors also share resources like tools, etc., typically co-housing situations involve 20-40 homes.

## House Sharing / Endless Girls' (or Boys') Nights

Another alternative that people don't often think of is sharing a home with some friends—*Golden Girls*-style. A recent UCLA study points out that 1-3 Baby Boomers are unmarried, making this a growing trend.[58] If you never married, are divorced, or widowed with several friends in the same situation, why not move in together? It will afford you companionship, fun, and assistance when needed. If one of you has a home that's conducive to home-sharing, the others can simply pay rent.

Or you can each sell your homes and possessions and find something that suits all of your lives perfectly. A large condo near the beach, perhaps? Let someone else do all the yard work and keep the pool sparkling. Your only job will be deciding what's for breakfast and how long to stay in the sun.

Don't have any suitable housemates? Check in to senior home share programs to find some. The obvious benefit of this type of arrangement is the lowered cost for each participant and companionship.

There's really no right or wrong way to do this. The key is being clear on the rules of engagement from the onset and then having a process in place to deal with them, when or if it goes awry. You know what I mean . . . when Blanche stays out all night and forgets to call so the others don't worry.

## Housing Co-ops

These are member-owned and run the gamut from apartments to single family homes. You'll find them in specific communities and even mobile home parks. These are less expensive than private-pay senior living and have less services but align you with people with the same needs.

## NORC (Naturally Occurring Retirement Community)

NORCs are multigenerational planned neighborhoods that have organized volunteer programs. These neighborhoods provide the structure to allow support services to be in place for all generations in a free volunteer format. (ghdc.generationsofhope.org/initiatives/)

## Niche Retirement

Similar to a CCRC (Continuing Care Retirement Community) but around a niche such as golf, religion, sexual orientation, or occupation. These are popping up all over and can allow you to age with your tribe.

## Village to Village

Neighbor helping neighbor with some paid help and organized events. The Village to Village Network was formed in 2010. Currently, there are over 200 of these villages and another 150 coming online in 45 states. They're similar to a NORC but are created to support aging in place and support reciprocity. Some volunteer services include wellness programs and transportation. Per their site, "VtVN energizes Villages, hyper-local neighborhood groups, of vibrant members engaged in their communities. Village members experience reduced isolation, increased independence, and enhanced purpose of life. These feet-on-the-street resources, focused on social determinants of health, positively improve population health." (vtvnetwork.org/)

## ECHOs (Elder Cottage Housing Opportunities) / Grand Pods or Flats / Micro Living

These are trailer homes that are attached to existing homes and removed when no longer needed.

You may not want to live like my family does in a multi-generational household, but you may want to be really close to your family without having to share the kitchen or be able to hear and see each other. A new option is the Grand Pod. Think of it like a small cottage placed in the backyard of your daughter or son's home. You have complete privacy but also security and can see the family whenever you want without getting into a car or plane. Several companies are making these backyard mini houses, and some have even worked through local permitting with the cities. They range in size from 140 sq. ft. on up and are typically one story. The cost ranges from $85,000-$250,000. These Grand Pods can be as disconnected or as connected as you want them to be, and some even sharing a patio, covered walkways, or garage.

MEDCottage is one of the few manufacturers of Grand Pods that has built-in features to age in place such as grab bars, night-lights, and emergency call systems. Per their website, "The MEDcottage is a mobile medical dwelling designed to be temporarily placed on a caregivers' property for rehabilitation and extended care." The cottage is delivered fully assembled and costs about $60 per day, which is very economical considering the options, and it Fis a rented model.

One of the great features of the Grand Pod is that if you decide not to use it in a micro living capacity, it can become a great art studio, workout studio, home office, or anything else you can imagine.

## Cruising Through Life

Amazingly, life on a cruise ship is a great way to travel while taking advantage of amenities quite similar to those of an assisted living facility (ALF). Nearly all cruise ships offer all-inclusive plans that include meals, and there are many entertainment and exercise opportunities. Swimming pools, well-equipped fitness rooms, live music, shows, and games are fixtures on most cruises, and each has on-board doctors.

Cruising costs are typically lower than what you'd pay in a private pay assisted living facility. Consider that the average cost of assisted living is about $4,300 per month, though the costs vary widely by state.[59] Cruises average less than $100 per night. Longer cruises offer even larger discounts, and often, a couple's discount can be offered for two people traveling together. There are also senior discounts, discounts for frequent cruisers, and points that you can stack up on a credit card. Be sure to check with the cruise line to see if they allow long-term passengers or sign up for an around-the-world voyage that lasts several months. For even more travel variety, you can try different cruises from the same departure point that travel to varied ports of call.

## Road Tripping

Love to get in the car and just drive? Did you ever consider making that your new retirement lifestyle? If nothing is holding you in the town where you live, why not get out the maps and plot your journey? The great thing about road trips is that they can be different things to different people. If you love camping, buying an RV and making friends in campgrounds around the country might be to your liking. Alternatively, if you enjoy creature comforts and hate bugs, driving your luxury SUV to well-appointed hotels around the country might work best. Either way, you can stop to see the sights on your journey that you've always wanted to visit. Better yet, the costs will most likely be less than living in a traditional assisted living facility.

## House Swapping

Have you always wondered what it would be like to live in a certain state, a particular town, or even overseas? House swapping for Baby Boomers gives you lots of options. After all, there's likely someone out there interested in finding out what living in your area is like, but not as a tourist. Swapping homes gives you the opportunity to stay where you want with limited or no added costs. Of course, most Baby Boomers are empty nesters with lots of flexibility, making it easier to work out exchanges. Some sites to look into for home exchange: (homeexchange.com/), (sabbaticalhomes.com/), and (homeexchange50plus.com/).

## Moving to Paradise

Aside from just visiting somewhere tropical or amazingly historical, you might decide you'd love to live there. Growing numbers of American Boomers are now opting to relocate outside of the United States to great tropical areas like the Bahamas, coastal Mexico, Belize, and Costa Rica. There are also large numbers of expatriates in countries like Germany, Japan, and the United Kingdom. Most seniors cite the cost of living in these countries as one of their biggest considerations before making a move, with rent and utilities averaging less. Additionally, many Boomers find that hiring help in some areas is quite affordable, allowing them to relax and let someone else do the cooking, cleaning, and laundry. Of course, you can't overlook the amazing scenery and culture in many of the places that are burgeoning with expats as well as the wealth of activities available.

With all of the options now available, look at which ones strike your fancy before deciding on moving to an independent or assisted living facility. You just might find that you'd prefer lying on a beach under swaying palms!

## Understanding Traditional Aging Housing Options

## CCRC

CCRC is a Continuing Care Retirement Community. Typically, you pay a large fee, anywhere from $100,000 to a $1,000,000, and buy into a community that has patio homes, independent living, assisted living, skilled nursing, and memory care. You lock into the monthly rates the year you buy-in and can move throughout the system as you need. This is a great system for those planners that saved lots of money, but sometimes the community can wear down 10 years into your stay. They offer less flexibility to leave due to your large investment.

## Independent Living

Age-restricted apartments, typically 55 and older, and may have dining facilities, activities, and some cleaning services. You can typically get a home health service that isn't provided by the community to come in and help with medications and health needs. Costs range from $1,500 a month to $20,000 a month, depending on the campus, design, location, and services.

## Assisted Living

Apartments that are smaller than Independent Living and have much smaller kitchens aren't usually equipped with a stove or oven. They're age-friendly and attach to lots of services that are part of the monthly rent cost such as dining, activities, game room, cafe, and transportation and van for rides to the doctor's office. They also offer a 24/7 nurse on-site in most states and assistance with daily living activities (ADLs) such as bathing, toileting, medications, and dressing. These may be over and above your monthly rent or included as a flat fee. These communities are typically a rental program.

## Memory Care

Purpose-built Memory Care homes have staff who are trained specifically to deal with cognitive issues or memory loss. This could be any form of dementia, which is the umbrella term for anything from Alzheimer's to vascular dementia or Lewy Body disease. Typically, they'll have an interior courtyard so that the resident can wander outside without getting into trouble. They utilize technology such as induction cooktops, trackers, circadian lighting, and others to help a resident with memory issues have as much freedom as possible while being safe. Costs range from $4,500 a month on the low end to $20,000 a month, depending on the home. Newer concepts are surfacing where early diagnoses are made, and corrective actions are taken with diet, exercise, and supplements to stop or reverse the disease if caught early enough.

## Skilled Nursing and Short-Term Rehabilitation

Skilled nursing typically arises due to a hospital stay or surgery. Stays may be long-term or short-term. Usually insurance is involved in this option as this is really a healthcare situation. It's not a choice but a need.

## The Biggest Question I Get Asked?

Some questions I'm often asked are, "If you were moving into AL (Assisted Living), which is the best *home* you'd choose?" and "What would you look for if you had to decide on an AL?"

So if it's for you, your spouse, or someone else you love, my advice is to look for which providers will give you the most choices, which equals flexibility and freedom.

Make the kinds of choices that will give you the freedom to live on your terms for your mind, body, and spirit. Because some private-pay assisted living places do—and some don't. There are many AL homes where it's a lot like the song "Hotel California," where you can check in but you can never check out. They watch your every move, make you sign in and out, and track all your guests and the times they come and go. Some even make you sign in and out the key to use the bathroom in the lobby, just like when you were in high school!

For me, I would look for an Independent Living or Assisted Living facility that will be able to customize things to you. They should give you a suite of options when you move in.

It's actually a lot like a menu, and if you want to choose the right restaurant, you need to know what you want (type of food) before you go. Right now, the menu for many senior living places is like a restaurant that offers appetizers, entrées, and desserts. You *may* be able to find a star rating on it for service, and you *may* be able to find the little dollar signs on it for affordability, but that's about it—that's about the amount of information out there in regard to senior living options. Talk to people, and do the research.

In choosing an AL, I'd want *MORE* than basic living services and a pretty living room. More information that tells me what they're offering in terms of the technology will help me have freedom to live on my terms. What I mean by technology isn't just Wi-Fi but also fitness, data mining, robots, IOT, lighting, and well building—all of it!

My final bit of advice is to get clear on what you want using the three foundational questions listed in every chapter, then do your research, and interview them all.

This is a decision that will impact the rest of your life, even if you're not the one living there.

Clarity creates confidence, and confidence creates freedom.

I've provided a simple checklist that will let you ask the right questions if and when you decide to move into senior living in the resource section in the back of the book.

# CHAPTER 13

## GAMIFICATION, AUGMENTED REALITY (AR)/VIRTUAL REALITY (VR), & LIFELONG LEARNING

You probably would never guess it, but AARP has one of the highest rankings for online games on Google. Playing games and competing against others are fun and healthy, especially when you add exercise. Fitbit and Wii Fit are fantastic examples of how games can help you to stay active without having to go into a home and sit in a large room while someone yells BINGO or tosses a balloon around!

Gamification is the process of applying games to tasks to encourage compliance or fun in doing an activity. You're already familiar with gamification if you or anyone you know has ever used Wii Fit. Basically, you're playing a game while exercising, which allows you to focus on the fun or the competition vs. the actual workout.

Another example of gamification that you may not be aware of is Fantasy Football, which is a multibillion-dollar-a-year industry. The NFL noticed that viewers weren't tuning in as much as they used to (probably due to the enormous amount of access to entertainment anytime, anywhere). Per Wikipedia:

> *In 1997, **CBS** launched the beta version of the first publicly available free fantasy football website. The game immediately became*

*widely popular. Today, it is estimated over 19 million people compete in public and private leagues online nationally.*[60]

Engagement is key. How do you get your parent or spouse involved and motivated? These are two of the keys to happiness and health. Games seem to be the Holy Grail of engagement but not just any games like Solitaire or working a puzzle. Games need to be highly interactive, flexible, and ever-changing, which is where gamification comes in. People want to not only immerse themselves in a game but also compete and get rewarded. I may be known to be competitive (Blame it on me having two older brothers.), but let's be honest, who would rather lose than win?

Why is this important to you? "You can't teach an old dog new tricks" was a saying I was brought up on, and it implied that once we become mature, the learning stops. We're forever cemented to be who we are, and our ability to learn becomes very difficult. To further this sad idea, we were taught, up until 2005, that if something catastrophic happened to one part of your brain (such as a stroke), that part was basically dead and couldn't be recovered. In other words, when your memory starts to go, the old school thinking was that you could never get back what you had lost, and it would only get worse over time.

However, in 2005, a study was released that found that when medical students were studied during a period of studying for their exams, their gray matter (the stuff that processes information in your brain) actually increased.[61] This then became known as a mainstream concept called neuroplasticity.

The concept, simplified, is that if you exercise your brain, you can keep it healthy just as you would if you exercise your body, and doing so also deters the effects of aging and can possibly even reverse them. Several doctors and futurists have written books on this concept and numerous companies are cashing in on brain games. A lot of Boomers are adopting this mindset. They fear they'll end up like their senile parents or grandparents, and if that's not reason enough, it's because to them it just makes good sense. The word "senile" is hardly used any longer, but it refers to a person having or showing weaknesses or diseases of old age, especially a loss of mental faculties. Now doctors are more specific with their diagnosis such as Alzheimer's/Dementia.

Lumosity is for athletes, kids, seniors, Boomers, and it's for you and me. It's a phone app that utilizes gamification to improve your memory, increase focus, and find calm. Elevate, which I actually play, is a free app, and it does the same thing as Lumosity, essentially. Brain Fit Life is software that not only helps your brain to stay fit by playing games, but it also provides support and creates a brain report.

"We are NOT just playing games with your brain"[62]
– Dr. Daniel Amen

A COMPREHENSIVE BRAIN HEALTH PROGRAM LIKE NO OTHER.

| BENEFITS | Lumosity | CogniFit | ?Brains | BrainFitLife |
|---|---|---|---|---|
| Brain Type Report | | | | ✓ |
| Memory & Attention | ✓ | ✓ | ✓ | ✓ |
| Stress & Mood | | | | ✓ |
| Monitors Progress | ✓ | ✓ | ✓ | ✓ |
| Personalized Meal & Fitness Plans | | | | ✓ |
| Motivational Tools | | | | ✓ |
| Positive Thinking Resources | | | | ✓ |
| Relaxation Resources | | | | ✓ |
| Community Support | | | | ✓ |
| Live Webinars & Online Coaching | | | | ✓ |

Dr. Daniel Amen, one of the leading psychiatrists on brain health, speaks about the fact that psychiatry is the only medical field that guesses to diagnose instead of using the technology we have today in imaging and blood work. Any other doctor would use the technology to help them create a proper diagnosis so they can create the most successful treatment strategy. According to Dr. Mehmet Oz, "Dr. Amen is one of the most gifted minds in medicine."[63]

He uses the example of Abraham Lincoln being diagnosed as depressed based upon his symptoms of depression. The astonishing fact is that 173 years ago, and the way diagnosis is made today by most doctors, is the same as it was then.

While Dr. Amen has been on the forefront of NFL concussion research and debate and helping to heal players from traumatic brain injuries, he's concerned about all brain health and has written books not only on ADD/ADHD but also aging, including *Use Your Brain to Change Your Age: Secrets to Look, Feel, and Think Younger Every Day*. Dr. Amen's book, *Memory Rescue,* is a must-read if you want to maintain your memory. He gives simple, actionable plans (with research to back it up) to keep your mind sharp through reducing sugar and increasing physical and mental exercises.

The relevance to anyone 45 years old and older is that Alzheimer's/Dementia is mostly diagnosed by symptoms. Rarely is a brain scan completed or labs taken to determine if there's another cause for the memory loss. It's just as rare for those scans and labs to be used to see whether memory loss could be reversed through supplements and/or medication, TMS, psychological testing, neurofeedback, lifestyle changes, bioidentical hormone replacement therapy, oxygen therapy, hypnotherapy, IV nutrient therapy, prolotherapy, or platelet-rich plasma therapy. Not all of these therapies are for memory loss—some are for depression, anxiety, joint aches, etc.

As I mentioned in Chapter 8, if you're in your 70s and you start to have memory loss, you're written off from really finding out what the issue is and if there's a possibility you could be *fixed* back to a higher level of cognitive function. SPECT scans that look at brain blood flow and activity patterns have been shown to change the treatment plan or diagnosis 78.9% of the time vs. just asking the patient for their symptoms.[64] This translates to almost 8 of out 10 treatment plans being wrong when not using the technology that we currently have at our disposal. I know this sounds crazy, but it's true. Why would you ever accept a brain diagnosis that's going to rob you of your memories and loved ones without having a brain scan first.

If you're anything like me, I don't always feel like my mind is as quick as it was in my 20s. Maybe it's because I'm less active, or maybe it's because my cells are dying and have become senescent, or maybe I'm developing a form of dementia. The thought goes through my mind, and frankly, it worries me.

Keeping your brain fit and even turning back the clock to when you felt like you were firing on all cylinders—thinking clearer and faster— is the goal of brain exercises through gamification. Dr. Amen has a brain-type assessment that you take online, and then they direct you to brain exercises and even diet to help you reduce your risk of Alzheimer's disease and stay your best you, mentally.

*There is a fountain of youth: it is your mind, your talents, the creativity you bring to your life and the lives of people you love. When you learn to tap this source, you'll truly have defeated age.*

— Sophia Lauren

An excellent example of the power of gamification is Volkswagen's Fun Theory. They're a group that sets out to change behaviors by utilizing fun or gamification. They've completed numerous experiments with throwing trash away, taking the stairs vs. the escalator, and even reducing speeding in your car. If you have flown lately on Delta Airlines, you would have noticed that their safety video is actually fun, and it helps you to pay attention. While we can't make everything fun, there's a lot more we can do to positively manipulate behavior to get the desired results we want, all while having fun. If you have children or have ever babysat, you know how to play this game . . . making the food on a spoon become an airplane or train with actual sound effects for the mouth to open and the food to go in. This is the basic concept of gamification.

Don't get me wrong; I'm not implying that we should treat others as toddlers. What I'm saying is if a process must be completed, such as exercising or taking medications, why can't we make it a little fun or gamify the process?

We can build in rewards to encourage the outcomes we want so that it becomes a win-win, something that isn't only fun but challenging and gets us excited. This one technology, if applied properly, could dramatically improve the results in almost every aspect of what you do. This isn't exactly brain surgery, but it could actually save your brain!

The Fun Theory site states:

> *This site is dedicated to the thought that something as simple as fun is the easiest way to change people's behavior for the better. Be it for yourself, for the environment, or for something entirely different; the only thing that matters is that it's change for the better.*[65]

They encourage participation by offering a Fun Theory award and testing the top winners' theories.

Some of Volkswagen's Fun Theory experiments in how to manipulate behavior for the better and to have fun, which is eye-opening to say the least. I would highly encourage you to watch the videos and brainstorm how you may engage the concept in your life.

The most famous of the experiments involves a piano staircase, in which folks are encouraged to take the staircase vs. the escalator out of the subway. They recorded data with cameras of how many individuals took the stairs vs. the escalators and then came in and installed a weight-activated piano on the staircase like the one in the Tom Hanks movie, *Big*. Sound would come out as people stepped on the keys of the stairs. Some would try to play a song on the way up and out of the subway while others tried to hold back a smile. The end result was there was a 66% increase in people taking the stairs vs. the escalator![66]

Another example of the Fun Theory was "The World's Deepest Bin." They took a trash can in a park and rigged a motion sensor sound to it so that when trash was thrown into the bin or can, it made a sound like it never hit the bottom. People would actually go looking for more trash on the ground to throw into the bin just to hear the sound again or to try and figure it out. In the end, 158 lbs. were collected in the trash bin in one day, which was 90 lbs.[67] more than the next-closest bin.

The final Fun Theory example was through a contest for Fun Theory ideas. The contest winner postulated that you could reduce speeding by entering those who obeyed the speed limit into a lottery that would allow them to gain some of the money from those who were speeding and issued tickets. The concept was simple: Get more people to obey the speed limit by giving them a chance to win money from those that broke the law. The results weren't surprising—speeding was reduced by 22%.[68] Apparently, positive reinforcement works better than negative.

Given the results, it seems ridiculous not to employ more of the Fun Theory in our lives. Who wouldn't want a 66% positive increase in participation of any item that we already do? Imagine what this could do to increase your quality of life.

## Augmented Reality and Virtual Reality

Take a moment to think about all the technologies that you use today that you didn't have when you were a kid. One technology that comes to mind is the cellular phone. Take this one step further to the smartphone. It cannot only call others, but you can text, look up anything on the Internet, have it remind you of appointments, and help you get to a location when you're driving. It's incredible what a smartphone can do today.

I recently was challenged to fast from my smartphone and computer and tablet from Saturday night until Monday morning. Easy peasy, right? Not really. I had no idea how much I rely on my electronics. Both my kids are in college, so they can fend for themselves, yet I was making up excuses in my mind of why I needed to keep my phone on in case they needed me and texted me. When I was in college, I had a phone in my apartment with no answering machine, and if I was not at home when my parents called, then they couldn't get ahold of me and vice versa. I know you understand this, but for the millennials reading this book, I felt the need to explain, LOL.

Technology has become part of me, and I couldn't have imagined when I was young that in the future, I would sleep with my phone, turn the car around and go back home if I forgot my phone, and rely on it for my access to the world, my money, and memories (all my photos). I can tell you that Augmented Reality and Virtual Reality are going to change how we live, and they'll help us much in the same way that our smartphones do today but at a multiple of 10 times!

So what is Augmented Reality (AR) and Virtual Reality (VR)?

If you have ever watched Monday night football on TV, AR is the line that's superimposed on the field to show you where first down should be. If you haven't watched Monday night football, maybe you have used your smartphone or tablet to go on a furniture or paint site such as Sherwin Williams. If you take a photo of your living room, you can change the paint color on the screen to see how it will look before you buy the paint and paint the entire room! Pretty cool technology, right?

VR is more immersive. It's like playing a video game, but you're inside the game. If you're unfamiliar with video games, the best analogy I can give you is being in a 3D movie theatre. You have special glasses on, and the room is dark, and you feel like you're in the movie.

## AUGMENTED REALITY (AR)

Think of Augmented Reality (AR) as your *life GPS*.

Here's what I mean: AR mixes your current reality with your *virtual reality.*

Think about what happens when you're using your GPS. Your GPS is reading your current reality on the actual street you're driving on, and at the same time, it's also telling you where to go—your virtual reality—but you're not actually there. That's where you'll be in the near future (traffic problems notwithstanding)! And it's doing it in a way that takes the stress out of driving because it's clear, straightforward, and not emotional. It's not like the days when you had to pull over and unfold a complicated map, or the passenger had to use the map and direct you; those were the days of emotional navigation!

**How AR might show up in your life:**

One of the ways you envision AR to show up in your life is that you'd have glasses that you use to see but also AR information, such as GPS. This way, you don't have to look down at your phone or GPS on your car. Advertisers are looking to leverage this technology by automatically popping up advertisements as you're walking down the street or through the mall. Imagine you're shopping and advertisers suddenly jump into your world. As you're walking past a Victoria Secret store, you get an ad in front of your glasses that says, "Buy two pair of underpants and get one free," or as you're walking past Golf Galaxy, there's a sale on the driver you've been wanting.

Another use for AR is being able to turn any surface into a game board. Just like when you're watching an NFL game and they overlay the first-down line on the field, your glasses would overlay a game onto a surface. Instead of playing Solitaire on my phone, I could play it on my coffee table or TV tray.

One of the more exciting applications for AR glasses is for travelers. Imagine being in Pompeii, Italy, and looking at the ruins. Your AR glasses show you what the areas looked like prior to the volcanic eruption! They give you facts and details that make the experience so much richer, augmenting the experience without the annoying struggle of hearing the tour guide.

AR is already available on your smartphone, and you may be using it. Ikea has an Augmented Reality app that you can use on your tablet or phone. This app allows you to see their furniture in your home without having to buy a thing! This way, you can make decisions without having to buy something and then possibly return it. Basically, your camera shows the room on your device, and then you drag furniture items from the menu into the camera view, and it augments the space to show you what it will look like with that piece of furniture in it—pretty neat!

Currently, most of the glasses are either still in development, used for business, or are being made for drone users, cyclists, or as sunglasses.

Some of the following products may be of interest to you.

- **AR Apps for your phone:**
  - **Google Sky Map**—This AR app lets you look at the sky, and it will point out constellations, planets, and stars.
  - **Pokémon GO**—If you have grandkids, you might already know about this AR game. Basically, you have the app open on your phone, and when your phone vibrates, you'll see a Pokemon (cartoon character that will look like it's on the street, etc., where your camera on your phone is

looking, and you throw a virtual ball at it to get points). The game is so popular—it's been downloaded over 800 million[69] times.

○ **Google Translate**—This is a great one for Boomer travelers. Basically, hold your camera phone so that it can see a sign in another language or menu, and it will be translated on your phone immediately through AR. Super cool, easy to use, and helpful!

○ **Google Lens**—Point your phone's camera at something, and it will read it and tell you something. Having a discussion with a loved one over who painted that painting? Just use Google Lens, and the mystery will be solved. It can also read QR codes, which can link you to other information.

○ **IKEA Place**—A Swedish furniture company has created an AR where you can try furniture prior to buying. You access the app and aim your camera at the room you wish in your home and then drag furniture pieces you like into the room, and magically, a chair looks like it is sitting in your living room! A must for anyone downsizing. Even if you don't want IKEA furniture (The seat heights are a bit lower than desired for Boomers.), you can get an idea of what works and fits in your new space.

o **Sherwin Williams Visualizer**—This tool helps you to see what your paint color looks like on your walls prior to all the cost and work of painting. Just upload a photo of your room to the visualizer, and select a paint, and voila! The room changes color. If you don't like it, just tap and choose a new color. Great tool if you want to freshen up where you live, get ready to sell, or if you just bought a new place.

• **Own a business that requires a lot of training or 3D communication:**

o **Microsoft HoloLens**—As an interior designer, this technology is very cool. Basically, I could walk into a home and place furniture from a catalog into the space and rearrange it until I get the look I want. This is similar to IKEA Place but can be anything I want and can also collaborate with others through the glasses. Onsite technicians such as an elevator repair guy can wear the glasses, and the home office can see what he's seeing immediately to help him with support and even tutorials, saving time and increasing safety.

○ **Google Glass**—These have been around since 2013, but Google pulled back and now is only selling them as an enterprise edition. While they look kinda like glasses, they really are just a very small screen attached to the frame of glasses that give information. Boeing and medical doctors are testing them now. I'm not sure of the relevance to Boomers but thought inquiring minds would want to know their status as they were the first ones on the scene.

○ **Magic Leap**—Technically, they're developing for both business (enterprise) and consumers (you and me). The only version available at this time of writing is the Magic Leap 1; it costs about $2,200 and is meant for developers. I had the pleasure of trying out the headset and found it comfortable and easy to use. Not sure how long you could wear them comfortably, but they do seem to work really well.

○ **Meta 2**—A similar product to HoloLens. If you're designing a product, this helps you to trouble-shoot issues prior to going into production, which is a huge win for any designer.

- **Cycle:**
  - ○ **Vara Vision**—This AR device attaches to your sunglasses or glasses and gives you information on approaching cars, your personal performance data, and directions.
  - ○ **Solos**—These sunglasses have built-in AR to give you data like that of Vara Vision and also your health metrics. It will also give you phone call notifications and allow you to stay connected while you keep your eyes on the road.
  - ○ **Raptor**—These sunglasses are for those who want to stay connected, know their stats, take video and photos, share, and keep their eyes on the road.
- **Out in the sun quite a bit:**
  - ○ **Vuzix Blade AR**—These sunglasses mirror whatever is on your smartphone so you can keep up with all the incoming emails and Facebook posts.
- **Fly Drones:**
  - ○ **Epson Moverio BT-300FPV Drone Edition**—I don't fly drones, but we

have one. These AR glasses allow you to see the controls while you're watching the drone fly vs. looking down at the controls, then back up again, then back down . . . well, you get the point. The experience is much more user-friendly and enjoyable.

**How VR might show up in your life:**

Want to learn a new language? Sculpt without the mess? Play a video game in 3D? Travel to distant lands or underwater? Meditate? Meet new people from around the world or take a tour of an ancient Egyptian tomb all from your living room sofa? Welcome to Virtual Reality.

I have to admit the thought of messing up my hair and putting on a headset where I couldn't see who was around me was daunting to say the least. I avoided it for quite a while until I learned all the positive aspects. Then I tried VR at a conference, and what I experienced was so immersive that I forgot all about what my hair looked like and who was in the room. It was wonderfully liberating and fun! I was able to connect with people in different countries and felt like we were together. I felt happiness just like it was a real situation. Think of going to the movies and multiplied by 100.

**How VR might show up in your life:**

There's a current movie out called *Ready Player One* (highly recommend watching this to understand VR). Plus, the movie is situated in Columbus, Ohio, where I live, so I have to promote the city that I love. The concept is that when you live in a not-so-great environment, Virtual Reality (VR) can help you to escape to a better virtual reality. This means if you're not able to travel anymore, don't have the funds, your body isn't as able as it used to be, or you're alone and want to experience more than books and TV, just put on the headset, and you're off to do whatever, wherever, with anyone you want.

And it feels real—so real—that your brain thinks it's real by the chemicals it produces.

This isn't a placebo effect; research was conducted by Tsinghua University and Immersive Lab regarding the Qinghua elderly study and their response to VR use. Per Qiyong Chen from Vive Immersive Lab:

*We measured the elderly's emotional sta-*
*tus using SAM (Self-Assessment Manikin)*
*scale before and after they used Vive Pro.*
*Then we compared the data and discovered*
*VR can effectively help the elderly to get*
*emotional arousal. We also used wristbands*
*to test EDA (Electro Dermal Activity) and*
*HR (Heart Rate) at the same time, which*
*will help us know if the subjects correctly*
*express their emotional state.[70]*

It's such exciting research that I am partnering with Vive and Research Square to reproduce this study worldwide.

If you don't want to play games, there are many applications that can let you learn, explore, create, and meditate. You could tour the tomb of Christ, paint and sculpt in 3D with Tilt Brush (I personally have used this and was inspired to paint again.), explore the sea (without getting wet) or Mars for that matter. Or you could just chill and meditate. The possibilities are endless and incredibly engaging. You're transported to another world while you sit or stand in your bedroom or living room. It's the closest thing to space and time travel. It's liberating for the mind, body, and spirit and can change your attitude in a second.

When I first started down the path of virtual reality, it was a bit overwhelming. Keep in mind it's a lot like having a car—I don't have to know how the engine works or be able to fix it to drive a car and have fun on a road trip. Virtual Reality Glasses (You need these to use virtual reality games and programs.) work with a computer system and typically the Internet. Like a TV, you still need to plug it in, have cable or Wi-Fi, and then pay for channels for your entertainment. Unlike a TV, you can go anywhere and do about anything! Think about the massive difference between radio and black-and-white TV, and then color TV. VR takes you INTO the entertainment and allows you to control where you go and what you do. Frankly, it's one of the most liberating things I've experienced, and I've driven a Nascar on the Brickyard (Indy 500 track), hang glided, scuba dived, and sculpted. And it's safe.

First, you'll need a gaming computer or PlayStation to use virtual reality. Then you need the glasses. Any big box store can help you with the right computer or your existing one may already work. The important thing to remember is you need to have a graphics card that will work for VR and gaming. The graphics card needs to be more powerful than a regular computer that you'd be using for email and Facebook. Basically, VR has more FPS (frames per second) so that you don't get motion sick. Trust me; I get motion sick on boats, cars, and planes, but I've been fine when doing VR.

Here's what to look for when you buy a computer:

- Strong graphics card
- HDMI video output, typically
- Computer engine has to be fast
- Memory 8GB or higher of RAM (it's like your short-term memory)

Please don't get worried about knowing what to get; whoever you buy from can easily help you out. Expect to spend a minimum of $600 for the computer.

**Some of the following products may be of interest to you.**

- **VR Glasses:**
  - o **Oculus Rift ($399)**—This is one of the best rated VR glasses out there, very powerful, and pretty easy to set up. It is tethered, which means that there will be a cord from the headset (glasses) to the computer. Personally,

I think being tethered isn't a big issue as I would recommend doing VR sitting down to start with until you get comfortable.

o **HTC Vive ($499)**—This powerful VR set has support hand LED controls and whole room VR. HTC is the leader in research on VR and seniors and has clinical studies showing an improvement of mood while using VR. It is tethered.

o **Sony Playstation VR ($399)**— This powerful VR set works with a Playstation gaming device vs. a computer. It is still tethered.

o **Samsung Gear ($99)**—This powerful VR set works with a Playstation gaming device vs. a computer. It is still tethered. Samsung Gear-99 works but difficult to find content.

o **Oculus Go ($199)**—This VR is standalone, meaning no cord tying you to a computer. It still needs one to work, but your movement can be more free, especially when playing games. Facebook acquired Oculus for 2.3 Billion—yes, billion. Oculus Go's low price is intended to get into everyone's home. In other words, VR is the TV of the future.

o **HTC Vive Pro ($799)**—The most awesome tethered VR tracks your movements to the millimeter in real-life movement 360 degrees and has built-in eye tracking.

o **Lenovo Mirage Solo with Daydream ($359)**—This VR is a standalone (non-tethered) VR.

o **Google Daydream View ($79)**—This VR is intended to work with a smartphone such as a Google Pixel or Pixel XL. It's basically goggles that you snap in your smartphone. While I have the phone and the goggles, I'm concerned about my data package on my phone going through the roof. Some of the apps are the *Washington Post* VR and Youtube VR. There are others but very limited.

o **R-9 Smartglasses ($1,999)**—While these are on a waiting list for release, they're much smaller than most VR sets and look like a pair of sunglasses. They'll also do both AR and VR.

o **Rendover**—These VR glasses are made specifically for senior living homes. These operate similar to other

VR glasses but the content delivered (what you can see) is tailored towards seniors. Imagine hiking up Machu Picchu or visiting your favorite park all virtually.

- **VR Games and Experiences:** Once you have your glasses, you can download various games and experiences. Think of it like this, the VR headset is your record player, and the downloadable games and experiences are your albums (music). Some will be free and others you'll need to purchase. Please note, not all apps work with all glasses.
    - o **theBlu**—This is a deeply immersive experience that transports you under the sea to a sunken ship. You'll see incredible sea life and even a whale. Explore the reef, travel to the bottom of the sea, and discover the iridescent sea life or explore a sunken ship.
    - o **Apollo 11**—Relive the full experience of Neil Armstrong and Buzz Aldrin from inside the cockpit, become an astronaut, and take the controls on the greatest journey of mankind.
    - o **Google Earth (FREE)**—Go anywhere you want with this app. You can fly, walk around, or easily pick

from preloaded locations such as the Giza Pyramids, Rome, or Iceland. Choose to stroll the streets of your hometown or watch a solar eclipse.

o **Rapid Fire: A Brief History of Flight**—This app transports you to the airstrip of an air show but not any air show—you'll see up close the history of all planes.

o **Tilt Brush**—Want to paint or sculpt without the mess or any spatial restrictions? Then Tilt Brush is for you. The first time I tried Tilt Brush, it was one of the most fun, liberating experiences I've ever had. You can zoom in on what you're creating and back out again, and if you make a mistake, you can easily erase. It's not just for art; you can create anything from a new invention to decorating your house.

o **Within (FREE)**—This app has content from around the world from NBC and the *New York Times* to watching a dance video or concert.

o **FirstHand Technology**—This VR experience isn't available to the general public. Opiates used to treat pain have been fairly unsuccessful as pain is just a signal to the brain. So VR is being used to rewire the brain to reduce and eliminate nerve pain. Basically, playing guided games and activities can help you to regain your life back, pain free.

AR and VR are here to stay and can help us to stay connected, create, collaborate, and explore new worlds through education and entertainment. I would highly recommend getting onboard with these technologies. They'll be as common in the near future as your computer or smartphone, but much more engaging and liberating.

## Lifelong Learning

Some Boomers are moving back to their alma mater college campus and signing up for one class so that they have full access to all the university has to offer, such as the cafeteria, library, fitness facilities, and tons of youth to engage with. Others are engaging in other ways such as traveling, VR classes, or simply listening to podcasts.

Want to give back, share, and learn? Check out: (lifeguides.com). This new platform connects people that have experienced an issue—such as those with aging parents—who now have wisdom to share with those in need of it. It's an incredible way to help others and learn more about yourself and the world. This is truly a multi-generational wisdom share.

As I've discussed in previous chapters, house swapping and Airbnb friendly services for seniors can give you the freedom to travel with ease, cost-effectively, and there's also the Evergreen Club, which allows you to stay in others' homes (like a mini bed and breakfast version) for around $20.00 a day! Imagine the museums, concerts, classes, and tours you could go on with this kind of savings on your stay. Heck, even if you stay with friends, you're still obligated to buy them dinner or bring them a gift. (evergreenclub.com) The Evergreen Club is probably cheaper than staying with friends and family. Also, check out a blog for Boomers that travel. (travellingboomer.com)

Want to travel the world, go on an adventure, learn something new, and meet new people? The Road Scholar experience is for you. (roadscholar.org) Learning doesn't always have to be on a campus or in a physical classroom. Osher Lifelong Living Institute offers many classes to pique your interest, keep your mind sharp, and have something to talk about that's more than the weather or your favorite game show. Other online class portals include:

o  **Udemy—<u>udemy.com</u>**
o  **Teachable—<u>teachable.com</u>**
o  **Ruzuku—<u>ruzuku.com</u>**
o  **WizIQ—<u>wiziq.com</u>**
o  **Educadium—<u>educadium.com</u>**
o  **SkillShare—<u>skillshare.com</u>**
o  **Coursera—<u>coursera.org</u>**

By the time you read this, there will probably be many more. Do your research and find out which ones will be best for what you're interested in.

Another great way to learn is through podcasts.

What's a podcast? I had the same question a couple of years ago. So I thought instead of you going through the pain of figuring this out like I had to, we're friends now, and friends help each other out, so I wrote you a podcast how-to.

"What the Heck Is a Podcast, and Why Should I Be Listening to Them?"

*Podcasts* are free, downloadable audio shows. There are thousands, if not millions, of podcasts available. While they've been around for over a decade now, podcasts are seeing a surge of popularity with independent shows like *Serial* and *Radiolab*, in addition to podcasts from the likes of *ESPN* and *National Public Radio*.

The beauty of listening to a podcast is that you can listen to whatever you want, whenever you want. Imagine having millions of radio shows on everything from health, sports, cooking, news, or entertainment at your fingertips. You don't have to worry about missing your favorite radio talk show or not being able to hear it all when you need to answer someone at the door.

Unlike traditional radio or television, podcasts require a bit of work to set up, but once you're there, a world of audio enjoyment awaits. It may seem a bit daunting at first, but once you get started, the process becomes second nature.

When it comes to lifelong learning, you can pick which areas you want to learn more about and go as shallow or as deep as you would like with podcasts.

A tool called a *podcatcher* is used to download podcasts. Think of a podcatcher like a TV or radio station where you get to choose all the programming. Most podcasts are available in all podcatchers, so in general, you won't have to worry about missing out on your preferred device.

There are a number of different podcatchers available for Windows computers, Macs, iPhones, iPads, Android phones, Kindle Fire tablets, and even some televisions. Each tool should have a directory included where you can search for podcasts by name, topic, or keyword. Many also come with recommendations or charts to let you know what's popular.

After you've found the podcast you want to listen to, you can subscribe to it (similar to subscribing to a newspaper or newsletter). This will download the most recent episode and make sure that every new episode downloads as well. You can also download individual episodes if you want to check the back catalog or if you just want one or two episodes before you decide to subscribe. Subscribing costs nothing and helps the show creators gain visibility, so if you like a show, you should subscribe!

Once the podcast you want to hear has downloaded, you can usually click or tap on it to play it. You can listen to it as many times as you want. Some podcatchers will delete a show after you listen to it, but you can always download episodes again whenever you'd like.

To sum up, the steps to get started with listening to podcasts are as follows:

1. Download a podcatcher.

2. Search the directory in that podcatcher to find the show you want to hear.

3. Download individual episodes or subscribe.

4. Play your podcast!

Using Apple Podcasts on iPhones and iPads

1. Go to your Apple App Store (unless the podcast is already showing on your device then skip to step 3).

2. Download and install the Podcasts app from the App Store.

3. Launch the app. You'll be greeted with a welcome screen with some basic info

about the app. Tap *Start Listening Now* to proceed.

4.  To search for a podcast, tap the *Search* icon in the lower-right corner.

5.  Tap in the text field under Search and type in whatever you'd like to search for. For example: seniors, Baby Boomers, etc. Then tap the blue Search button in the lower-left corner.

6.  The search results will load. Shows will appear at the top, and swiping them to the left will reveal more results. Individual episodes that match your search term will appear below.

7.  Tap on an episode to reveal its details. You can press the *Play* button to stream the episode or the + button to add it to your library then tap the download icon to listen on the go.

8.  If you tap on a show in your results, you'll then see the info page for that show, along with recent episodes. You can tap the + on an individual episode to add it to your library or tap *Subscribe* to have the app automatically download the most recent episode and all future episodes.

9. You can find unplayed and recently listened-to podcasts by tapping the *Listen Now* icon in the lower-left corner. To see all your subscriptions, tap the *Library* icon to the right of the Listen Now icon.

Using Podcast Addict on Android:

1. Go to the Google Play Store on your phone.

2. Download and install Podcast Addict or other podcatcher from the Google Play Store.

3. Launch the app. You'll be greeted with a *Get Started* screen. To add a podcast, tap the + icon in the upper-right corner.

4. Tap the Search Engine tile in the upper-left corner.

5. Tap the text field and type in whatever you'd like to search for. For example: seniors, Baby Boomers, etc. Check the box for "Use iTunes Search Engine." Then tap Search.

6. Your search results will load in two tabs: Podcasts and Episodes.

7.  To subscribe to a listed podcast, tap the check mark next to it. This will have the app automatically download the most recent episode and all future episodes.

8.  You can also tap the Episodes tab to see episodes that match your search. Tap on the episode's name to stream it or tap the Download button to save it to your device for listening on the go.

# Pod catchers

A comparison chart is a helpful tool in decision making. In one glance, the features and qualities

| NAME | SYSTEM | STREAMING | DOWNLOAD | PLAYBACK OFFLINE | AUTO UPDATES | SEARCHABLE | TRENDING FEATURE | COST | PROS | CONS |
|---|---|---|---|---|---|---|---|---|---|---|
| Spotify | 🤖 🍎 | ✓ | ✓ | ✓ | ✗ | ✓ | ✓ | | Built into Spotify app. | Ads inserted into audio unless on Spotify Premium plan. No options to subscribe to podcasts. |
| Stitcher Radio for Podcasts | 🤖 🍎 | ✓ | ✓ | ✓ | ✓ | ✓ | ✓ | | Customizable playlists. Great for discovery. Exclusive shows. | Ads inserted into audio unless on Stitcher Premium plan. |
| TuneIn Radio | 🤖 🍎 | ✓ | ✓ | ✓ | ✓ | ✓ | ✓ | | Upgrade to TuneIn Premium for live play-by-play of NFL, MLB, and Barclays Premier League games, commercial-free music stations, and an audio book library | Preroll ads unless on TuneIn Premium. Banner ads without Premium or a one time Pro unlock. |
| Podbean | 🤖 🍎 | ✓ | ✓ | ✓ | ✓ | ✓ | ✓ | | Also includes an audio recorder. Free. | Discovery might be focused on shows using Podbean hosting, their primary product. |
| Spreaker Podcast Radio | 🤖 🍎 | ✓ | ✓ | ✓ | ✓ | ✓ | ✓ | | Free. | No speed adjustments. Similar to Podbean. |
| Pocket Casts | 🤖 🍎 | ✓ | ✓ | ✓ | ✓ | ✓ | ✓ | $3.99 | Trim Silence, Volume Boost | Paid app. |
| Podcast Republic | 🤖 | ✓ | ✓ | ✓ | ✓ | ✓ | ✓ | | Free with ads. Playlist support. | Ad Supported; can be removed with one-time purchase. |
| Player FM | 🤖 | ✓ | ✓ | ✓ | ✓ | ✓ | ✓ | | Free. Optional features via subscription. | Reserves the right to show ads in the future. |
| Podcast Addict | 🤖 | ✓ | ✓ | ✓ | ✓ | ✓ | ✓ | | Supports video podcasts, YouTube channels, audiobooks, streaming radio and other media sources. | Ad supported. |
| Beyond Pod | 🤖 | ✓ | ✓ | ✓ | ✓ | ✓ | ✓ | $6.99 | Fine-grain download settings give users control of how much the app downloads in the background. | Paid app. Features are lost after 7 days unless full version is purchased. |
| Dogg Catcher | 🤖 | ✓ | ✓ | ✓ | ✓ | ✓ | ✓ | $2.99 | Plays video as well. Variable speed playback. | Paid app with no trial. |
| AntennaPod | 🤖 | ✓ | ✓ | ✓ | ✓ | ✓ | ✓ | | Variable speed playback. Ability to tip podcasters. Open source application. | Maintained by volunteers. Designed for power users. |
| Google Play Music | 🤖 | ✓ | ✓ | ✓ | ✓ | ✓ | ✓ | | Included on most Android devices by default. | Lacks additional features offered by most third-party apps. |
| Apple Podcasts | 🍎 | ✓ | ✓ | ✓ | ✓ | ✓ | ✓ iCloud | | Easy to use. Syncs across iOS devices. | Lacks additional features offered by most third-party apps. |
| Overcast | 🍎 | ✓ | ✓ | ✓ | ✓ | ✓ | ✓ | | Smartspeed and Voice Boost features. Playlists. Great developer support. Upload your own audio files for later listening with optional patronage. Recommended podcasts from Twitter and the author. | Slightly more complex than Apple Podcasts. |
| Castro | 🍎 | ✓ | ? | ✓ | ✓ | ✓ | ✓ | $3.99 | Triage feature to organize podcasts for playback. | Paid app with no trial. May be difficult to learn Triage. |
| iCatcher! | 🍎 | ✓ | ✓ | ✓ | ✓ | ✓ | ✓ | $2.99 | Gesture support for eyes-free use. | Paid app with no trial. |
| Downcast | 🍎 | ✓ | ✓ | ✓ | ✓ | ✓ | ✓ | $2.99 | Variable speed playback. Gesture support. | Paid app with no trial. |
| RSSRadio | 🍎 | ✓ | ✓ | ✓ | ✓ | ✓ | ✓ | $3.99 (Remove Ads) | Free with ads. Playback speed adjustment. | No list view. Difficult to find search for new podcasts. |

# CHAPTER 14
## PETS

As you know by now, our family loves animals, and they're an integral part of unconditional love, stress relief, and keeping active. While our family has had dogs, chickens, and bees, I felt it was critically important to find the best source for you. Luckily, America's favorite veterinarian, and the #1 Amazon best-selling author, Dr. Gary Richter, was kind enough to write this chapter. If you'd like to know more information from Dr. Gary Richter, please check out his website (drgaryrichter.com) and books on Amazon.

## Unconditional Love:
## A Boomer's Guide to Pets
### Dr. Gary Richter

Relationships can be complicated. Whether it's marriage, family, or friendship, maintaining healthy relationships with people takes time and effort. Despite the work involved, nurturing connections with those who care for us is one of the things that keeps us healthy and give us purpose. There are times, however, when what we really need is someone to walk with, talk with, and share affection with in a way no human can offer. There are times when what we need most is the unconditional love only a pet can provide.

In addition to love and affection, did you know that pets are good for your health? Studies indicate pet ownership can be associated with improved cardiovascular health, lower blood pressure, and cholesterol.[71] [72] In addition, owning a pet leads to increases in daily activities and decreases loneliness.[73] [74] [75] All in all, pets are good for our bodies and our spirits.

The following chapter provides a guide to pet ownership at all stages, from choosing the right pet to geriatric care. Taking a proactive approach helps prevent illness and, if illness does occur, provide for early diagnosis and more successful treatment.

## What Pet to Get and When

Choosing a pet may be the only time in our lives we get to pick a relative. Caring for a pet should begin even before you bring him or her home. Possibly the single most impactful decision you'll make during the entire time you have a pet is choosing the right one. Variables to navigate include choosing a dog or cat, young or adult, and purebred or mixed.

Making these kinds of decisions really is about lifestyle. The best pet to get is one that will be comfortable living in the environment and at the pace of life that's comfortable to you. The following are some important lifestyle considerations to keep in mind as you decide on your pet:

- What is your level of health and mobility?
- How much time are you at home vs. working?
- Are you an *outdoorsy* person, or do you spend more time at home?
- How large is your living space?

- Do you have an enclosed yard?
- If you have other pets, how do they get along with other animals?
- Do you have the time and resources to brush and groom long hair, or would you prefer something lower maintenance?

When most people consider getting a pet, they generally are considering a dog or cat. Other types of pets such as birds, guinea pigs, reptiles, etc., have very specific (and frequently high maintenance needs), so it is critical to do your homework before committing to any kind of pet. Failing to consider these kinds of factors can lead to a very stressful experience.

Look for a pet that naturally agrees with your pace of life. Make your decisions based on personality, not aesthetics. Forcing a square peg into a round hole is asking for trouble. Countless pets have been taken to shelters because their natural behaviors were at odds with their owner's lifestyle. For example, the person who is at work for 12 hours per day might not want to get a high-energy dog that needs lots of exercise. A bored dog cooped up by himself leads to a pretty good chance the couch is going be eaten when you come home.

The best advice for someone looking for a pet is to do research about breeds and look before you leap. If you've decided to adopt from a shelter or rescue, spend some time with the animal before you make a decision. If you choose a pet from a breeder, check references and make sure the dog or cat was bred responsibly and has excellent genetics.

## Pet Insurance

The healthcare options available to pets are more effective now than they've ever been. Top-notch care, however, can get pricey. Many of the drugs and supplies used in veterinary medicine are exactly the same as those used for humans, and pharmaceutical companies don't discount a drug just because it is used on animals.

The solution to the rising costs associated with better health care is pet insurance. Like any insurance, what suits you best has to do with what kind of coverage you want, deductibles, coverage limits, etc. As a veterinarian that practices both Western and alternative medicine, I always encourage new pet owners to look for a policy that covers holistic treatment. When health issues arise, most pet owners are ready to do whatever is necessary to help their friend feel better. The last thing you ever want to do is make a treatment decision based on finances.

Insurance plans change all the time, so the best advice is to do your due diligence when shopping for a policy. Ask your veterinarian which policies their clients seem most happy with. Consult with trusted friends and colleagues and do an Internet search for "Pet Insurance Comparisons." As with any insurance plan, make sure to read the fine print.

## Introducing New Pets to Old

Bringing a new pet into a household with existing pets has the potential to be a stressful experience, depending on the personality of the new and existing pets. (In many cases, introductions of pets of the opposite sex seem to go more smoothly than having two of the same gender.) There are, however, ways to smooth out rough spots in the transition. The name of the game with introductions is to take it slow and be patient. There are excellent resources out there to help guide new pet introductions. Books, articles, and videos by the renowned veterinary behaviorist Dr. Sophia Yin are a great place to start.

**Dog Introductions:** The best way to introduce dogs is on neutral ground. To prevent territory aggression, have the dogs meet at the park or some other place where neither of them are on their home turf. Have the dogs meet several times over several days before bringing the new dog home (If this isn't possible, even a single meeting in neutral territory can be helpful). Once home, be sure to supervise interactions until you feel comfortable a workable relationship has developed.

**Cat Introductions:** Cats are tricky when it comes to introductions because they don't like change of any kind. When bringing home an additional cat, keep it in a room with the door closed and allow the cats to sniff each other under the door. Allow the new cat to explore the house while the *old* cat is in the room. Do this for several days and then reverse the arrangement.

It may take as long as a couple of weeks before the cats can be allowed full contact with one another. Even then, there may be some hissing and spitting. However, most cats will find a way to get along or, at least, peacefully coexist.

**Dog-Cat Introductions:** When introducing dogs to cats, take it slow. Unless the animals are particularly tolerant of the other species, it's going to take time. Cats typically feel threatened and scared, while dogs may either feel scared or want to chase the cat.

Allow the dog and cat to sniff one another under a closed door as in cat introductions. Consider keeping the dog on a leash even in the house whenever the animals are in the same room until you feel comfortable that a relationship has been established. Sometimes it takes a few good swats from the cat for a dog to realize it's in their best interest to keep some distance.

## Puppy and Kitten Socialization

The first weeks and months a puppy or kitten is at home lay the foundations of behavior for their entire lives. Your veterinarian can direct you to good local trainers if you need one. Books and videos from veterinary behaviorist Dr. Sophia Yin are excellent resources in this field as well.

**Puppy Socialization:** Socialization of young dogs is critical, especially for dogs with a tendency toward nervousness or anxiety.

The optimal window for socialization is before they're 14 weeks old, so get started early. Introducing puppies to new experiences at a young age expands their horizons and creates a well-adjusted dog. However, this must be done under controlled conditions to prevent disease transmission and inadvertently traumatizing your dog.

Early puppy socialization classes with a trainer and taking your pup to meet friends' dogs are good ways to encourage social behavior. Any dog the puppy comes in contact with should be healthy and current on his vaccines. To prevent serious illness, never take an unvaccinated puppy to dog parks, sidewalks, or anywhere there's dog traffic you aren't in control of. The risks of disease are too great.

**Kitten Socialization:** Kittens kind of socialize themselves. Since they aren't out and about like dogs, there isn't the same concern for disease transmission. Kittens can get a little aggressive with their play tactics, though. Even though it may be cute when they bite you when they're small, it's not so great when they weigh 15 lbs. Discourage this behavior by disengaging play when they get too rough. Then once they calm down, you can play with them again.

## Choosing a Veterinarian

Different people have very different perspectives on medicine and health care. Some people are very conventional in their approach to health care, where others prefer a more natural approach to medicine. Personally, I prefer to look for the benefits in both Western and holistic medicine and provide integrative solutions for my patients. Whatever approach you're looking for, it's important to find a veterinarian who shares your health care philosophy. You should feel confident that their treatment recommendations fit with how you want your pet's care managed.

If you're unsure what your best choice is, see what the *word on the street* is. Ask for recommendations at pet stores in your area, dog parks, and trusted friends and colleagues. If you prefer a more natural or integrative approach, the American Holistic Veterinary Association has a listing of holistic practitioners on their website: (AHVMA.org). Just click on "Find a Vet."

## Schedule Regular Physical Examinations and Diagnostic Testing

Beyond everything you do at home, regular veterinary visits are among the most important way to make sure your pet stays healthy. As your pet gets older, you'll want to move from annual examinations to semiannual (twice yearly) examinations. The following is a general guideline, and your veterinarian may make other recommendations based on your pet's health and lifestyle.

- Cats (1-10 years old): annual examinations
- Cats (10 plus years old): semiannual examinations
- Small to medium breeds of dog (1-10 years old): annual examinations
- Small to medium breeds of dog (10 plus years old): semiannual examinations
- Large to giant breeds of dog (1-7 years old): annual examinations
- Large to giant breeds of dog (7 plus years old): semiannual examinations

During the physical exam, your veterinarian will want to run routine lab work on your pet to make sure they haven't been exposed to parasites and everything is okay systemically. In many cases, the early onset of disease can be detected in blood or urine before symptoms arise. Just as with physical examinations, you'll want to move to more frequent screenings as your pet gets older from biannual (every two years) to annual testing. The following is a general guideline, and your veterinarian may make other recommendations based on your pet's health and lifestyle.

## All Pets, All Ages: Annual Fecal Screening for Parasites

- Cats and small to medium breeds of dog (1-10 years old): biannual blood and urine testing
- Cats and small to medium breeds of dog (10 plus years old): annual blood and urine testing
- Large to giant breeds of dog (1-7 years old): biannual blood and urine testing
- Large to giant breeds of dog (7 plus years old): annual blood and urine testing

## Choosing the Right Procedures for Your Pet:

## Vaccines and Routine Surgical Procedures

Being a pet owner requires taking preventive steps to make sure your pet (and the pet population at large) stays healthy. While certain procedures involve short-term discomfort, the long-term benefits they provide are substantial—just like having your child vaccinated. Since pets don't plan for the future, pet owners and veterinarians must make the decisions that will provide them with a lifetime of good health.

## Declawing Cats

Let's get this procedure out of the way right now. In short, there's absolutely no legitimate reason to declaw a cat. Please don't do it.

The process of declawing cats is equivalent to a person having their fingertips amputated at the last knuckle. The procedure itself is painful, and it may lead to lifelong chronic pain. Declawed cats frequently become biters after having lost their ability to use their claws. Alternatives to declawing are scratching posts, nail trimming, and placing soft rubber caps on the nails.

## Microchipping

Implanting a microchip in pets is commonplace in most veterinary practices. It's a tiny device about the size of a grain of rice that's implanted with a syringe. After the microchip is placed, you register the chip number with your address and contact information. Should a lost pet be brought into a veterinary hospital, shelter, etc., the chip can be scanned and the owner contacted.

There are a couple of common misconceptions regarding microchips. Microchips cannot be used to track a pet because the scanners work only when they're a few inches away from the animal. Claims of cancer and other severe complications from microchips are vastly exaggerated. Some isolated incidences may have occurred but the benefits far outweigh any perceived risk.

Should a fire or natural disaster occur, owners and pets may become separated, and there's little chance for animal control to reconnect them without some kind of positive identification like a microchip. In fact, according to the Humane Society of the United States, of the 15,000 animals rescued after Hurricane Katrina, only 3,000 were reunited with their owners.[76]

In short, microchips are recommended for all pets.

## Routine Parasite Prevention

### Fleas and Ticks

The relative necessity for flea and tick products depends on geographic location, season, and pet's lifestyle. In hot and humid areas, the presence of these parasites can present major health problems, so good medical care necessitates regular treatment to prevent infestation. In more temperate areas, however, fleas and ticks are more of a nuisance.

There are many flea and tick products on the market, and more are coming and going all the time. Which product to choose for your pet and how often to use it depends on the pet's sensitivity to fleas and how bad the fleas are in your area. Natural flea and tick control products can be useful in some situations but are generally only somewhat effective. For more comprehensive control of these pests, a more conventional treatment is generally recommended. As some over-the-counter products are ineffective (and sometimes toxic), please consult with your veterinarian about the best flea and tick control method for your pet.

## Gastrointestinal Worms and Deworming

Deworming generally refers to gastrointestinal worms such as hookworms and roundworms. Like all parasites, prevalence is a function of climate, with warmer, more humid areas having more severe issues. There are several ways to address GI parasitism in pets.

Regardless of where you live, an annual fecal examination is recommended to screen for parasites. If a pet is on heartworm preventive, they're likely getting dewormed regularly as part of that product. Otherwise, deworming can be accomplished on an as-eeded basis.

When GI parasites are confirmed via fecal testing, the best bet is to deworm your dog or cat through conventional medical means and be done with it. Although there are natural dewormers such as diatomaceous earth, they're often unreliable in the treatment of worms. They may, however, be helpful as preventives.

Pharmaceutical dewormers generally take 1-3 days to be effective. It is commonplace and relatively safe to use dewormers on puppies and kittens, but it may not be necessary. During the course of the puppy or kitten vaccines, your veterinarian should ask for a stool sample to check for parasites. If the test is positive, deworming is appropriate and safe. If the test is negative, however, it may be just as well to hold off. Since parasites cannot always be found in every sample, it is best to have two fecal screenings done during the course of the puppy or kitten vaccines. If both are negative, there should be no need to deworm.

## Heartworm

Heartworm is a parasitic disease where worms literally live in the heart of an infested dog. (Although cats can also contract heartworm, it is rare.) Mosquitoes transmit heartworm, so disease prevalence is dependent on weather. Warm, humid climates have more heartworm cases.

Depending on where you live, you may or may not have options regarding heartworm for your dog. Temperate climates, like where I live in Oakland, don't have much heartworm. We do have it but it's relatively rare. The options here are to put the dog on heartworm preventive and test dogs annually. Albeit highly unlikely, if a dog comes up positive, we will have caught the infestation very early making treatment easier.

In high heartworm areas such as the Southeastern U.S., heartworm prevention for dogs is a necessity. The odds are just too great to try and go without protection. These pets should be on heartworm prevention year-round and receive an annual heartworm test.

There are many brands of heartworm preventives on the market. They all use some version of drugs like Ivermectin or Milbemycin. These drugs kill the larval forms of heartworm before they become adults and set up shop in the heart. While high doses of these drugs can be dangerous to dogs, the doses used for heartworm prevention are very safe. Any risk is far outweighed by risk of contracting heartworm.

One final note regarding heartworm prevention: There's no such thing as effective, natural, or holistic heartworm preventive. Please don't attempt this. If a dog gets heartworm due to ineffectual prevention, the results can literally be fatal.

## Spay and Neuter

The decision when (or if) to spay or neuter a pet weighs heavily on some pet owners. If you or someone in your family is hesitant to spay or neuter your pet, you aren't alone. Many people are a little hesitant. There are, however, plenty of great reasons to spay or neuter and very few reasons not to. Saying yes benefits your dog or cat from a physical, behavioral, and safety standpoint. It also benefits you financially and socially. Let me explain:

Spaying or neutering pets eliminates the chances of unwanted reproduction, cancer of the testicles, ovaries, and uterus, and decreases the chances of mammary (breast) cancer. In addition, neutering dogs prevents enlargement of the prostate in male dogs as they age. All of these factors improve the quality and quantity of life of dogs and cats.

Behaviorally, the reduction in testosterone and estrogen after spaying often makes pets better pets. Behaviors like aggression between animals, urine marking or spraying, and a tendency to roam looking for mates are all minimized. Pets are safer since they get into fewer fights, are less likely to be hit by cars, and there's far less of a chance they'll be surrendered by their owners because of behavioral issues.

In addition to benefits to your pet, having them spayed or neutered benefits you as well. The decrease in fighting and elimination of medical issues as described below makes their health care easier and less expensive. It's also cheaper to license a spayed or neutered pet. Lastly, there's a social stigma to having an intact pet. If your pet is trying to mate or your female cat in heat is keeping the neighborhood awake with her howling all night, you aren't winning any popularity contests.

## Perceived Drawbacks of Spay and Neuter

There are purebred dogs and cats that are left intact in order to continue their breed. Even within this narrow field, however, breeding of pets should be done very judiciously and only as often as is necessary. These pets can and should be spayed or neutered after they're successfully bred.

Perhaps the argument with the least validity is "I want my pet to experience having a litter" or "I want my children to experience the miracle of our pet having babies." There's absolutely no evidence to suggest dogs or cats are longing for the joys of parenthood. Under most circumstances, their offspring are separated from them eight weeks after birth anyway. It's not like they have the joy of watching their kids grow up!

Parents who want to breed their pets for the benefit of their children's experience would be better served to think it through a little more. A more educational alternative is for the family to volunteer at the SPCA or a local rescue group. This allows children to enjoy puppies and kittens and also realize the reality of pet overpopulation. The ASPCA estimates 2,700,000 dogs and cats are euthanized in shelters every year.[77] There's no reason to breed more.

## What to Do and When

Classically, veterinarians recommend spaying and neutering before pets are six months old. The goal here is to perform the surgery before they hit puberty. This eliminates most hormonally-associated behavioral issues and, in females, eliminates the chances of mammary (breast) cancer later in life. Although this has been written in stone in the veterinary community for many years, new research is about to shake things up.

Recent studies, however, indicate certain breeds of dogs have lower incidences of specific cancers, orthopedic disease, urinary incontinence, and age-related cognitive decline if they're spayed or neutered later. In other words, waiting longer leads to better health in the long term. While there are definitely differences between the breeds, there does appear to be a trend towards better health in pets that were spayed or neutered later. To date, the published studies have only evaluated Golden Retrievers, Labrador Retrievers, and German Shepherds, and it is unknown if these trends will hold true with all breeds of dogs.

There have been no similar studies done in cats, and the behavioral issues associated with intact male and female cats is so significant, it would be unrealistic to expect the majority of pet owners to stick it out and wait to spay and neuter.

In the final analysis, the question is really not if you should spay or neuter your pet, but when. Based on what we know as of 2018, recommendations for spay and neuter are as follows:

- Small to medium dogs: Spay or neuter at 12-18 months of age.
- Large or giant breeds: Spay or neuter at 18-24 months of age.
- Cats: Spay or neuter on or around 6 months of age.

Lastly, if an intact male dog doesn't have behavioral issues, there's no absolute necessity to neuter him. Careful veterinary monitoring for the development of testicular cancer or prostate enlargement as he gets older may necessitate neutering down the road. Outside of these concerns, leaving males intact poses no major

health risks. The same cannot be said for females who run the risk of ovarian, uterine, or
mammary cancer as well as uterine infections,
which can be life-threatening. They should be
spayed as described above.

## A Guide to Appropriate Vaccination

Dog and cat owners are often unclear about
what to vaccinate their pets for and how often. In truth, the veterinary community isn't
in complete agreement on the topic. There are
several reasons for the disparity amongst veterinarians that range from disagreement between
researchers to simple unwillingness to change.

It is true that vaccines aren't benign drugs.
Under normal circumstances, vaccines stim-
ulate the immune system, leading to antibody
production and effective immunity against
disease. However, the body might respond to
a vaccine with excessive or aberrant immune
stimulation, and this may lead to medical issues
in your pet. Although the research is ongoing
and not conclusive, vaccines in pets have been
implicated in the onset of autoimmune diseases
and cancerous processes. Cats are susceptible
to a cancer called feline injection-site sar-
coma, which are aggressive tumors that require

extensive treatment. However, the risk to your cat is as low as one in 10,000.

Despite any controversy, appropriately administered vaccines are absolutely necessary. The fact is, without protection from diseases like canine distemper and parvo, many dogs would die before reaching adulthood. The same is true for cats with panleukopenia, and both species are susceptible to rabies.

Vaccines are effective and have saved countless pets. Like every other drug, however, vaccines should be used judiciously.

## Vaccine Dos and Don'ts

The big *don't* when it comes to vaccines is: **Don't over vaccinate**. To that end, in the following sections, I discuss the difference between core and non-core canine and feline vaccinations as well as vaccine titers.

Core vaccines are the ones that should be given to all pets to protect them from life-threatening diseases. The only exception are pets with an underlying medical condition that precludes the ability to safely vaccinate; such decisions should be made with your veterinarian based on what's safest for your pet.

Non-core vaccinations are available for pets whose lifestyle may put them in contact with specific diseases. These non-core vaccines are recommended for certain animals based largely on lifestyle and geographic location.

Vaccine titers are a means by which your pet's level of immunity can be measured through a blood sample. It measures the level of antibodies that the animal's immune system has produced in response to a vaccine against a specific disease. Through this method, we can determine whether your pet is protected.

The bottom line is, vaccinate for what's absolutely necessary based on core vaccination protocols, legal necessities, and your pet's lifestyle. Don't vaccinate for diseases your pet will never come in contact with.

To prevent adverse reactions, it is best if pets receive no more than two vaccines at any one time, and wait at least one month before giving the next vaccinations. As they get older, dogs and cats may need fewer vaccines. Older pets tend to be outside less and have less direct contact with other animals. Talk with your veterinarian about what's necessary for your pet at the stage of life he or she's currently in.

## Core Canine (Dog) Vaccines

The vaccine schedules discussed below are guidelines for safe and effective vaccination. Timing and protocol variation based on the needs of an individual pet are commonplace. Consult with your veterinarian about what's best for your dog.

**Canine distemper and parvo vaccination:** Canine distemper and parvo (short for canine parvovirus type 2) are deadly viruses that commonly affect younger, unvaccinated dogs. Distemper often causes severe respiratory infection and sometimes neurologic disease; it is most commonly transmitted through coughing dogs. Parvo causes severe gastrointestinal disease, including vomiting and profound bloody diarrhea that's infectious to other dogs.

Because parvo is so contagious, it is critical that puppies not be allowed to go anywhere with a lot of dog traffic or stray dogs. Until they're fully vaccinated, keep their interactions restricted to controlled environments like puppy class or friends' houses.

There are many vaccines available that protect against distemper and parvo. However, Nobivac made by Intervet/Merck is the only one that contains only distemper and parvo. All others are combined with vaccinations against diseases such as leptospirosis, canine adenovirus, and parainfluenza. I believe that vaccines combining three, four, or even five different diseases are unnecessary because they may increase the chances of adverse reactions.

Canine distemper and parvo titers can be used to determine the necessity of further vaccinations after the initial core vaccine series. Dogs who show adequate antibody levels to distemper and parvo are presumed to be immune and need no further vaccinations; however, they'll need to be retested every three years.

- Puppies need 3 doses at 3-4 week intervals starting at 8–10 weeks of age—for example, at 8, 12, and 16 weeks of age.
- One-year-old dogs should have a distemper-parvo titer (see below) or a single vaccine. The Nobivac vaccine will have a 3-year duration.
- Starting at 1 or 4 years old, distemper-parvo titers are recommended every 3 years.

**Rabies vaccination:** Most people are at least passingly familiar with rabies. This virus, which is transmitted through the saliva of an infected animal, is 100% fatal to pets. Only a handful of humans have ever survived a rabies infection, and because of its transmissibility to humans, rabies vaccinations in dogs are legally required. Depending on where you live, rabies vaccinations may be required for cats as well. Medical exemptions can be granted based on approval of the local animal services or public health departments.

The legal specifics of when rabies vaccines need to be given vary by geographic location. Your veterinarian will let you know what the requirements are.

Rabies vaccine titers are available and often required for the transportation of dogs overseas. Although a rabies titer does indicate protection from the rabies virus, it isn't acceptable as an alternative to vaccination in the eyes of the law.

There are two different kinds of rabies titers. If you're traveling overseas, the Fluorescent Antibody Virus Neutralization (FAVN) test may be required. If the titer is being used to demonstrate immunity for reasons other than travel, Rapid Fluorescent Foci Inhibition Test (RFFIT) is recommended. It can take weeks to get rabies titer results back, so be sure to plan ahead with regards to travel.

- Puppies should have a rabies vaccine between 16 and 20 weeks of age, as per local ordinance.
- A one-year booster is required in most areas, and then the vaccine is required every three years.
- Rabies vaccine titers are often required for overseas transport of your pet. They aren't a legal substitute for vaccination.

## Non-Core Canine Vaccines

**Leptospirosis:** Leptospirosis is a bacterial disease transmitted through the urine of infected animals. It is contracted when a dog drinks from a contaminated water source such as a puddle. Leptospirosis infections can be quite serious and lead to liver or kidney failure (see Chapters 18 and 19). It is also transmissible to humans. Dogs spending a lot of time outdoors may be at greater risk for leptospirosis. Your veterinarian can discuss with you the relative incidence in your area. It is possible for vaccinated dogs to get leptospirosis.

- Initially, dogs are given two vaccines, approximately one month apart.
- A booster vaccine is required annually to maintain immunity.

**Bordetella**: Bordetella bronchiseptica is a bacterium that causes the disease colloquially known as *kennel cough*. However, saying a dog has kennel cough is like saying a person has a cold. Kennel cough is simply a description of symptoms that can be caused by many different organisms. The Bordetella vaccine protects against only the one bacterial organism.

Kennel cough is transmitted through the air when infected dogs cough, which is why transmission is most common in enclosed areas such as boarding facilities. To help prevent outbreaks, the vaccine is frequently required by boarding, daycare, and grooming facilities.

The vast majority of dogs who get kennel cough recover with no treatment or with a short course of antibiotics and cough suppressants. Severe disease from kennel cough caused by secondary pneumonia is rare, and the vaccine doesn't prevent all dogs from getting sick.

- Bordetella vaccines can be oral, intranasal, or injectable. The oral or intranasal forms are best.
- Vaccination is needed every 6-12 months, depending on risk assessment and the requirements of any facilities that you frequent.

**Canine Influenza:** Canine influenza is a strain of flu that specifically infects dogs. As is the case with the flu in people, most dogs will recover, although a small population of them can get very sick and even potentially die. Much like Bordetella (above), canine influenza is frequently transmitted in enclosed, high population density environments like boarding facilities, groomers, etc. If canine influenza is prevalent in your geographic area, your veterinarian may recommend vaccination.

- Initial vaccination with canine influenza requires 2 vaccines given 2-4 weeks apart.
- Booster vaccinations for at-risk dogs are given annually.
- Note: Canine Influenza is NOT transmissible to humans.

**Lyme:** Lyme is a bacterial disease transmitted by ticks, so along with vaccination, tick control is a major part of Lyme prevention. The disease affects both dogs and humans, although humans tend to get the worst of it. The prevalence of Lyme disease varies greatly by geographic region. Depending on where you live, a Lyme vaccination may be considered a core vaccine.

- Initial vaccination is a series of 2 vaccines given 1 month apart, and then a third given 6 months later.
- Annual boosters are recommended to maintain immunity.
- Vaccinated dogs will sometimes show a false positive on Lyme testing.
- Note: Lyme cannot be transmitted from dogs to humans. A bite from an infected tick is required for an individual to get Lyme disease.

**Rattlesnake Toxoid:** Obviously, there's no vaccine that's going to prevent a snake from biting a nosy dog. The rattlesnake toxoid was developed to help minimize the severity of rattlesnake bites in dogs. Vaccinated dogs tend to have less severe reactions to rattlesnake venom and may need less antivenin. However, any dog bitten by a rattlesnake needs immediate medical attention, regardless of vaccination status.

- Dogs living in rattlesnake endemic areas or those who travel to the backcountry may benefit from vaccination.
- The rattlesnake vaccine is initially given as a series of two vaccines, one month apart. Boosters are recommended every 6-12 months, depending on the level of risk.
- If the booster is given annually, it is best to give it in the spring when snakes have the most venom and bites are potentially the most dangerous.

## Core Feline (Cat) Vaccines

The vaccine schedules discussed below are guidelines for safe and effective vaccination. Timing and protocol variation based on the needs of an individual pet are commonplace. Consult with your veterinarian about what's best for your kitty.

**FVRCP**: FVRCP is a combination vaccine that protects against feline viral rhinotracheitis (FVR), feline calicivirus (C), and panleukopenia (P). Rhinotracheitis and calicivirus cause upper respiratory symptoms rather like bad head colds and are rarely life threatening. Panleukopenia, however, is similar to parvo in dogs, a potentially fatal disease that causes severe GI distress.

Feline panleukopenia titers can be used to determine the necessity of further vaccinations after the initial core vaccine series. Cats who show adequate antibody levels to panleukopenia are presumed to be immune. There's no titer for rhinotracheitis or calcivirus.

- Kittens are usually given three doses at 3- to 4-week intervals, usually at eight, 12, and 16 weeks. Alternatively, 2 vaccines can be given when they're eight or nine weeks old, and then at 12 or 13 weeks old, as long as they stay strictly indoors so their disease exposure prior to completing their vaccine series is minimal.
- A booster vaccine at 1 year of age is effective for 3 years. You may use a panleukopenia titer afterward to determine whether further vaccinations are needed.
- Adult cats who are allowed outdoors may benefit from an FVRCP booster every 3 years, as protection against upper respiratory viruses.

**Rabies**: Most people are at least passingly familiar with rabies. This virus, which is transmitted through the saliva of an infected animal, is 100% fatal to pets. Only a handful of humans have ever survived a rabies infection, and because of its transmissibility to humans, rabies vaccinations in cats are legally required. However, medical exemptions can be granted based on approval of the local animal services or public health departments. The legal specifics of when rabies vaccines need to be given vary by geographic location. Your veterinarian will let you know what the requirements are.

There are several rabies vaccines available. Purevax made by Merial seems to cause the fewest reactions. Purevax vaccines are available as both 1-year and 3-year protection duration.

Rabies vaccine titers are available and often required for the transportation of cats overseas. Although a rabies titer does indicate protection from the rabies virus, it isn't acceptable as an alternative to vaccination in the eyes of the law.

There are two different kinds of rabies titers. If you're traveling overseas, the Fluorescent Antibody Virus Neutralization (FAVN) test may be required. If the titer is being used to demonstrate immunity for reasons other than travel, Rapid Fluorescent Foci Inhibition Test (RFFIT) is recommended. It can take weeks to get rabies titer results back, so be sure to plan ahead with regards to travel.

- All kittens should be given a rabies vaccination between 16 and 20 weeks of age.
- Strictly indoor cats don't need a rabies booster. (The single vaccine as a kitten may help provide some immunity in case the cat gets outside.)
- Cats allowed outdoors should have a booster at 1 year, and then every 1 or 3 years, depending on the vaccine used.
- Rabies vaccine titers are often required for overseas transport of your pet. They aren't a legal substitute for vaccination.

## Non-Core Feline Vaccines

**Feline leukemia:** Feline leukemia virus (FeLV) is a retrovirus much like human immunodeficiency virus (HIV) in humans. Despite the name, the virus rarely causes leukemia, but it can lead to immune dysfunction and secondary illness in much the same way HIV progresses to acquired immune deficiency syndrome (AIDS). Also similar to HIV, it can take years for cats infected with FeLV to show any symptoms of disease.

FeLV is contracted through the bite or scratch from an infected cat. *Casual* contact isn't generally considered a major risk for contracting the disease, and cats living in the same household for years may not transmit the virus from one to the other. Regardless, infected cats should be kept strictly indoors to prevent transmission. Outdoor cats and cats living with an FeLV-infected cat should be vaccinated.

- Kittens should initially be given 2 vaccines, approximately 1 month apart.
- A booster vaccine is needed at 1 year of age and every 3 years afterward.

**Feline Immunodeficiency Virus:** Feline immunodeficiency virus (FIV) is a retrovirus like FeLV. Over time, the virus suppresses the immune system, leading other conditions like infections and organ disease. Just like FeLV, FIV infection can take years to show symptoms. FIV is usually contracted through the bite or scratch from an infected cat, and casual contact isn't generally considered a risk for contracting the disease.

There are two problems with the FIV vaccine: (1) It isn't particularly effective, and (2) FIV-vaccinated cats will test positive for FIV. Unfortunately, this can lead to FIV-vaccinated cats that turn up at shelters being euthanized under suspicion of being FIV positive. For these reasons, vaccinating for FIV isn't recommended.

## Feeding Dogs and Cats for a Lifetime of Good Health

### Deciphering Dog and Cat Diets

"Let food be thy medicine and medicine be thy food."[78] When Hippocrates said this around 2,500 years ago, food and medicine were largely one and the same. The miracles of modern science have since created a separation between our food and medicine. While no one can deny how humans and animals benefit from the current state of our medical care, we have, in some respects, lost our way with regard to how critical nutrition is to preventing and treating disease.

All animals evolve to function optimally when they're provided with a specific set of nutrients. We all need water, proteins, fats, vitamins, minerals, etc., to survive. The closer an animal comes to consuming these nutrients in the quantities, formats, and varieties that satisfy biological requirements, the healthier their body tends to be.

Back in Hippocrates' day, certain foods (and thus certain nutrients) may have been scarce based on season, weather, and demand. The result could have been ill health related to poor nutrition. In the modern era, we don't have to search far and wide for our basic nutritional requirements. We have our own issues, however, such as excessive intake of calories, carbohydrates, and fats. Highly processed foods deplete nutritional value. The general state of our food industry may be providing foods with fewer inherent nutrients, and genetically modified foods create a whole additional layer of complexity and concern. The result of the modern diet is often obesity, chronic inflammation, and the onset of disease related to imbalanced nutrition.

As an integrative practice veterinarian, one of the most frequent questions I encounter is, "What's the best food to feed?" The answer to this question depends on many factors such as age, breed, current state of health, and lifestyle. That said, one generalization can be made: The closer we get our pets to eating a fresh, whole food diet, the better their health tends to be.

Hopefully, this isn't a shocking statement to anyone. We all evolved to eat fresh, whole foods. It doesn't take a PhD in nutrition to realize that the biological *machine* functions best with this kind of fuel. While not all pet foods on the market provide optimal nutrition, thankfully there are quite a few good options available.

There are multiple formats of foods out there to offer our pets. Nutritionally speaking, some are better than others. Let's look at them 1 by 1 and discuss their merits and potential short-comings. Remember, some individual pets will do better on certain food than others.

## Dry Food (Kibble)

Kibble is by far the most popular format of food. Most kibble is manufactured through the process of extrusion.

**Pros**

- You can't beat the convenience. Just open the bag and pour into the bowl.

- It is inexpensive.
- The food has a long shelf life.

## Cons

- It's made in a high-temperature process, which may affect the nutrient profile.
- This method of production leads to the presence of toxic by-products like Maillard reaction products (MRPs) and advanced glycation endproducts (AGEs).
- The level and type of preservatives used in dry food varies. Some foods use natural preservatives such as mixed tocopherols and rosemary extract. Others use artificial (and potentially harmful) preservatives such as ethoxyquin.
- Kibble is, by definition, high in carbohydrates, even the low-carb and grain-free varieties. High-carbohydrate diets can lead to weight gain and chronic inflammation. Note: Some smaller companies have begun to introduce baked (rather than extruded) kibble that's lower in carbohydrates.
- The low-moisture content in kibble may also lead to pets (particularly cats) having chronic mild dehydration, which can affect health in both the short and long term.

## Canned Diets

There's a range of canned diets from super premium to very low quality. It is important to read ingredients labels and know what you're buying.

**Pros**

- Canned foods are convenient and have a long shelf life.
- The high moisture content helps provide extra water in the diet (which is a benefit over dry foods).
- Canned foods are lower in carbohydrates than kibble. (Note: Canned foods containing grains such as rice will have higher levels of carbohydrates.)

**Cons**

- Canned foods are by necessity processed at very high temperatures, which leads to the presence of MRPs and AGEs. The process may also result in the loss of micronutrients and enzymes that are beneficial for your pet.
- Metals or plastics (from the can or the can liner) can potentially leach into the food.

## Low-Temperature Processed Foods

These diets are generally freeze-dried or de-hydrated versions of fresh, whole-food diets. Many pet stores carry them.

**Pros**

- Freeze-dried diets retain many of the benefits of the fresh, raw diets. The low-temperature processing preserves micronutrients that might be lost in higher temperature methods. (Note that dehydration is a somewhat higher temperature process than freeze drying but is far more preferable to kibble or cans.)
- Since water is added to the diet before feeding, moisture content is controlled, which helps make sure pets are getting enough water.
- As with the fresh-food diets, these diets tend to be made with high-quality ingredients.
- These diets have a long shelf life at room temperature.
- Several freeze-dried pet foods are certified pathogen-free when packaged. (This means they're tested and found free of bacterial contamination.)

## Cons

- Freeze-dried raw products carry the risk of cross-contamination. Be careful in households with small children or immune-compromised people. (Cross-contamination refers to exposure to bacteria from secondary contact. In other words, the dog eats his raw food and then licks someone in the face or someone touches the plate the food was on and then puts their finger in their mouth.)
- These products tend to be more costly than kibble and cans, which can sometimes present a financial challenge for people with a large dog or multiple pets.

## Fresh-Food Diets

These diets include either raw or lightly cooked foods purchased fresh or frozen or made at home using a balanced recipe.

## Pros

- A balanced, fresh, whole-food diet contains excellent nutrition and high-moisture content while minimizing exposure to artificial ingredients and preservatives.

- The lack of high-temperature processing preserves micronutrients and enzymes that may be lost in other food formats. Many pets with chronic inflammatory conditions, such as allergies or inflammatory bowel disease (IBD), fare better on fresh-food diets.
- These diets tend to be made with high-quality ingredients.
- Several raw pet foods are certified pathogen-free when packaged. This means they're tested and found free of bacterial contamination.
- When made at home, fresh-food diets can be reasonably cost effective.

**Cons**

- Fresh food is perishable and requires frequent preparation and significant freezer space for storage.
- Appropriate precautions should be taken when handling and feeding raw meat regardless of prior testing for bacteria. Potential cross-contamination to humans should be considered. Be careful in households with small children or immune-compromised people.

- Homemade fresh food diets can be cost effective but time-consuming to prepare.
- When purchased, premade in stores, these diets can be expensive for larger dogs or in multiple-pet households.

## The Bottom Line: Good vs. Optimal

Most good-quality pet foods, regardless of format, provide good nutrition. The *super premium* brands of food use excellent ingredients. Once it is processed into cans or kibble, though, some of the nutrition is lost. Optimal nutrition can only be achieved through fresh, whole-food diets. While the particular ingredients and nutrient profiles of optimal diets will vary with species, age, and medical conditions, the future is leaving kibble and canned diets behind in the distance.

In our quest for optimal nutrition, practicality must play a role. (This is the real world, after all.) No doubt we'd all be healthier if we had a private chef preparing all of our meals with the best and freshest ingredients. Sadly (for me, at least), this isn't reality. When it comes to our pets, store-bought foods are practical. In these cases, frozen raw, freeze-dried, or dehydrated foods that are readily available provide excellent options that are far superior to kibble and cans.

For those with the time and interest, well-constructed, home-prepared diets are usually the best way to feed a dog or cat. Preparing food at home means you're in control of the quality and freshness of ingredients and the food can be custom-tailored to your pet's needs. Recipes must, however, be properly nutritionally balanced by a trained nutritionist. The road to poor nutrition is often paved with the good intentions of loving pet owners. Long-term feeding of an unbalanced diet can lead to serious medical consequences. Thus, creating a home-prepared diet is absolutely not the time to wing it.

## Technology for Pets

Regardless of how you may feel about it, we live in a technological society. Cell phones, computers, and gadgets of all kinds regularly govern our lives. While our pets are far less dependent on tech than we are, there are some new innovations that your pets might really benefit from and even enjoy.

**Chips and Trackers:** Microchips (as described above) have been around for years and are responsible for thousands of pets being reunited with owners after being lost. The shortcoming of microchips, however, is that to read the chip, a scanner has to be within inches of the animal. Thus, microchips only help once the lost pet has been found and scanned.

More recently, however, GPS tracking devices for pets have been developed. These products are small enough to be put on a pet's collar. Once set, the tracker allows pet owners to locate their pet on their cell phone or computer. They can also be set to alert owners when the pet leaves a predesignated area such as your yard.

**Feeding:** Automatic food bowls are available for pet owners that may have to miss feeding time. These bowls, however, generally only work for dry food. As we discussed previously, dry food isn't optimal nutrition, and thus their application is limited for pet owners feeding fresh, whole food diets.

**Entertainment:** Did you know there's TV for pets now? Yes, your dog can tune in to programming specifically designed for animals.

Dog TV (dogtv.com) will give your pet something to watch while you're out of the house.

**Exercise:** One of the great health benefits of owning a dog is walking. The act of walking your dog provides emotional, social, and physical benefits. There may be times, however, when you're unable to get your dog out for a walk. Internet-based services like Rover.com can schedule a dog walker to come and walk your dog(s) for you. The company does all of the background checking for you. And if that isn't enough, prototypes are in development for robotic dog walkers. Yes, I'm serious.

**Medical Technology:** At-home and point of care medical devices are the future of medicine, and veterinary medicine is no exception. Many of the same GPS locating devices described above also help monitor your pet's health. They can keep track of activity and alert you if there are any changes in his or her patterns. In addition, technology now exists for pet owners to monitor their pets for the presence of urinary tract infections, diabetic monitoring, and even EKG monitoring for pets with heart conditions.

## Ensuring Your Pet's Future

Having a pet provides us with unconditional love in ways only they can provide. In exchange, we provide them with love in return as well as safety and security. Depending on the breed and species, life expectancy of dogs and cats tends to be between 10 and 20 years. That's a long time, and a lot can happen with our health during that time. It is important to consider your pet's future should something happen that would make it impossible for you to care for them.

As with all issues of estate planning, deciding what will become of your pets ahead of time is, by far, your best course of action. In many cases, family members or close friends will take on pets when their primary owner can no longer care for them. In circumstances where this isn't possible, making a contingency plan for your pet could literally be a life or death decision for them. Middle-aged to older pets frequently don't get adopted from animal shelters.

If there's no family or friend who can take care of your pet, consider making an arrangement with a shelter or rescue group. If you're able, you might make arrangements to leave a grant or endowment to a rescue group in exchange

for them agreeing to see that your pets are
well taken care of. Alternatively, you may consider volunteering at a shelter or rescue group.
Beyond being a rewarding experience and a
way to help animals, you may be able to make
connections to ensure your pets are cared for
should something happen to you.

## End of Life Care and Moving Forward

## Why Is This So Difficult?

It's inevitable. We pretend every day that it
isn't . . . but it is. Our pet's physical bodies (not
to mention our own) cannot go on forever. The
illusion that the day will never come is just that,
an illusion. Unless we, as pet owners, are very
old or very unlucky, we will have to face end of
life issues with our pets. For many people, the
emotional complexities of the experience are
more than they're prepared for.

Given these circumstances, is it any wonder
that we have such a hard time letting go?

## The day you find out what it is going to be

It's a surreal moment when you find out what
your pet is likely going to die from. With the
initial diagnosis of cancer, kidney failure, or

some other incurable condition, the illusion is dispelled and the veil is lifted. Their life is going to end, and you're going to have to figure a way to deal with it. While the details of the process tend to be specific to the individual patient and pet owner, the general plan is fairly constant: Maintain quality of life for as long as possible, decide when to say *when*, begin to cope, and move on once they've passed.

## Quality of Life Care

For most veterinarians and pet owners, quality of life is really the only parameter that matters. We can talk all day about blood work and biopsies, but none of it holds a candle to the discussion of quality of life. Quality of life can be roughly divided into two categories:

1. The level of physical pain anddiscomfort the pet is experiencing.

2. How a pet's day-to-day experience is compared to what it was prior to their getting sick.

## Assessing and Treating Pain

Assessing pain and discomfort in animals can be difficult, even for veterinarians. Although they've been domesticated for thousands of years, our pets retain much of their ancestor's sensibilities. A wild animal that looks sick or injured is going to be targeted by predators. As such, animals are very good at hiding their symptoms. This is why many animals are diagnosed in the later stages of their illness. They're doing everything they can to project the image that they're okay. It is often only when they can no longer maintain the charade that we're able to see outward signs of them being sick or being in pain.

Given their hard-wired nature, we can't count on our pets to cry out in pain or give us other obvious cues when they're hurting or uncomfortable. Fortunately, there are subtle changes in behavior we can look for that will let us in on some of their secrets. In the case of dogs and cats, pain may be manifested as behavioral changes such as hiding or isolating themselves from people or other animals. In many cases, a pet will lay in places they've never gone to before. Lack of appetite can also sometimes be a sign of discomfort. Increases in respiration rate and heart rate are also possible indicators of pain.

There are many options for treating a pet in pain. On the pharmaceutical side, we have non-steroidal anti-inflammatories (Rimadyl®, Metacam®, etc.), steroids (prednisone), opiates (fentanyl, morphine, buprenorphine), and other pain-relieving drugs such as tramadol and gabapentin. Which medication or combination of medications is appropriate is a discussion to have with your veterinarian.

Traversing beyond the pharmaceutical, complementary and alternative care can be very helpful in managing pain and with the hospice aspect of veterinary care in general. Acupuncture, for example, can help with pain as well as with anxiety and in supporting appetite in ailing pets. There are many Chinese and Western herbal formulas that can be beneficial in alleviating pain and supporting quality of life as well. For those who are interested in exploring complementary and alternative care options, finding a veterinarian with experience in these areas is the best way to go. The website for the American Holistic Veterinary Medical Association (ahvma.org) is an excellent resource for finding a trained veterinarian in your area.

## Evaluating Quality of Life

Quality of life evaluation can be challenging. Our judgment may be clouded by emotion, unrealistic hopes, and *seeing what we want to see*. That said, however, making this determination is a vital component of providing our pets with the soft landing they deserve.

Begin by determining your definition of quality of life. It is different for everyone. Quality of life should be defined by the level of pain and discomfort the animal is in (see above), and what their day-to-day existence looks like. Specifically, ask yourself the following questions:

- What activities is my pet doing during the day?
- Is he or she eating and drinking normally?
- How does his or her day now compare to what it looked like prior to him or her getting sick?
- Considering the things he or she used to do for fun, how many of those things are still going on?
- Is he or she interactive or withdrawn?
- Is he or she *living* or just eating, drinking, and sleeping?

One of the most common questions pet owners ask in these situations is how to tell when it's time to consider euthanasia. My recommendation is to consider their pet's quality of life at this moment and decide what parameters will lead them to conclude their quality of life has become overly compromised.

While there are no right or wrong answers, it is advisable (if possible) to consider these parameters while your pet is stable and feeling relatively good. This allows you to consider the situation with a relative minimum of emotion. The goal is to determine *a line in the sand,* which, once crossed, would indicate that euthanasia should be considered. Remember, none of this is written in stone. You can change your mind and your parameters along the way. It's just a good idea to have a starting point that was made during a calm, rational moment.

## When Quality of Life Deteriorates

There will come a time when medical options are exhausted, the line in the sand has been crossed, and decisions have to be made. This is the toughest part of the journey: the decision of when to say, *When.*

There's perhaps no more personal decision someone can make than the decision of when to euthanize. It cuts to the core of our philosophy, religion, and our ability to end the suffering of a loved one despite the level of emotional pain it causes us. Clearly, this isn't a decision that's made lightly, and to the extent that it is possible, it should be a decision you feel good about. Remember, our pets provide us with unconditional love for their entire lives. They deserve not to suffer. This is the last, best favor you can do for them.

Once the decision has been made, there are just a few secondary considerations. The first is location. The veterinary office is always an option although many people prefer in-home euthanasia due to more comfortable surroundings for the pet and the entire family. The second is deciding to be present during part or all of the process. This is a very personal decision. Do what feels right for you. Lastly is the question of what to do afterward. Most veterinarians provide services for cremation of pets. People can either request the ashes returned or to be scattered. Burial at home is also an option although it is advisable to check local ordinances prior to doing so.

The process of euthanasia generally involves two steps. Usually, the pet is sedated with an appropriate sedative as determined by the veterinarian. The goal is to minimize any stress or anxiety the pet may be experiencing. We want this to be as peaceful a process as possible. Once the sedation has taken effect, an intravenous injection is given. This injection is a very large dose of anesthesia. The result is the pet becomes so deeply anesthetized that their body systems stop. The process takes only a matter of seconds, and they're unconscious well before their heart stops beating. There's no pain—only peace.

## Immediately After

The moments immediately following euthanasia have been described as "surreal," "sudden," and occasionally, "relief." For most people, being witness to the end of the life of a loved one is sacred and profound. If you're compelled to, take a few moments and appreciate with gratitude the love and joy you have experienced with your pet. Thank them for all they've given you and be assured you gave them the same in return.

## Moving Forward

Even in situations where euthanasia has long been discussed, the finality of it all can be over-whelming. One moment they're with us, and in the next moment, they're gone. The reality that we as pet owners had a hand in when and how that happened affects people in different ways. The only constant is, we must go through it.

Grieving is part of life. We all lose loved ones along the way. How to cope with the loss depends on people's individual preferences and communication styles.

Being a veterinarian, I've had the opportunity to speak with many pet owners over the years and hear how they've found closure after the loss of a beloved pet. In many cases, people rely on family members and friends to help them through the loss. For those who have other animals in their lives, the consistency of unconditional love from them can provide a great level of comfort. In addition, many com-munities have pet loss support groups that offer a place for people to find one another and share their experiences.

As is the case with the loss of a human fam-ily member, a ceremony of remembrance can provide comfort and solace. Ceremonies can range from the highly spiritual to something resembling an Irish wake. Some people choose to scatter their pet's ashes in a favorite spot while others take advantage of a biodegradable urn containing a tree seed. The urn is buried and a tree grows up from the ashes. Caring for the young seedling as it grows into a tree is a wonderful way to remember a lost pet and continue a relationship with them through nature.

There may come a day when you're ready to consider allowing another loving pet into your life. For some of us, it takes longer than others to be ready. The reality is, in many cases, we have nothing to do with it. Your new pet may find you when you least expect it. Regardless of the steps one takes through the grieving process, it is vital to remember all of the love and joy that you and your pet provided one another.

# CHAPTER 15

## THE CRAZY, BUT VERY POSSIBLE FUTURE

- **Avatar—Anywhere is possible (ANA) XPRIZE** per the site "The $10M ANA Avatar XPRIZE is a four-year global competition focused on the development of an Avatar System that will transport a human's sense, actions, and presence to a remote location in real time, leading to a more connected world."[79] Imagine having an avatar suite in your home (think of a robot that looks human), various people could sign in to the avatar suite to help you with cooking, therapy, cleaning, and even companionship. You'd only pay for the services they offered, and your safety is maintained at all times as they're never really in your house; they're only operating the avatar robot remotely. While this technology is several years away, I would expect avatars to be the new appliance of the future. Just as a washing machine, oven, and vacuum cleaner improved our lives, so will this technology.

- **Fallskip**—Fallskip, developed in Spain, allows for a risk assessment to be quickly and accurately completed using a belt that you put around your waist with a smartphone (Android). Healthcare professionals can objectively measure your risk of falling, which isn't only a huge fear as we age, but according to the Centers for Disease Control and Prevention (CDC), **falls** are the number one cause of fatal and non-fatal injuries in Americans aged 65 and older. Precision medicine or personalized medicine can then be increased to help you with customizable therapy or exercise to reduce the risk of falling.

- **Spider Silk**—Spider silk is stronger than steel but has yet to be able to be mass-produced like silk; however, this is changing. Bolt Threads has finally cracked how to mass-produce it. This will change forever what our clothes, furniture, wall coverings, and flooring, etc., are made of and how durable—similar to when nylon was introduced. Currently, Adidas has used spider silk in a prototype running shoe, the U.S. Army is testing for ballistics protection, and Northface is using it for a lightweight coat.

- **Brown Algae Memory Booster**—This memory boosting drug just completed Phase 3 clinical trials (which is right before it hits the market and can be purchased by the public) for Alzheimer's/Dementia. GV-971 (the memory boosting drug) was developed by Ocean University of China's Shanghai Institute of Materia Medica and is extracted from brown algae. The drug has also shown that it can regulate the immune system, reduce neuro-inflammation, and improve cognition.

- **Facial Recognition**—Facial recognition looks at 30,000 separate infrared points that can determine you from another. The technology is nothing new as Las Vegas casinos have used this for years as well as China who is currently working to identify its 1.4 billion citizens in seconds. The positive implications are personalized concierge shopping, going to a restaurant, hotel, or the doctor. In this situation, facial recognition allows others who are there to help, diagnose, and serve you to have information of your likes, dislikes, health issues, etc., in milliseconds without even having to ask you, look something up, or have a photographic memory. Imagine having your glasses fitted with facial recognition automatically telling you the names of everyone at the party. Chinese police officers already use these glasses.

- **Alzheimer's and AI**—uMETHOD Health has developed artificial intelligence (AI) for precision medicine to treat and diagnose Alzheimer's.
- **Tooth Sensor**—A wearable, on the tooth, could improve your health. Tufts University has developed a millimeter sized sensor that can detect sugar, salt, and alcohol. "The team plans to refine the sensor to the point where it will be able to detect and measure all kinds of nutrients, and maybe even biochemicals too," per Singularity Hub.[80] This wearable tooth sensor could help you refine what you need to eat more of, less of, and the supplements you need to take to improve your well-being and be your best you.

- **Memory Boosting Cells**—Wake Forest Baptist Medical Center has produced results where they were able to boost memory by 37%.[81] Essentially, the researchers identify and take out an individual's brain cell pattern for memory and then reinsert it back in; this increases the strength of the memory and makes it easier to recall.
- **Cancer detecting AI**—Artificial intelligence has been proven to detect skin cancer, metastatic breast cancer, colorectal cancer, and other cancers better than doctors. As the technology becomes more widely available, precision medicine along with early detection should substantially increase the positive outcomes of treatment.
- **Muse EEG sunglasses**—Sunglasses with built-in EEG will be able to help you count your steps, record your EEG, and document your heart rate, creating a biofeedback so that you can have better quality of life.
- **NanoDrops**—Researchers in Israel are developing Nanodrops that would correct vision for most eyesight problems such as nearsightedness, farsightedness, astigmatism, and presbyopia—making glasses obsolete.

## GE 2025 Future of Appliances

I had the honor of interviewing General Electric's (GE) chief designer for appliances, Paul Haney, regarding the vision they've laid out for how technology will impact the home through appliance design.

In GE's Home 2025 Appliances of the Future, in their vision, they created personas explaining the needs and then the technology that could help those needs for each persona. Multi-tasking Maria and Reluctant Roberto are GE's senior personas. Maria is 61 years old, has raised her family, and has her 84-year-old father living with her. The vision is that the technology can ease Maria's burden and Roberto's guilt of having his daughter take care of him.

While interviewing Paul regarding how quickly these technologies will be available, it was clear that market demand, which will reduce cost, will be the key. The technology isn't farfetched. Most of it exists today in various forms. Tying the various technologies together into a seamless system that's cost-effective will be the key to mass adoption.

For instance, GE already has an oven that's a four-in-one unit that uses Advantium technology. Sounds like something out of *Star Trek*, but it's been around since 1999.

According to GE:

> *Advantium technology harnesses the power of light. The outside of the food is cooked like a conventional oven, with radiant heat produced by halogen bulbs above and below the food. This halogen-produced heat receives a boost of microwave energy. The result? Foods brown and cook evenly and fast, while retaining their natural moisture.*[82]

Advantium combines a speed cook oven, convection oven, sensor microwave oven, and warming, proofing oven all in one. Imagine cooking food anywhere from half to three-quarters of the time it would normally take with a convection oven vs. the issues involved with microwave cooking. The issue as to why this technology isn't in everyone's home is a simple one, price. As with any new technology, research and development gets paid for by the first adopters, who are either wealthy or just have to have the latest and greatest and are willing to pay the price. The issue is, this isn't a new smartphone that gets changed out every two years, and with new house sales declining, it seems that this technology is destined to stay in the homes of the rich and famous.

While I'm sure this technology will start to become more mainstream, let's focus on the future and exciting new possibilities that GE believes will shape how we live.

Coming back to Maria and Roberto, GE imagines how food is grown, delivered, and prepared, and how medicine is delivered and monitored, and how we can better connect through everything from our smartphones to our furniture.

Items not identified with the Maria and Roberto personas, but other personas that GE created, address additional technologies that will have huge value to Baby Boomers.

They are:

- 3D food printer
- Induction units
- Smart faucet
- Laundry and clothing storage

Paul states that GE hasn't only worked with ADA guidelines but also Universal Design for their aging-in-place vision. They've engaged in the use of empathetic tools such as sight. Paul explains,

> *We have a lot of small, little graphics. How do we approach that? One is arthritis, obviously being able to turn the knobs, open the doors, just simple things like that. The other is reaching up very high or having to get on a step stool. If we design the kitchen from a holistic standpoint, how do you bring things down more into, say, the nose, top of the head, or to the waist areas? Picking up heavier loads is another issue. We're looking at the big picture. Obviously, we aren't going to be able to solve every problem. We're going to tick off as many as we can.*[83]

These are GE's more near-term concerns vs. the 2025 product. They found through their ergonomic studies that seniors can't bend over and get in the back of a dishwasher or get in the back of a laundry machine. They're trying to help seniors achieve their goals around cooking and cleaning to stay independent longer.

One of the largest concerns for aging and staying in your home is cooking and forgetting to turn the stove off. GE has this issue front and center on their radar. Paul states,

*We have a couple of ideas around if you think of a sensor over a stove to where it'll actually have some sort of smoke detector in it that will, if it starts smoking or the heat builds up too high, somebody just leaves it on, automatically shut off the system. That's one idea. Another one is real light . . . we have a couple of stoves with light bars over the handle, and those are out now to where they can notify people when things are done. The other is sound. It is obviously a big issue if you lose your hearing; you don't want a siren going off. That's a little bit of a tricky one. What we're doing is exploring, as this generation of Baby Boomers will move into the last part of their lives, and some of them are really tech-savvy and some of them are still not.*[84]

Paul doesn't feel it's realistic to think that we can just push all of these notifications to smartphones, as some just won't be that tech-savvy at the point they need help.

One of the other factors that GE is taking seriously is the need to downsize: making appliances the right size for the situation vs. a one-size-fits-all methodology. The challenge is that smaller used to be perceived as lower quality. Think of an apartment-sized refrigerator, 22" wide vs. a 48" wide GE Monogram side-by-side refrigerator. GE believes that while Baby Boomers will downsize to smaller spaces, they won't give up on quality. It seems we're finally hitting the issues that space-tight countries, such as Japan and Europe, have been dealing with for decades. How do we not give up on quality and services yet make our spaces more flexible and functional?

*One of GE's micro-kitchen concepts—dubbed the Monoblock—is an integrated unit with cooking, dishwashing, and refrigeration in a single standalone enclosure that would become a seamless part of the cabinetry.*

GE's press release for FirstBuilt states:

> *'Boomers will have a huge impact on smaller
> living, and it is GE's bet that they won't
> want to lose any of the luxury or conve-
> nience they've had in their lives,' said Lenzi.
> 'Whether they need a micro kitchen for their
> downsized dwelling, vacation home, refur-
> bished man cave, or boat . . . Boomers have
> always wanted the best.'*[85]

In developing what would be the ideal smart
kitchen, GE utilized the concept of crowdsourcing that was detailed out in a previous chapter. They basically built a micro-factory called
FirstBuild and then engaged a co-creation social media community to help them design the
first prototypes.

"Through FirstBuild and its global online community, GE Appliances is able to create, design, build, and sell new innovations for your
home faster than ever before," says Venkat
Venkatakrishnan, director of research and development for GE Appliances and mentor for
FirstBuild.[86] "We launched a **micro-kitchen
challenge** in May, and everyone from enthusiasts to experts can join FirstBuild.com to

contribute their ideas to make the concepts a reality."

Who better than your clients to help you design and develop the product they'll eventually buy? As my mentor Dan Sullivan of Strategic Coach says, "Always test your ideas out on check-writers." It seems that GE has done just that.

Concepts range from putting nice cabinetry doors on the front of washers and ventless dryers so that they can be in open view, eliminating the need for a laundry room or the awkwardness of having a stackable in a closet that's sandwiched behind cheap bi-fold doors, to a "monoblock," which is an entire kitchen in a single standalone unit that looks like cabinets.

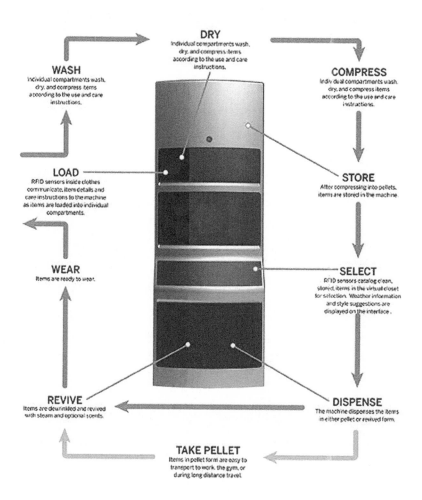

**DRY**
Individual compartments wash, dry, and compress items according to the use and care instructions.

**WASH**
Individual compartments wash, dry, and compress items according to the use and care instructions.

**COMPRESS**
Individual compartments wash, dry, and compress items according to the use and care instructions.

**LOAD**
RFID sensors inside clothes communicate item details and care instructions to the machine as items are loaded into individual compartments.

**STORE**
After compressing into pellets, items are stored in the machine.

**WEAR**
Items are ready to wear.

**SELECT**
RFID sensors catalog clean, stored items in the virtual closet for selection. Weather information and style suggestions are displayed on the interface.

**REVIVE**
Items are dewrinkled and revived with steam and optional scents.

**DISPENSE**
The machine dispenses the items in either pellet or revived form.

**TAKE PELLET**
Items in pellet form are easy to transport to work, the gym, or during long distance travel.

One of the more applicable future technologies GE has involves laundry. Imagine washing, drying, and storing clothes in a single unit.

While GE's concept of an all-in-one washer and dryer has been around for years, the storage component of clothing due to fabric being compressed into a pellet makes this the perfect fit for a senior.

I've used a Korean all-in-one washer and dryer for over 12 years at a lake house. It has one opening you place the clothes in and then it washes and dries them, all in one space. It seems to take quite a bit more time per load because the activities are combined. It works great for beach towels—to set and not have to worry about switching the load, so it won't get mildewed. While the all-in-one washer and dryer would be perfect for a senior doing one load a day at the most, I can't see this working for a family with kids as you aren't able to multitask and handle large quantities of clothing.

GE's vision is that this type of laundry application would take up less room and add more convenience. According to Paul Haney, "It came from the idea that, if you've ever been to a sporting event where they shoot those tightly packed T-shirts out at people." It's interesting how simple things can spark creativity that will create a new invention. This is only now possible due to new technology in wrinkle-free fabrics. The implications for downsizing, travel, or senior living are immense . . .

Imagine for a moment that your seasonal clothing would fit into a shoebox! One of the largest obstacles for downsizing is the lack of storage space. This could reduce the size of a closet by 50%–75%, which would free space up for the room and allow you to not have to choose what clothes you'll have to get rid of, which can be a very dramatic event.

Let's develop this further: Think of towels and linens taking up 75% less space in your home. Mind-blowing, isn't it?

**Laundry Pellets**

After washing and drying your clothing, the laundry machine in GE's Home 2025 compresses items into pellets and stores them in the machine. When ready to select your outfit, the machine dispenses the items in either pellet form for on-the-go or in revived form to wear now.

This is really not new technology, as much as it would be applied in a more commercialized format that's easier to use. The home shopping networks made mainstream the vacuum-seal bags for clothing that allow you to place your clothes and bedding into a plastic bag, then suck the air out, and then seal, so that you can get triple your storage space. At the very least, senior living should be utilizing this basic technology for their residents to help them manage their space easier.

**Smart Faucet with Hydration Sensor**
The smart faucet in GE's Home 2025 not only dispenses filtered water, but also ice and carbonated water, vitamins and various beverages. Just place your finger on the faucet and the built-in hydration sensor lets you instantly see your hydration level.

GE's smart faucet envisions that not only would your faucet properly filter your water, but it would also be able to read how hydrated you were and if you needed vitamins, etc., added for optimum health.

The fact is that Google is currently developing health-sensing technology such as a *diabetic contact lens* that can read your glucose levels through your tears, and the XPRIZE's Qualcomm Tricorder contest announced its final 10 teams to build the world's first handheld smartphone medical diagnostic tool that can take vitals as well as oxygen saturation. It's not too hard to imagine that by placing a finger on the faucet sensor, your hydration levels and vitamin and mineral levels could be accessed. Having reservoirs of vitamins and minerals hidden under the sink, you could add them to your drink (no different than adding drops of vanilla to a recipe) along with flavoring if needed or desired.

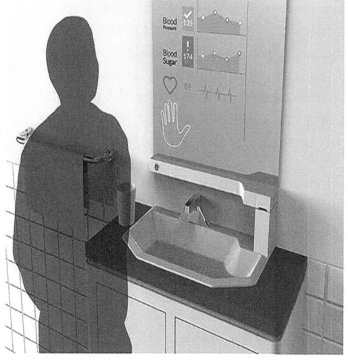

**Medical Dispenser**

No need to remember what medications to take when living in GE's Home 2025. Just place your hand on the mirror, and the Medical Dispenser reads your vital signs and decides the amount of medication needed for the day. The machine combines, processes and dispenses the medication in liquid form. Medication cartridges can be easily reloaded.

Taking this concept one step further, GE has reimagined the medicine cabinet to be a combination of the GE imagined faucet and the Qualcomm Tricorder diagnostic tool!

Imagine placing your hand on the mirror so that it recognizes you and takes your vitals, which are then sent to your doctor, or your loved one doing this to see if they need monitoring or if something isn't as it should be. The medicine cabinet would then dispense the medications you need in liquid form through the sink. Medication cartridges would be easy to change, and medication compliance would be much easier to monitor with constant vitals being taken. No need to be reminded to take this or that; it's all there for you.

Of course, if Roberto dumps his meds down the sink or won't place his hand on the cabinet, you could get a notification of this also.

The best way to imagine this is as a very sophisticated vending machine of sorts. The key will be monitoring of the vitals to ensure medication compliance. Taking too many meds due to forgetting what you have already taken would be a thing of the past.

Paul Haney feels this is more than plausible and not far out. He states:

*As we went through our research, we found medicine is gigantic and only growing, and how much medicine these seniors are taking is enormous. Whether they need them or not, the idea was instead of having to remember all that; you don't have to worry as much. It's a little bit of a different paradigm, where the senior says, it's okay because I'm going to get up in the morning, I brush my teeth, I'm by my mirror, and it dispenses . . . it's a smart dispenser. It dispenses for that day in something I drink right there instead of sitting there on the counter. My mom has one of those Monday, Wednesday, Friday pill things that never seems to work, and she dumps them out all over the place, but this would be taking a different look at the issue.* [87]

The burden would be placed on the technology vs. the senior, with built-in reminders and safety features to ensure the best results.

Paul's mother isn't alone. If you're over 50, you can identify with trying to manage your prescriptions and supplements. It's easy to forget what you took when, especially when so many of these pills look alike, and then you take them out of their containers, and unless you're highly organized and disciplined, you overtake or undertake weekly.

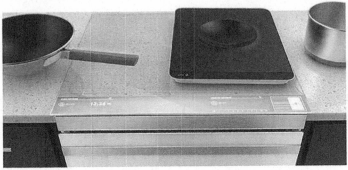

**Induction Cooking**

Packed in a 27-inch-wide design, the oven in GE's Home 2025 exhibit combines the efficiency of an induction cooktop, Advantium® Speedcook oven, sensor cooking, and a traditional thermal oven into a single unit. The interchangeable and integrated induction accessories allow for unlimited and exciting culinary exploration, as well as more cabinet space when stored in the integrated storage drawer below.

Induction cooking has been around since 1900 but not used by consumers until the 1970s through Westinghouse. Senior living, but especially memory care neighborhoods, has been utilizing induction units for safety and to be able to provide a more home-style dining experience than using steam tables as seen in a skilled nursing facility or cafeteria.

For those not familiar with the basics of an induction cooking unit, I've referenced Wikipedia:

**Induction cooking** heats a cooking vessel by electrical induction, instead of by thermal conduction from a flame or an electrical heating element. For nearly all models of induction cooktops, a cooking vessel must be made of or contain a ferromagnetic metal such as cast iron or stainless steel. Copper, glass, and aluminum vessels can be placed on a ferromagnetic interface disk, which functions as a conventional hotplate. According to the U.S. Department of Energy, the efficiency of energy transfer for an induction cooker is 84% vs. 74% for a smooth-top non-induction electrical unit and an approximate 40% for a gas cooktop.[88]

So why does GE see this as a future technology? Paul Haney explains that while this isn't a new technology, it hasn't caught on. "Partially due to Americans' love of cooking with gas; another issue is the lack of understanding and thinking that it's radiating the food. The final is it requires new cookware."

The benefits to induction cooking are immense.

- The obvious benefit is the energy savings.
- Seniors and senior living have the ability to safely cook and then remove the pan or cookware, and the surface is safe to touch.

- Homestyle cooking can be performed in a safe environment that's non-institutional and eliminates the need for steam wells.
- When the induction units are mounted under a granite surface, the space looks just like a regular counter when not in use and, therefore, can be placed on an island and not hurt the aesthetics of the space.
- Finally, the countertop where induction cooking takes place can be dual purpose. Space is always limited, whether in an apartment or performance kitchen, so being able to utilize the cooktop space as a prep area or serving space when not in use allows the countertop to be more flexible.

With all of these benefits, we still see both existing senior living environments and new-build homes miss the return on investment that induction cooking units provide. It's amazing to see a $17 million project value engineer out the induction units because they'll have to buy more expensive pots. Silly, I know, but it happens every day.

**Thermal Nightstand**

In GE's Home 2025, a thermoelectric nano material allows a user to activate a designated area on the nightstand using their body heat, such as from a finger, and leave a reminder. The thermoelectric nano material also recognizes the temperature difference between the surface and any object you set on it, such as a cup of coffee, and will adjust to keep your beverage warm (or cool).

While I love the idea of smart furniture and Corning Glass, "Day in the Life" video makes a hard case for all of our surfaces becoming interactive computer screens; this nightstand seemed a bit out there. Think of a digital Etch A Sketch that's able to warm or cool your drink and know which one it should do.

GE assures me that this isn't so out-of-the-real as both the thermoelectric and nanotechnology exists as well as the heating and cooling technology. It's the combining of these technologies that will take some time.

Being able to leave notes for a loved one or resident to start their day off with a smile or reminder is a wonderful idea. Corning would also have this surface light up and become the alarm clock.

Under-Cabinet Mounted 3D Printer
GE's Home 2025 comes equipped with an under-cabinet mounted 3D printer where homeowners can constantly print their own houseware, home décor and dry toys.

Roberto gets a notification that his meal is ready, it will stay hot and fresh for 8 hours.

The GE future kitchen has everything from ultra-smart appliances (something out of *The Jetsons*) to the induction cooktop technology that's been used by the public since the 1970s. The key is that the appliances are integrated into your food delivery system, your smartphone technology, and 3D printing.

If anyone is familiar with PeaPod (mostly in large cities), which started in 1990, it delivers groceries to your door from your online order for a nominal fee. GE envisions the future kitchen as a step up from this, having the appliances have storage units, similar to a freezer case in the grocery store that can be stocked from outside the house and accessed from inside the house. The stocking method would be completely secure and medications could be delivered this way as well. You'd determine your basics, order them up, and then meal-plan, and the appliance would calculate how much you need of what for your recipes and servings and order the proper amounts. GE envisions you'd possibly have a personal micro-garden to grow items that you enjoy growing yourself or aren't available at your store.

The appliances would be a combo refrigerator and oven that would allow you to prep a meal for cooking (plate up), similar to a crock pot, and then start cooking at the appropriate time.

They also envision that leftovers could be utilized with a 3D food printer for pet treats. Although the technology is currently available to 3D print meat, they feel it will take some time for people to adapt to this technology.

The focus is on how we can have fresh food, without it going bad, when you're only cooking for one or two. The analogy was given of making tacos for one, and the whole head of lettuce would go bad, as the persona only needed a small amount. Seniors tend to reduce cooking due to the issues of cooking for one with leftovers. If we could reduce this and engage cooking with interactive learning, the whole process would become enjoyable again.

In summary, Paul Haney says:

> *Looking back, I think that one of the interesting things about this 2025 project was we were grounded in current technology or technology that's either pretty far developed or pretty far in it. We couldn't just say your kitchen is going to float, or your clothes are going to automatically be clean by solar light or some new element." "Everything had to be grounded in a technology that we either A, know it's worked or B, is right there. I think that gave the designers a little bit more of a challenge, but I think you come out with better ideas when you do that kind of stuff.*

So people aren't like, 'Yeah, hovercraft,' or whatever it is. I don't get it. This kind of stuff is out there. As I mentioned before, the little T-shirt things that they shoot out at sports games, our laundry concept uses that same technology.

We are living in the opposite world of you, by the way. That's why these projects are so fun for our designers. Our teams include industrial designers, user interface designers, UX and engineers and researchers, and our internal user insight team. It was good to stretch everybody's wings and see what's possible instead of trying to make the millionth dryer of the year."

In January of 2015, after this interview, GE unveiled smartphone appliances that let you do everything from preheat your oven to send a warning to you when your clothes have been left in the dryer too long and will wrinkle soon.

*We need not be afraid of the future, for the future will be in our own hands.*
                                —Thomas E. Dewey

# CHAPTER 16
## SUMMARY, BONUS, & RESOURCE LINK

Summary:

*The Jetsons* aired in 1962 and was set in the future, 2062; they gave 100 years for this imagined world to become reality, yet it's only taken 53 years. While some of the technology on the show isn't as mainstream today as others (flying cars), we can expect that as the past 10 years have felt like technology was created at light speed, the next 10 will fundamentally change how we all live.

We've discussed technology that can help the blind to see, the deaf to hear, and the disabled to walk again. Self-driving vehicles and other mobility devices increase our freedom and safety. Lighting has become interactive and aids in our well-being as well as the planets. Crowdsourcing and gamification can help to complete simple tasks to complex tasks by leveraging our connection to others through the Internet.

Behavior modification through gamification can make you physically and mentally healthier, increase the compliance of your team and residents, or save lives. Robots reduce stress on caregivers' bodies, engage with residents, or deliver their medications via drone.

While data mining and artificial intelligence run as a part of most of the technologies presented, they deserve their individual kudos for diagnosing medical conditions and helping to learn our behavior and patterns so that we aren't inundated with information that isn't relevant to us.

We've been introduced to 3D printing that will change how our goods are delivered to us similar to having a computer and printer in your home. 3D printing will also increase the dignity we can provide for our residents by appealing to the look of food, not just the taste, without causing a choking issue.

Finally, we looked to the future with GE's 2025 Home and saw how the need for clothing storage could be substantially reduced, and furniture and appliances becoming dynamically integrated with technology will help us stay in our homes longer.

Some future technologies to think about that we haven't completely covered in this book but have interesting implications are: LED lit highways, a breathalyzer that can detect disease, nanotechnology, virtual reality, We:eX Navigate Jacket and Corning's Day in the Life video, which features how important glass will be in the application of technology in our surroundings.

**Bonus:**

As part of a group Peter Diamandis runs, called Abundance 360, I get access to not only the top technology geniuses in the world but also Peter's brain. He's truly one of the great thinkers of our day and freely shares his knowledge with all. While not all of these may apply, I hope you'll find it as thought-provoking and exciting as I have. Enjoy!

## Proof We're Living in 2019
## by Peter Diamandis, Founder
## of the XPRIZE

**Communications Abundance:** We're living in a time where there will be no person disconnected. Everyone will have access to the world's information. We've seen Facebook and Microsoft wire the entire globe. 5G networks have begun deployment allowing us to download movies in seconds rather than minutes. In 2017, about 3.8 billion people were connected; that's half of the world's population. In the next 5-6 years, it will be the entire world at even faster speeds, which means doubling the consumer base for businesses, and spreading information to everyone as quickly as possible.

**Cryptocurrencies:** In 2017, we saw a 5,000% increase in the cryptocurrency marketplace hitting $800 billion units on its way to a trillion dollars in 2018.[89] From Bitcoin to Ethereum and Coinbase, these companies sell tokens to raise capital in large amounts. Try $6.4 billion in 2016 and 2017.[90] Institutions are starting to invest, which only validates further the direction of cryptocurrency and its effect on the world marketplace. It's growing too fast to ignore and soon, numerous businesses like UPS are going to partake. Even Estonia has used this new borderless currency to create their own E-Residency program.

**Energy Abundance:** Our energy innovation is at an all-time high. We're constantly setting records for energy creation from renewable sources. The cost of coal is 5–6 cents per kilowatt hour, but solar energy in Mexico is at 2.7 cents.[91] That's a big difference in electricity bills for not just families but entire countries. Coastlines of various countries, like Scotland, are turning into wind farms that supply power to homes. Costa Rica went 300 days in a row with 100% renewable energy.[92] Even cloudy Germany was able to do 33% for the entire year.[93] We're going to have so much energy production in the next few years, we won't need petroleum or coal to create that anymore. Even car companies see the wave and are investing in batteries to make more cars electric by 2022. The energy world as we know is shifting and doing it quickly.

**Healthcare Abundance:** Healthcare is finding advances in all kinds of areas to help with the diagnosis of disease to sequencing genomes to help people stay healthier. The Tricorder XPRIZE winners created a handheld mobile device that could diagnose 15 diseases on the spot. This puts more power into our hands to be able to help ourselves. We're starting to use technology, such as Abilify, that utilizes sensors to tell whether you're compliant with your medication and can even warn your doctor when you aren't. The real ticket is being able to sequence your own DNA and even that of food you're eating to know exactly what's going on inside of your body. CRISPR is a software that allows us to accurately and easily change nucleotide sequences in our DNA that could decrease our chances for diseases.

**Transportation Abundance:** In 2018, we saw the autonomous car happen. We saw test runs and videos, and in many cities, you can ride in an autonomous car right now. Uber announced a 24,000-car deal with Volvo with cars operational by 2019.[94] These are cars with steering wheels, gas pedals, or brake pedals—just an onboard computer that gets you where you need to go. This will make the biggest difference in the world in countries and cities like Sao Paulo, Mexico City, and China. It's going to completely change the truck driving game.

Today, it's about giving the truck driver a break and him not falling asleep at the wheel. Next, it's fleets of trucks without human drivers. And the next step is coming from places like Airbus and Boeing creating the air taxi business. Uber Elevate is going to be taking over parking garages near you sooner than you think. Not to mention, we have the Hyperloop that can connect entire cities and maybe rocket travel in the near future as well. Soon, it will be so easy to see the world or get from one place to another in minutes.

**Robotics and Drones:** Robots are becoming a part of everything we do and making life easier. We spend so much money as our aging parents go to old age homes. $80,000 a year is the average.[95] Imagine if you can have a robot that gives them the dignity to stay in their own homes and helps them get up, make their meals, and go to the bathroom. We're starting to see robotics in farming and construction. In New York, LA, and Seattle, we're seeing Amazon Go open up a store without any employees. The AI knows who you are, what you took, and charges your Amazon account when you leave. Drones are being utilized to do anything from forecasting the weather to planting trees in deforested areas.

**AI and Computation:** We're seeing a vast improvement in AI across different dimensions of our lives. AlphaGo Zero is a computer program that's taught itself how to play the game Go. The original AlphaGo defeated the top ranked player in the world 4-1. AlphaGo Zero beat that program 100-0. It learns completely from its own experience and continues to play itself to get better. We have AI programming that can do facial recognition while you're moving. In the future, this could mean you walk into a store, they see you coming in, know exactly who you are, what you're likely to be looking for, and what questions you might ask. There are new virtual desk assistants from Google and Soul Machines that are able to hold conversations. AI is helping us predict difficulties in mental and physical health from suicidality to heart failure.

**Space and Physics:** You can put a deposit down for a flight on Blue Origin and New Shepard, suborbital flights that go up and fly back down. SpaceX had 15 consecutive landings of their first stage rocket. Something that 2 years ago people said couldn't be done is now a routine. The Kennedy Space Center has Falcon Heavy ready for launch to take astronauts to the moon and with plans for humans on the surface of Mars by 2024! Even with these steps, we've seen so much more of our universe. We discovered a solar system reasonably close to our home with 7 earth-like planets. We've seen early signs of life on Saturn! The Logo Observatory witnessed colliding neutron stars, and scientists discovered massive binary black holes. This is truly the days of science fiction.

I want you to feel how fast things are going. The water is boiling; it's getting hotter and hotter, and a lot of us are focused on our businesses, focused on our customers, focused on our kids and our family, and we lose track of how fast it's going. I don't want you blindsided. And so my goal here is to give you a sense of what I'm seeing as the trends. You should walk away realizing, *there's real stuff happening here, and I need to pay more attention to it.* Not all of it. Pick one or two things that are important for your future, for your investments, and for your life.

Find resource links at <u>LisaMCini.com</u>.

# ABOUT THE AUTHOR

 Lisa M. Cini is a globally renowned thought leader in the transformational living industry, having won many design awards over her 25-plus years developing interiors for senior living. The author of several books on the subject, including *Boom, Hive: The Simple Guide to Multigenerational Living*, and *The Future is Here . . . Senior Living Reimagined.*

Lisa has received numerous awards, which span multiple industries. A sought-after speaker, Lisa has been featured on radio and CNN, CBS, FOX, and NBC. She also appeared on *Today in America* with Terry Bradshaw and is quoted frequently in *The New York Times.*

As the nation's leading provider of design services for senior living, long-term care, and healthcare institutions, Cini's Mosaic Design Studio has worked with such high profile clients as the NHL, the U.S. Military, Brio Bravo Restaurants, PGA Tour Country Clubs, and various hotels.

Lisa shares from personal experience. Her family designed and thrived in a multigenerational home with her aging parents, her grandmother who struggled with Alzheimer's, her husband and children. That social experiment helped Lisa learn and create designs to help those aging in place. She founded www.BestLivingTech.com to provide products to help seniors embrace living as they age with the help of simple technology.

Her most recent venture, Infinite Living, is a live, senior-friendly, 10,000-square-foot, historic mansion that she is converting into an Airbnb model, which showcases the latest tech, creates multigenerational connections, and moves people from fear to freedom as they age.

A resident of Columbus, Ohio, Lisa supports her community through her dedication to volunteer work. She believes that we are all here to add value to this world using our God-given talents and treasures.

# TURN YOUR VISION INTO A REALITY AND DESIGN A SPACE THAT IMPROVES YOUR QUALITY OF LIFE!

Mosaic Design Studio is a global Award-Winning Aging, Alzheimer's, and Senior Living Interior Design, project management, and procurement company with the mission to Improve Quality of Life by Design.

Mosaic is dedicated to helping each client create spaces that serve their unique needs, mission, vision, and values. With a diverse clientele, ranging from senior-living clients and healthcare systems to the US Air Force, Mosaic prides itself in staying on the cutting edge of design, technology, and service.

Mosaic specializes in making the complex simple. With seven copyrighted processes that leverage technology and tools to reduce the time it takes to renovate, reposition, or design a new project. Mosaic saves you time and money, which allows you to focus on your core mission.

Our greatest joy is creating award-winning and cost-effective environments that address the needs of families and residents dealing with the issues of aging.

**Take your next step today at MosaicDesignStudio.com**

# AGING ON YOUR TERMS

**Products that allow YOU to control your destiny**

 **Best Living Tech**

Leading Alzheimer's and Senior Living Design expert, Lisa M. Cini, created Best Living Tech to bring you curated products from around the world to increase your freedom and quality of life as you age.

*Think Sharper Image meets AARP!*

## Discover Solutions for Every Area of Your Home and Life

**For Your Home**

- Bathroom
- Kitchen
- Sleep Space
- Lighting

**For Your Life**

- Healthy Living
- Memory Assistance
- Companion Devices
- Fitness & Mobility
- Safety Products

Explore your options at **BestLivingTech.com** today.

# THE WERNER HOUSE,
## AN INFINITE LIVING COLLABORATION

Senior-living design expert Lisa M. Cini has designed the first-ever Aging-in-Place living-tech lab. Making the most of the historic, 1914 Henry C. Werner House, Cini integrated the latest interior design while showcasing technology that safely enables independent living as we age, and offers AirBnB availability for seniors to test the products by using them.

**Do You Ever Wonder...**

- Whether aging in place or moving into a senior living community is right for you?
- If you could save money aging in place?
- If there is technology that could help you age without being a burden on others or breaking the bank?
- If you could try out this technology and fully experience it before you take the plunge to purchase it?

The Werner House allows you to explore options and experience a variety of technology and spaces designed to aid in independent living.

**Features Include**

- A full-service spa with fitness technology straight from NASA's space program for seniors
- Ballroom/education space with the latest technology for presentations and collaboration
- Bedrooms and bathrooms with the latest tech to age in place
- A creation studio where guests can record their legacy, music, video, or podcast

Learn more at Infinite-Living.org

# Connect with International
## Aging & Senior Living Specialist

LISA M. CINI

Lisa M. Cini is regarded as the leading Aging, Alzheimer's, and Senior Living Interior Design and Technology expert in the nation and has often been recognized for her contributions in the field.

Lisa's mission is to improve the lives of seniors and their families through design, speaking, writing and consulting, helping millions move from fear to FREEDOM.

Book a consultation, learn more about Lisa and her mission, access her appearances on television, radio, and podcasts at LisaMCini.com

# Other books by Lisa M. Cini

# There's nothing dull about aging.
## Your next event shouldn't be either!

International Aging &
Senior Living Specialist

# LISA M. CINI

utilizes her extensive practical knowledge and experience to
ignite, inspire, educate, and engage audiences
with the latest technology, information, and designs for aging.

Customized to your audience's needs, Lisa's presentations deliver
a unique blend of hope, happiness, and humor.

Help your participants incorporate proven changes into their lives
and the lives of the seniors they know and love.

A sought-after speaker, Lisa has been featured on CNN, PBS, CBS, FOX,
and NBC and is a regular guest on podcasts and radio shows across the
nation. She has appeared on Today in America with Terry Bradshaw and
is quoted frequently in The New York Times.

*Lisa Cini's speech was exceptional. Our attendees were actively engaged
throughout due to her interactive presentation style and her dynamic
speaking ability. She has an amazing ability to connect with her audience
and stay connected for the duration of the presentation.*

**—Rich Viola**
Chief Executive Officer, Hotel Interactive, Inc.

## Book Lisa today for your next event at LisaMCini.com

# REFERENCES

1   *Merriam Webster Online*, s.v., "Retire."

2   Alissa Sauer, "Why Do Seniors Want to Stay in Their Homes?" *Senior Living Blog* (blog), *LeisureCare*, August 7, 2018, https://www.leisurecare.com/resources/why-do-seniors-want-to-stay-home.

3   "The Common Sense Consensus: Media Use by Tweens and Teens," 2015, https://www.commonsensemedia.org/sites/default/files/uploads/research/census_researchreport.pdf.

4   "The Hoover Company," *Wikipedia*, last modified March 16, 2021, https://en.wikipedia.org/wiki/The_Hoover_Company #Development.

5   Peter H. Diamandis, *Abundance: The Future Is Better than You Think* (New York: Simon & Schuster, 2015).

6   Peter H. Diamandis and Steven Kotler, *Bold: How to Go Big, Achieve Success, and Impact the World* (New York: Simon & Schuster Paperbacks, 2015).

7   Ian Steadman, "IBM's Watson Is Better at Diagnosing Cancer than Doctors," *Wired*, February 11, 2013, https://www.wired.co.uk/article/ibm-watson-medical-doctor.

8   Maggie Fox, "Healthcare System Wastes up to $800 Billion a Year," Reuters, October 25, 2009, https://www.

reuters.com/article/us-usa-healthcare-waste-idUSTRE 59P0L320091026.

9    "Seniors Regain Mobility, Quality of Life with Portable Oxygen Concentrators," MSN, October 26, 2018, https://www.idahoseniorindependent.com/poc-oxygen-concentrators/.

10   "Aging in Place: A State Survey of Livability Policies and Practices," *National Conference on State Legislators and AARP*, December 2011, https://assets.aarp.org/rgcenter/ppi/livcom/ib190.pdf.

11   "Cellvation," https://cellvation.com/.

12   "The Science behind Fold-It," *Fold-It: Solve Puzzles for Science*, https://fold.it/portal/info/about.

13   Steve Barber, "Hearing Aid 'Sticker Shock' and Things to Consider When Purchasing," *Audiology Online*, June 20, 2005, https://www.audiologyonline.com/articles/hearing-aid-sticker-shock-and-1026.

14   Lisa M. Cini, *The Future Is Here…Senior Living Reimagined* (Bloomington, IN: iUniverse, 2016).

15   Dan Schawbel, "53 of the Most Interesting Facts about Baby Boomers," *Dan Schawbel* (blog), February 3, 2017, https://danschawbel.com/blog/53-of-the-most-interesting-facts-about-baby-boomers/.

16   "Robotic Lawn Mower," *Wikipedia*, last modified February 24, 2021, https://en.wikipedia.org/wiki/Robotic_lawn_mower.

17   Peter von Stramm, "The Chef of the Future Could Be a Robotic Kitchen," *Peter von Stramm Travelblog & Travel News* (blog), December 19, 2017, https://petervonstamm-travelblog.com/moley-the-chef-of-the-future-could-be-a-robotic-kitchen/.

18   "Workshop on Portable Androids and Its Application," *JST CREST/Patient@home/SOSU Nord Future Lab*, http://hil.atr.jp/projects/CREST/DenmarkSymposium/program.html.

19   "The World's 100 Most Influential People," *Time*, 2012, http://content.time.com/time/specials/packages/completelist/0,29569,2111975,00.html.

20   Amanda Ngo, "Israel's Next Top Robots," July 12, 2017, *The Next Wire*, https://thenextweb.com/syndication/2017/07/12/from-robot-companions-to-wall-climbing-machines-the-israeli-companies-advancing-robotics-worldwide/.

21  Peter Hancock, "Are Autonomous Cars Really Safer than Human Drivers?" *Scientific American, The Conversation US*, February 3, 2018, https://www.scientificamerican.com/article/are-autonomous-cars-really-safer-than-human-drivers/.

22  Bryan Thomas, "Proposed Rule Would Mandate Vehicle-to-Vehicle (V2V) Communication on Light Vehicles, Allowing Cars to 'Talk' to Each Other to Avoid Crashes," *NHTSA*, December 13, 2016, https://one.nhtsa.gov/About-NHTSA/Press-Releases/ci.nhtsa_v2v_proposed_rule_12132016.print.

23  "A First Drive," by Google Self-Driving Car Project, May 27, 2014, YouTube video, 2:52, http://bit.ly/3c3Bc4k.

24  Ibid.

25  Ryan Jaslow, "Paralyzed Patients Hope ReWalk Gets Approved by FDA," CBS News, March 4, 2014, https://www.cbsnews.com/news/paralyzed-patients-hope-rewalk-exoskeleton-gets-approved-by-fda/.

26  Irene Maher, "Peripheral Neuropathy's Pain Grips 20 Million Americans," *Tampa Bay Times*, June 12, 2014, https://www.tampabay.com/news/health/pain-of-peripheral-neuropathy-grips-20-million-americans/2184144/.

27  "Genomics and Personalized Medicine Empower People to Save Their Own Lives," *BIOtech Now Blog* (blog), June 23, 2017, https://biotech-now.org/blogs/genomics-and-personalized-medicine-empower-people-save-their-own-lives.

28  "David Karow, MD, PhD," *Health Nucleus by Human Longevity, Inc.*, https://healthnucleus100plus.com/doctors.

29  Mika Kivimäki and Archana Singh-Manoux, "Prevention of Dementia by Targeting Risk Factors," *The Lancet* 391, no. 10130 (April 21, 2018): 1574-1575, https://www.thelancet.com/journals/lancet/article/PIIS0140-6736(18)30578-6/fulltext.

30  Cromwell Schubarth, "Palo Alto Startup Is Looking for the Fountain of Youth in a Vial," *Silicon Valley Business Journal, Technology – The Pitch*, September 10, 2018, https://www.bizjournals.com/sanjose/news/2018/09/10/elevian-biotech-regenerative-anti-aging-medicine.html.

31  "Prospectus Summary," *Unity Biotechnology, Inc.*, April 5, 2018, https://ir.unitybiotechnology.com/node/6396/html.

32  Megan Forliti, "Mayo Researchers Extend Lifespan in Mice by as Much as 35 Percent," *Mayo Clinic News Network*, February 3, 2016, https://newsnetwork.mayoclinic.org/discussion/mayo-clinic-researchers-extend-lifespan-by-as-much-as-35-percent-in-mice-2/.

33  Dr. Joan Mannick, quoted in Todd F. Eklof, *Evolution's Way: Toward Exponentially Higher States of Complexity, Consciousness, and Unity*, (Spokane: Oakleaf Press, 2020), https://books.google.com/books?id=ZuTiDwAAQBAJ&pg=PA201&lpg=PA201&dq=joan+mannick#v=onepage&q=joan%20mannick&f=false.

34  "Osteoarthritis," *Centers for Disease Control and Prevention*, July 27, 2020, https://www.cdc.gov/arthritis/basics/osteoarthritis.htm#:~:text=OA%20affects%20over%2032.5%20million%20US%20adults.

35  Helen King, *Hippocrates Now: The "Father of Medicine" in the Internet Age*, (n.p.: Bloomsbury Academic, 2019), https://www.bloomsburycollections.com/book/hippocrates-now-the-father-of-medicine-in-the-internet-age/ch6-let-food-be-thy-medicine.

36  *BookBrowse*, s.v., "One Man's Meat Is Another Man's Poison," https://www.bookbrowse.com/expressions/detail/index.cfm/expression_number/442/one-mans-meat-is-another-mans-poison.

37  Kristen Ciccolini, "If Your Gut Could Talk: 10 Things You Should Know," *Healthline*, September 17, 2018, https://www.healthline.com/health/digestive-health/things-your-gut-wants-you-to-know.

38  "SPECT (Single Photon Emission Computed Tomography) Scan," *Mayfield Brain & Spine*, March 2019, https://mayfieldclinic.com/pe-spect.htm#:~:text=Overview,and%20tumors%20in%20the%20spine.

39  "What Is Alzheimer's Disease? Questions and Answers," *Texas Department of Health and Human Services*, last modified March 1, 2021, https://dshs.texas.gov/alzheimers/qanda.shtm.

40  "Baby Boomers," *Wikipedia*, last modified March 19, 2021, https://en.wikipedia.org/wiki/Baby_boomers.

41  Teachmitra, "Anyone Who Keeps Learning Stays Young—Henry Ford & Research," *Medium*, August 27, 2017, https://

medium.com/teachmitrahq/anyone-who-keeps-learning-stays-young-henry-ford-research-19c21b2a07ed.

42  Neil E. Klepeis, William C. Nelson, Wayne R. Ott, John P. Robinson, Andy M. Tsang, Paul Switzer, Joseph V. Behar, Stephen C. Hern, and William H. Engelmann, "The National Human Activity Pattern Survey (NHAPS): A Resource for Assessing Exposure to Environmental Pollutants," *Journal of Exposure Science & Environmental Epidemiology* 11 (2001): 231-252, https://www.nature.com/articles/7500165.

43  "Research behind the HumanCharger®," *HumanCharger®*, https://humancharger.com/research/.

44  Kit Fox, "The Distance Run Per Game in Various Sports," *Runner's World*, June 29, 2016, https://www.runnersworld.com/runners-stories/a20805366/the-distance-run-per-game-in-various-sports/.

45  Katherine Griffin and Katherine Bouton, "Hearing Loss Linked to Dementia," *AARP, Health*, July 2013, https://www.aarp.org/health/brain-health/info-07-2013/hearing-loss-linked-to-dementia.html.

46  "Hearing Loss Facts and Statistics," *Hearing Loss Association of America*, May 2018, https://www.hearingloss.org/wp-content/uploads/HLAA_HearingLoss_Facts_Statistics.pdf?pdf=FactStats#:~:text=experience%2C%20including%20physical%20health%2C%20emotional,some%20degree%20of%20hearing%20loss.

47  Janice Schacter Lintz, "How New York City Hears People with Hearing Loss," *Forbes*, August 8, 2016, https://www.forbes.com/sites/janicelintz/2016/08/08/new-york-city-hears-people-with-hearing-loss/?sh=1e08ee571f3e.

48  Lisa M. Cini, *The Future Is Here*, https://books.google.com/books/about/The_Future_Is_Here.html?id=7dOTCwAAQBAJ.

49  "CBD Consumer Market Expected to Reach $2.1 Billion by 2020," *Hemp Victory Garden*, https://hempvictorygarden.com/news/cbd-consumer-market-expected-to-reach-2-1-billion-by-2020/#:~:text=Now%2C%20a%20recent%20report%20by,coming%20from%20hemp-based%20sources.

50  "Alzheimer's Disease," *Centers for Disease Control and Prevention*, last modified June 2, 2020, https://www.cdc.gov/aging/aginginfo/alzheimers.htm.

51   Elizabeth Burns, MPH, and Ramakrishna Kakara, MPH, "Deaths from Falls among Persons Aged ≥ 65 Years—United States, 2007-2016," *Morbidity and Mortality Weekly Report* 67 (May 11, 2018): 509-514, https://www.cdc.gov/mmwr/volumes/67/wr/mm6718a1.htm#:~:text=Falls%20are%20the%20leading%20cause,deaths%20from%20falls%20is%20increasing.&text=The%20rate%20of%20deaths%20from,and%20among%20men%20and%20women.

52   "Prevent Falls and Fractures," *National Institutes of Health, National Institute on Aging,* last modified March 15, 2017, https://www.nia.dnih.gov/health/prevent-falls-and-fractures.

53   Matthew Frankel, "9 Baby Boomer Statistics That Will Blow You Away," *Lincoln Journal Star,* July 29, 2017, https://journalstar.com/business/investment/markets-and-stocks/9-baby-boomer-statistics-that-will-blow-you-away/article_67f661bc-293c-55fb-b762-4f0e1c9e48e6.html.

54   Erin Blakemore, "These Women Taught Depression-Era Americans to Use Electricity," *The History Channel,* March 29, 2018, https://www.history.com/news/new-deal-great-depression-rural-electrification#:~:text=These%20tactics%20worked%3A%20By%201939,percent%20of%20farms%20had%20electricity.

55   "Light Requirements," *AAA, Senior Driving,* https://seniordriving.aaa.com/understanding-mind-body-changes/vision/light-requirements/#:~:text=A%20driver%20aged%2060%20needs,change%20from%20light%20to%20darkness.&text=The%20light%20adapted%20eye%20of,of%20an%2080%20year%20old.

56   Hannah Chenoweth, "Can the Well Building Standard Thrive in Healthcare?" *HealthSpaces,* April 10, 2017, https://info.healthspacesevent.com/blog/is-the-well-standard-the-future-of-healthcare.

57   Mark Michaud, "Study Reveals Brain's Finely Tuned System of Energy Supply," *University of Rochester Medical Center,* August 7, 2016, https://www.urmc.rochester.edu/news/story/study-reveals-brains-finely-tuned-system-of-energy-supply#:~:text=In%20fact%2C%20the%20brain's%20oxygen,brain%20activity%20and%20blood%20flow.

58  I-Fen Lin and Susan L. Brown, "Unmarried Boomers Confront Old Age: A National Portrait," https://www. bgsu.edu/content/dam/BGSU/college-of-arts-and-sciences/ NCFMR/documents/Lin/Unmarried-Boomers.pdf.

59  "Financial Assistance, Costs and Payment Options for Eldercare in Ohio," *Paying for Senior Care*, January 27, 2021, https://www.payingforseniorcare.com/ohio.

60  Nate Williams, "Fantasy Football Draft Strategy 2014: Tips and Tricks," *Fansided*, July 26, 2013, https:// detroitjockcity.com/2014/08/29/fantasy-football-draf t-strategy-2014-tips-tricks/.

61  Anthony J. Krafnick, D. Lynn Flowers, Eileen M. Napoliello, and Guinevere F. Eden, "Gray Matter Volume Changes Following Reading Intervention in Dyslexic Children," *Neuroimage* 57, no. 3 (August 1, 2011): 733-741, https:// www.ncbi.nlm.nih.gov/pmc/articles/PMC3073149/.

62  *Amen Clinics*, https://www.amenclinics.com/.

63  "Daniel G. Amen, MD," *About Dr. Daniel Amen*, https:// danielamenmd.com/about/.

64  "SPECT Scan," *Mayfield Brain & Spine*, https:// mayfieldclinic.com/pe-spect.htm#:~:text=Overview,and%20 tumors%20in%20the%20spine.

65  Emma Webber, "What Does 'Fun Theory' Mean and What Does It Matter?" *Lever Learning*, October 29, 2009, https:// transferoflearning.com/what-does-fun-theory-mean-and-what-does-it-matter/.

66  "The Fun Theory 1 – Piano Staircase Initiative," by Volkswagen, November 12, 2010, YouTube video, 1:47, https://www.youtube.com/watch?v=SByymar3bds.

67  Lisa M. Cini, *The Future Is Here*, https://books.google.com/ books/about/The_Future_Is_Here.html?id=7dOTCw AAQBAJ&source=kp_book_description.

68  "The Speed Camera Lottery – The Fun Theory," by Rolighetsteorin, October 26, 2009, YouTube video, 2:08, https://www.youtube.com/watch?v=iynzHWwJXaA.

69  Mansoor Iqbal, "Pokémon GO Revenue and Usage Statistics," *Business of Apps*, March 8, 2021, https://www. businessofapps.com/data/pokemon-go-statistics/.

70  Skarredghost, "HTC Immersive Labs Shows That VR Can Already Benefit Various Sectors of Our Lives," *The Ghost*

*That Howls* (blog), August 16, 2018, https://skarredghost. com/2018/08/16/htc-rd-department-shows-that-vr-can-already-benefit-various-sectors-of-our-lives/.

71 Kanish Arhant-Sudhir, Rish Arhant-Sudhir, and Krishnankutty Sudhir, "Pet Ownership and Cardiovascular Risk Reduction: Supporting Evidence, Conflicting Data and Underlying Mechanisms," *Clinical and Experimental Pharmacology and Physiology* 38, no. 11 (August 8, 2011): 734-738, https://onlinelibrary.wiley.com/doi/full/10.1111/j.1440-1681.2011.05583.x.

72 Pamela J. Schreiner, "Emerging Cardiovascular Risk Research: Impact of Pets on Cardiovascular Risk Prevention," *Current Cardiovascular Risk Reports* 10, no. 2 (February 2016), https://link.springer.com/article/10.1007%2Fs12170-016-0489-2.

73 Cheryl A. Krause-Parello, "Pet Ownership and Older Women: The Relationships among Loneliness, Pet Attachment Support, Human Social Support, and Depressed Mood," *Geriatric Nursing* 33, no. 3 (May-June 2012): 194-203, https://pubmed.ncbi.nlm.nih.gov/22321806/.

74 Parminder Raina, David Waltner-Toews, Brenda Bonnett, Christel Woodward, and Tom Abernathy, "Influence of Companion Animals on the Physical and Psychological Health of Older People: An Analysis of a One-Year Longitudinal Study," *Journal of the American Geriatrics Society* 47, no. 3 (March 1999): 323-329. https://pubmed.ncbi.nlm.nih.gov/10078895/.

75 Jitka Pikhartova, Ann Bowling, and Christina Victor, "Does Owning a Pet Protect Older People Against Loneliness?" *BMC Geriatrics* 14 (September 2014), https://pubmed.ncbi.nlm.nih.gov/25240250/.

76 "Hurricane Katrina Rescue Facts," *Louisiana SPCA*, https://www.louisianaspca.org/about-us/hurricane-katrina/animal-rescue-facts/#:~:text=Of%20the%2015%2C500%20animals%20rescued,ever%20reunited%20with%20their%20owners.

77 "Pet Statistics," *ASPCA*, https://www.aspca.org/animal-homelessness/shelter-intake-and-surrender/pet-statistics#:~:text=Each%20year%2C%20approximately%201.5%20

million,670%2C000%20dogs%20and%20860%2C000%20 cats).

78 Helen King, *Hippocrates Now*, https://www.blooms-burycollections.com/book/hippocrates-now-the-father-of-medicine-in-the-internet-age/ch6-let-food-be-thy-medicine.

79 "XPrize: Anywhere Is Possible," *XPrize Foundation*, https:// www.xprize.org/prizes/avatar.

80 Vanessa Bates Ramirez, "Tiny Tooth Sensor Tracks What You Eat, and It Could Help You Be Healthier," *Singularity Hub*, April 15, 2018, https://singularityhub.com/2018/04/15/ this-tiny-tooth-sensor-tracks-what-you-eat-and-it-could-help-you-be-healthier/.

81 Brian Wang, "Recording Memory Patterns and Feeding Back Can Boost Memory by up to 37% in Alzheimer's Patients," *Next Big Future*, March 30, 2018, https://www.nextbigfu-ture.com/2018/03/recording-memory-patterns-and-feedin g-back-can-boost-memory-by-up-to-37-in-alzheimers-patients.html.

82 "Advantium Ovens," *GE Appliances*, https://www.geappliances. com/ge/advantium-oven.htm.

83 Lisa M. Cini, *The Future Is Here*, https://books.google.com/ books/about/The_Future_Is_Here.html?id=7dOTCwA AQBAJ.

84 Ibid.

85 "General Electric: Live Large in Small Spaces with GE's New Micro-Kitchen Concepts," *Market Screener*, https://m.marketscreener.com/quote/stock/GENERAL-ELECTRIC-COMPANY-4823/news/General-Electric-Live-Large-in-Small-Spaces-with-GE-s-New-Micro-Kitchen-Concepts-18629661/.

86 Ibid.

87 Lisa M. Cini, *The Future Is Here*, https://books.goo-gle.com/books/about/The_Future_Is_Here.html?id= 7dOTCwAAQBAJ.

88 Micah Sweeney, Jeff Dols, Brian Fortenbery, and Frank Sharp, "Induction Cooking Technology Design and Assessment," *ACEEE*, https://www.aceee.org/files/ proceedings/2014/data/papers/9-702.pdf.

89  "Proof We Are Living in 2019," *Abundance Digital*, https://www.a360.digital/proof-were-living-in-2019-sc.

90  Ibid.

91  Ibid.

92  Ron Brackett, "For 300 Days, Costa Rica Generated Electricity from Renewable Resources Alone," *The Weather Channel*, December 21, 2018, https://weather.com/news/news/201 8-12-21-costa-rica-300-days-energy-renewable-sources#:~:text=2018%20is%20the%20fourth%20year,eliminate%20 fossil%20fuels%20from%20transportation.

93  "Proof We Are Living in 2019," *Abundance Digital*, https://www.a360.digital/proof-were-living-in-2019-sc.

94  Darrell Etherington, "Uber Orders up to 24,000 Volvo XC90s for Driverless Fleet," *Tech Crunch*, November 20, 2017, https://techcrunch.com/2017/11/20/uber-orders-24000-volvo-xc90s-for-driverless-fleet/#:~:text=Uber% 20has%20entered%20into%20an,vehicles%2C%20according% 20to%20Bloomberg%20News.

95  "Proof We Are Living in 2019," *Abundance Digital*, https://www.a360.digital/proof-were-living-in-2019-sc.

Made in the USA
Coppell, TX
29 January 2022

72615366R00298